D1602624

THE MEANING OF CULTURE

THE
MEANING
— OF —
CULTURE

Moving the Postmodern
Critique Forward

Kenneth Allan

Westport, Connecticut
London

Library of Congress Cataloging-in-Publication

Allan, Kenneth, 1951–
    The meaning of culture : moving the postmodern critique forward /
Kenneth Allan.
      p. cm.
    Includes bibliographical references and index.
    ISBN 0–275–96124–9 (alk. paper)
    1. Culture. 2. Postmodernism. I. Title.
HM101.A565   1998
306—dc21   98–9941

British Library Cataloguing in Publication Data is available.

Library of Congress Catalog Card Number: 98–9941
ISBN: 0–275–96124–9

First published in 1998

Praeger Publishers, 88 Post Road West, Westport, CT 06881
An imprint of Greenwood Publishing Group, Inc.

Printed in the United States of America

The paper used in this book complies with the
Permanent Paper Standard issued by the National
Information Standards Organization (Z39.48–1984).

10 9 8 7 6 5 4 3 2 1

For David and Emily,
from whom I am learning what is really real.

Contents

Illustrations

THE
MEANING
— OF —
CULTURE

Introduction

Culture, Reality, the Demon of Reflexivity, and Theory

The work of social scientists and philosophers has progressively moved through the labyrinth of human reality. From Plato's notion of the ultimate Idea to Durkheim's argument concerning social reality *sui generis*, we have taken our experience of reality to be peculiar and a phenomenon to be explored and explained. For the social scientist, a major breakthrough came with the work of Peter Berger and Thomas Luckmann. In the *Social Construction of Reality*, Berger and Luckmann demonstrate that our reality is the result of the externalization of human nature into the environment, its objectification through institutionalization, and the subsequent internalization of this produced culture. They, like Alfred Schutz, put special emphasis upon the objectification process: it is only as culture is institutionalized that it can appear to us as a separate and viable reality. For Schutz, it is the existence of a broadly accepted language system, built upon sets of typifications and stocks of knowledge, that produces a feeling of "factness" about our culture and a sense of intersubjectivity. For Berger and Luckmann, it is the institutionalization of ultimate meanings through religion that, in the end, stave off the nightmare threat of chaos: a meaningless existence in a meaningless universe. Thus, through the work of social constructivists and phenomenologists, we found that cultural reality can confront us as a separate entity having its own ontology and facticity only because we work collectively to objectify our subjective and social experiences of the world.

Ethnomethodologists took us yet another step deeper into the maze. Through the work of such people as Hugh Mehan and Houston Wood, we came to understand that this cultural reality is reflexively constructed. Every culture system is built upon a foundation of cultural assumptions that are never questioned and are protected through a set of legitimized secondary elaborations of belief. For example, part of the conceptual foundation of science is that the universe operates according to law like principles and that these processes may be empirically discerned and discovered by humans, allowing us to manipulate the universe for our own benefit. However, it is not the case that scientifically controlled experiments and applications always work—the universe sometimes misbehaves. But rather than question their assumptions about the world, scientists use a legitimated set of reasons that not only elucidate why the universe did not behave as predicted, but also preserve the incorrigible assumptions that undergird science. The same is true for religion: the sovereignty and grace of God is never seriously questioned by the Christian when prayer goes unanswered; there are a myriad of accepted reasons that explain why the "heavens are as of brass" and that function to preserve the Christian's faith in his or her cosmology. Mehan and Wood thus argue that all reality systems are superstitious and founded upon belief.

Further, the proof of any culture system is determined by the culture system itself. In other words, how do we know science is true? By using the scientific method we are able to create a body of knowledge that substantiates our belief in a law-driven universe. How do we know that religion is true? Each religion provides a set of criteria (e.g., faith, scriptural knowledge, meditative practice) that will provide "eyes to see and ears to hear." For example, many Baptists feel that they are saved through faith, and that the validity of their faith is demonstrated by the presence of Biblically prescribed good works; on the other hand, some Pentecostal Holiness movements believe that faith is authenticated by the presence of the Holy Spirit through the gift of glossolalia. Thus for science, religion, and every knowledge system, the proof that a cultural system is real is provided by the culture itself, not an outside "objective" source. This reflexive construction also extends to such mundane occurrences as saying "hello." Saying "hello" to someone both presupposes and creates the social world wherein the gesture can exist.

Ethnomethodologists have shown us that human reality is not moored to any obdurate, brute world but, rather, it is thoroughly cultural in all its postulates, proofs, and practices. Postmodernists have taken us the next logical step into the heart of the labyrinth and have drawn back the curtain to expose the wizard. If reality for humans is reflexively constructed, then it has no outside reference point—it is not tied to any spiritual or physical world—and reality is therefore nothing more than a text, a set of signs that are read contextually. The reading of this text produces yet another text that is again available for interpretation, and so on. Taking their cue from poststructuralists, the postmodern concept of the text indicates that even the sign elements used within the text exist only by referencing one another. And since these signs can exist only as they reference one another, there can be no center or beginning point of reference for signs and their texts.

Postmodernists also inform us that, due to certain social processes, the overall structure of culture has become fragmented. Although culture has always had this element of reflexivity about it, in times past the structure of culture provided stable and consistent reality experiences for people. And the intact structure of a dominate culture functioned to effectively exclude considerations of alternative realities. Thus people were centered and secure in their culture—reality was experienced as fact and obvious to all. But the processes of modernity (e.g., markets, commodification, advertising, mass media, transportation technologies, structural and social differentiation, science and institutionalized doubt, and so on) have produced a threshold point wherein culture, and thus reality, has become fragmented and is no longer modern. Culture is not centered, competing realities are no longer censored, and the signs and symbols that make up culture have become free-floating entities unto themselves. Postmodernists have thus shown us the true nature of our own reality: texts chasing after texts in an endless field of play. And the curtain surrounding the search for an ultimate center has been pulled down and the truth of the search revealed: "emptiness, emptiness, all is emptiness and chasing after wind." But there is more to the story, processes involved in the production of reality that have been largely ignored by postmodernists, ethnomethodologists, and social constructivists. Postmodernism represents a point of conclusion for a number of lines of argument, taken from art, architecture, social constructivism, philosophy, structuralism, and so on. But, as is often the case, this conclusion becomes a premise for another argument. It is time to move the postmodern critique forward and exorcise the demon of reflexivity.

This book is a beginning effort at explicating the next step in understanding our reality. As such, it contains a theoretical look at culture in postmodernity. Having made such a statement, I must admit that it includes some of the more controversial terms to be found in the social sciences—theory, culture, and postmodernity. The field of cultural studies in sociology experienced unusually rapid growth between 1988 and 1990 (Peterson, 1990, p. 498). As Hall and Neitz (1993) state: "At the end of the twentieth century, culture once again has become a central focus of sociological theorizing" (p. 1). But the meaning of the word "culture" remains as problematic today as when Raymond Williams (1976) stated that "culture is one of the two or three most complicated words in the English language" (p. 76).

The term "culture" does indeed cover a broad range of topics: ideas, language, recipes for action, tools, products, norms, values, beliefs, art, and so forth. The term has also been used in conceptually polarized extremes: referring to either material or nonmaterial objects, and as being either an epiphenomenon or the center of the social system. My intent in the use of the term "culture" is to emphasize its function as a symbolic reference system whereby humans manufacture and reproduce a meaningful, real world in action and interaction. This definition stresses human agency in the creation of meaning: it is my position that signs and symbols and discourses are cultural artifacts. They themselves do not produce meaning; humans produce meaning in concert with the cultural system. Significance must be enacted and experienced, or else it simply remains a potential. Meaning is only produced by human beings acting and interacting through two primary mechanisms: the focus of psychic or emotional energy and the process of association.

The term "meaning" can have two distinct connotations: it may be used to refer to sense-meaning or to affect-meaning. Sense-meaning refers to the content of culture, and it is informed by the cultural structure and how the different sign elements are arranged together. For example, a sentence makes sense because the words are arranged in an accepted order, or categories make sense because of their structured relationships one with another, like good/bad or male/female. Although the sense-meaning of culture and its content have an explicit relationship to the structure of the culture system, it must be recognized and enacted to be subjectively meaningful to humans. And while this point may seem obvious to some, it is an assumption that is missing from much of the contemporary cultural analysis and theorizing; in particular, postmodernism. Affect-meaning is also dependent upon human interaction; affect-meaning is most explicitly related to ritual performance and thus requires a particular kind of enactment to be meaningful. Affect-meaning refers to the emotional response that a sign, symbol, or discourse can elicit. Yet the emphasis here is not on the emotional content but on the emotional impact; an element of culture may have a strong or weak affect on an individual or group. So, for example, some people may react strongly to the American flag or to the Christian cross, whereas others may not. The importance of affect-meaning is that it lies in back of the motivation for action and the experience of reality.

Many of the contemporary perspectives of culture view meaning as a function of the system, almost exclusively as sense-meaning, arguing that meaning arises from the semiotic relationships among the different sign elements. On the whole, contemporary cultural theory has been unduly influenced by a fundamental error that originated with structuralism: the structure of the sign system is posited to be the dynamic upon which human action and interaction are dependent. This error has resulted in a general overemphasis on the signification system and the neglect of agency and affect-meaning. This assumption can also lead to conclusions concerning the cultural "text" that have little to do with the meaning experienced by the people viewing or using the symbols.

The definition of culture that I have proposed also emphasizes the place of culture in producing human reality, in terms of both the subjective experience of people within a given culture and the feeling of facticity that may be achieved. This book, then, is about the human experience of reality; it is not a philosophic inquiry into the nature of reality, nor is it an explanation of how we form the psychological, cognitive frameworks that inform our view of the world, but, rather, it is a theoretical exercise that seeks to explain in a general fashion the subjective experience of a social actuality. Human reality is a produced reality. That is, it is nearly impossible for us to experience the world apart from culture; the thing-in-itself is not available to us because our culture tells us what an object or experience means, and that meaning becomes our reality. And because this meaning is not the thing-in-itself and is not anchored in the physical world but the social world, the reality of it is contingent and dependent upon human action and interaction for its stability and reification. Because human reality is a cultural construct, it is, by definition, impossible to predict the content of that reality with any certainty (hence a tree may become a sacred, commercial, or sentimental object, or an instrument of death). But, because it is cultural and humans must stabilize and reify its meaning, the form and processes that allow a reality to exist and influence human perception and behavior are explicable and may be stated in such a manner that predictive statements concerning the variability of reality for humans are possible.

However, this kind of project is at odds with postmodernism, and much of the contemporary field of cultural studies. At the core of the postmodern perspective is a philosophical critique of knowledge. This critique focuses on the problem of representation: to what degree do signs and language systems provide a true mirror through which reality may be viewed and, in the case of science, controlled? To the degree that signs are social constructions related to groups and their interests, the relationship between brute reality and its signification is rendered problematic. In its critique of science, postmodernism claims that scientific theory is simply a linguistic text that may be read and reread in distinctly different ways during different periods of time, and that this text is informed at least as much by values and politics as it is by the

obdurate world. Because science is based on the assumption of representation, postmodernists assert that the adulteration of scientific knowledge disqualifies it from having a privileged place among other
knowledge systems. Critiques of science, and of social science in particular, are not new. But, as Seidman and Wagner (1992) point out, it is the
critique of the assertion that science can be a "privileged form of reason
or the medium of truth" (p. 6) that sets the postmodern report apart.
But how much damage does this critique do to the production of scientific knowledge? Should we, as some have exhorted, abandon the project of social science and the production of positivistic theory?

In one sense, I consider the debate surrounding science and theory to be
metatheoretical and the issues ultimately decided by faith. All human knowledge is a component and a function of culture, whether scientific, critical, or postmodern. As Mehan and Wood (1975) argue,
cultural reality is founded upon incorrigible assumptions that are protected through secondary elaborations of belief. Further, the methods
through which any cultural knowledge is proven correct or discounted
are dictated by the culture itself. Hence, cultural reality is reflexively
constructed and the foundations of that production are never questioned
or themselves put to the test. But is the knowledge thus produced real
and valid? In the final analysis, there is no answer to these kinds of
questions, because both the method through which the answers are
"found" and the answer itself are bound by and contained within the
culture system that is under question. So, are the answers that science
proposes real? In the long run it does not matter, for the important
thing for science, and those of us using the fruits of scientific knowledge,
is that the answers work—science is driven by the pragmatic motive.

Although I do understand the problems associated with a positivistic approach to understanding social phenomena, and I do endorse and
give place to the use of different kinds of approaches in producing
knowledge, I have not despaired in the quest to find positivistic answers to human dilemmas, unlike some of my colleagues (e.g., Wuthnow, 1995). Nor have I been convinced that positivistic knowledge is by
definition any more oppressive than other knowledge systems—as I
will argue, all knowledge systems must engage in the process of exclusion. It is thus my intent in this book to state in propositional form the
general processes associated with creating meaning and reality; and it
is my hope that these propositions will tested and our understanding of
how human behavior is influence by the presence of cultural reality can
grow and become more robust. It is ironic to note, in view of the postmodern concern with reality and the critique of positivistic knowledge,
that the behavior of humans around the issues of meaning and reality
appear to be among the most predictable and governed by lawlike processes. Unfortunately, it is the dogmatic resistance to positivistic

knowledge that has blinded many postmodernists to the processes with which they are most concerned.

For example, Jean-François Lyotard (1984), one of the founding post-modern thinkers, argues that the goal of postmodernism is to produce a system of legitimated knowledge based on paralogy. This kind of le-gitimation occurs through two steps. The first step is a recognition that language is heteromorphous. This recognition implies the cessation of the use of exclusionary practices or what Lyotard refers to as terror. Second, any consensus that does exist must be locally agreed upon by the actors in the here-and-now and must be subject to cancellation at any-time. The value upon which this vision for society is predicated con-tains both a desire for justice and a respect for the unknown. While Lyotard's vision and value are admirable, he has sidestepped the twin problems of culture: meaning and reality. Luhmann (1985) makes the point that these problems originate from a paradox: culture both cre-ates and makes contingent meaning and reality. This contingency cre-ates questions of ultimate meaning and "makes 'religion' (whatever that means) unavoidable. Social life, therefore, has a religious qual-ity" (Luhmann, 1985, p. 8). This religious quality does not have to be religion per se, but the self-referential character of culture and human-ity's essential reflexivity inexorably push people to question culturally created meaning and reality to the point where they can cease to exist. But the answers to these questions are not ultimate answers, nor does the content of the answers matter, but, rather, they represent forms of coping that "deparadoxize" the world, generally through rituals.

Two essential elements of the coping mechanisms that people use to substantiate their world are denied in Lyotard's vision of justice and equality. First, Lyotard's formulation increases rather than reduces contingency. Consensus for Lyotard must be in the here-and-now and subject to cancellation. But a consensus of belief is a primary means of affirming meaning and reality. This belief must always entail the con-cept that meaning and reality extend for some distance in terms of both space and time, in that the essence of constructed meaning and reality extends beyond the immediate, sensate experience; that is, meaning always entails something other than the thing-in-itself and the here-and-now. The level at which this consensus must function is a theoreti-cal question that has yet to be answered; but to deny that it is needed, as postmodernists appear to do, is to misunderstand the fundamental nature of culture. Second, Lyotard naïvely wants to do away with ex-clusionary practices, but it is through the process of exclusion, opposi-tion and difference, that meaning and reality are created—it is not the case that a knowledge system can contain all meanings and still main-tain any meaning. Additionally, exclusion implies borders, and borders are a principle means of demarcating and protecting signs and symbols.

The stronger the borders between systems or discrete bits of knowledge, the more real will the knowledge appear and be experienced. All narratives, grand or mini, imply exclusion, bordering, reification, and consensus; without these processes culture has no meaning whatsoever and can convey no sense of reality. Thus all knowledge systems, even postmodernism, must exclude some considerations from the infinite possibilities facing humans and must produce borders around the categories and types that are used to limit human perceptions into knowable units. No where is this process of bordering and exclusion more apparent than in the argumentation that some postmodernists present concerning the meaning and place of theory in the study of social phenomena (e.g., Brown, 1987; Gottdiener, 1990; Lemert, 1990, 1992, 1994; Seidman, 1992).

Charles Lemert (1992), a postmodernist, states that "reality is discussible—not much more than this" (p. 23) and that "reality is figurative, available only within language" (p. 24). I disagree. Reality is experienced, and it is experienced as a variable; that is, some cultural objects and meanings appear more real than others. The content of the reality is discussible and a function of text, but the experience or the impact of reality, that which makes the meaningful content seem undeniable and factual, is produced by human beings in interaction, the processes of which are universal and discoverable. It is my position that postmodernism has identified some important factors influencing culture and meaning in technically advanced, capitalistic societies. But postmodernists have overstated the effects of these processes—in particular, the death of the subject and the decisive break between the sign and reality. Based on the nature of culture and reflexivity, I challenge these conclusions and argue that the dynamics of postmodernity create pressures at the micro-level to produce, stabilize, and reify cultural meaning. Thus, in contrast to many critics of postmodernism, I accept and generalize the factors posited by postmodernists and place them in a theoretical context that explicates the micro-dynamics of culture and the production of meaning.

The principal aim of this work is to advance cultural theory by arguing for a sociological theory of cultural meaning. Most contemporary sociological approaches to culture, including postmodernism, have missed crucial issues concerning the way in which meaning in culture is produced. The most important issue overlooked is the effect that reflexivity has on people in constructing culture. Reflexivity is at once the boon and the bane of humanity. Reflexivity allows us to create a cultural system through which the environment may be manipulated and controlled, but it also allows us to question the ontology of a constructed, symbolic world that has no essential relationship with the brute world. Culture intrinsically separates an object from its experience and demands an act of interpretation, that is, reflexivity; and, by extension, reflexivity implies the problem or paradox of meaning: humans can create questions concerning the ultimate meanings behind culture. Culture thus both creates and makes contingent meaning and reality. This self-referential character of culture and humanity's essential reflexivity inexorably create a sense of uncertainty and insecurity about reality and meaning. People are motivated then to "dampen" reflexivity, both individually and collectively, and to create a sense of directly experienced reality. Thus, even if the structure of culture is fragmented, as postmodernism argues, the nature of culture and reflexivity will tend to pressure people to participate in certain kinds of micro-level interactions that will mitigate the cultural problems associated with postmodernity.

My theory is thus based upon a need assumption: I posit that the presence of culture will, without fail, produce the needs for facticity and ontological security and that those needs will drive humans to certain kinds of behaviors that, in turn, both create and meet those needs. Although the place of need assumptions has constituted one of the criticisms of functional theory—the problem of teleology—it is not the case that people or social systems operate apart from requisite needs. For example, people have certain biological requisites that must be met in order for them to survive. For any society to endure, it must, in turn, have certain mechanisms in place to ensure the biological survival of its inhabitants. The theoretical problem, then, is not that a relationship is teleological—the presence of a need bringing about the factors that produce the need—but, rather, whether the relationships form a legitimate teleology; in other words, the logic of the connections must be made clear and the intervening steps from need to process and back to need again must be explicated, an issue I address in the remaining sections of this work.

In the course of this book, I argue that both sense- and affect-meaning are important to the study of culture but that affect-meaning, and its impact on the production of intersubjective reality, has, on the whole, been slighted by the different perspectives of culture. This general tendency has been exacerbated by the influence of linguistic-structuralism whose focus is entirely on sense-meaning, and this overemphasis on the signification system is most discernible in the postmodern view of culture. What constitutes postmodernism and who is counted as being a postmodernist are questions that have produced, at best, ambiguous answers. I have offered a definition of postmodernism elsewhere (Allan & Turner, 1998, p. 597) that indicates that it is essentially concerned with two linked elements: a critique of science and reality. These two are connected in that they are both culturally constructed. It is important to note that this work does not address the question of whether or not a new, postmodern age exists. I do use the terms "postmodern" and "postmodernity" to refer to certain social factors and dynamics throughout the book, but I use them only as orienting terms. The issue of the reality of a postmodern age must be addressed by researchers; a beginning step toward that goal is taken in this book by rendering the postmodern argument amenable to empirical testing.

In brief, I argue that the pressures of postmodernity have indeed brought about a macro-level fragmentation of culture, but, in contrast to postmodernism, I posit that the microdynamics of culture and meaning thus take on increased importance. Building on Heidegger and Giddens, I posit that people have a basic need for ontological security and for imposing facticity upon their experienced world (in Schutz's and Garfinkel's sense); hence actors seek out another level of experience beyond the fragmented, meaning-overturning arena of macro-cultural production—the level of increased interaction intensity that produces higher levels of affect-meaning and reification. But at the same time, the purely local, personal arena of primary groups, once grounded in family and community, cannot be the sole source of cultural stability, and thus I posit and explicate an arena of "secondary culture," a meso-level between mass-produced culture and personal interactions, where today's actors may perhaps seek their strongest affectual meanings. This secondary culture is used within social movements and organizations expressly oriented toward stabilizing meanings and identities in a world in which both macro-cultural production and personal relationships are in high levels of flux.

It is my position that many of the problems contained within the postmodern model are due principally to the inclusion of the basic error of structuralism: the structure of culture is privileged over agency, and affect-meaning is neglected in favor of sense-meaning. This structuralist turn is not restricted to postmodernism, but most contemporary approaches to culture take a linguistic-structuralist stance with regard to culture. I thus have two goals in this book. First, I present a critical reading of the major theories of culture within the sociological tradition. I generally divide the field into four main perspectives—structural, moral, subjective, ideological—based on how culture itself is conceptualized. I present both the classic and contemporary expressions of those perspectives for each of these positions, with the structuralist position subsumed under my discussion of postmodernism. My basic argument is that, on the whole, contemporary cultural theory has been unduly influenced by the linguistic/semiotic approach to culture. This emphasis has resulted in a general overemphasis on the signification system and the neglect of agency and affect-meaning. And the second purpose of this book is to generalize the dynamics posited by postmodernists and to place them in a theoretical context that explicates the microdynamics of culture and the production of meaning, in particular affect-meaning. Chapters 2, 3, and 4 contain my reviews and critiques of the moral, subjective, and ideological perspectives. At the conclusion of each chapter, I extract the general elements that would inform a theory of meaning and reality. Chapter 1 is a concise statement of postmodernism as developed by some of the more prominent authors. In that chapter I try to remain as true to the original expression as possible, while still explaining the position in more general terms. In Chapter 5, I generalize the theoretical elements proposed by postmodernists and bring them together with a general theory of meaning construction in order to move postmodernism forward and add to our general understanding of how culture works in advanced capitalist societies.

1

The Postmodern Problem and Linguistic-Structuralism

> *Referential value is annihilated, giving the structural play of value the upper hand.* The structural dimension becomes autonomous by excluding the referential dimension, and is instituted upon the death of reference. The systems of reference for production, signification, the affect, substance and history, all this equivalence to a "real" content, loading the sign with the burden of "utility," with gravity—its form of representative equivalence—all this is over with.
>
> —Jean Baudrillard (1976/1993, p. 6)

Defining postmodernism is a difficult task. Hall and Neitz (1993) note that "it is not possible to consider any specific viewpoint as representative of postmodernism and thus it is difficult to discuss postmodernism in general" (p. 247). From the subjective standpoint of the postmodernist, it is not only an impossible task, it is a task that should not be undertaken at all. Advocates claim that the quality of ambiguity is an essential attribute of the moment—the postmodern is a *fin-de-siècle* crisis—and attempts to categorize the movement are by definition modernist and thus deny the very phenomenon they try to capture. A definition of postmodernism is perhaps an oxymoron: at the core of the postmodern is the irreversible breakdown of categorical distinctions; reality is the sign, and the sign is free-floating and a reality unto itself. Even the word itself refuses to define the period: that which is "post" has not yet been defined as a separate thing in and of itself.

Even so, there have been attempts by postmodernists at staking the conceptual parameters of the perspective (e.g., Denzin, 1991, p. 27; Lemert, 1992, pp. 23–24) and at grounding postmodern theory in the works of Simmel (e.g., Weinstein & Weinstein, 1990), Weber (e.g., Turner, 1990), Mills (e.g., Soja, 1994), and Goffman (e.g., Battershill, 1990). These attempts by postmodernists to define the field and to link the concepts of postmodernism to prior theorists are a bit ironic. The act of finding the conceptual roots of one's theory in the classics is generally associated with theory cumulation, a tenet of positivistic social science. This grounding of theory has been derided by postmodernists as "logocentrism" (Gottdiener, 1990), the domestication and legitimization of new ideas, and is seen as a political ploy by established theorists to maintain their privileged position.

Zygmunt Bauman (1994) makes the point that the definition of modernity against which postmodernity makes its stand is defined within the postmodern discourse itself. Thus the distinction between postmodernism and modernism may be due to perception rather than actual conditions: "It is my view that the pair of concepts under discussion is important first and foremost (perhaps even solely) in the context of the self-awareness of the intellectuals" (Bauman, 1994, p. 195). Bauman also claims that postmodernity, for the intellectual, is a sense of anxiety that arises from the feeling that the kinds of services that created the status of the academic in modernity are no longer needed. This demand for intellectual services stems from the need of modern states for cognitive and normative legitimations for domination and the need for a huge system of social management.

Whether or not postmodernism is basically a conceptual problem for academics, the movement has captured the attention of the academy and the public alike. And in order to talk about a subject, the terms under discussion must have some agreed-upon meanings. Admittedly, I am not a postmodernist and the definition that I use is from an outsider's position. But it is not the case that I reject all that postmodernists have to say. It is my position that postmodernism has identified many important dynamics and processes at work in advanced capitalist societies; but, as will be seen, I do disagree with some of the conclusions reached. In this book, I use the following understanding of postmodernism (for an alternative definition, see Ritzer, 1997, pp. 8–9): Based on a critique of capitalism and mass media, postmodernism is essentially a critical stance that posits a break between signs and lived reality. This critique is complex and has various and nuanced permutations, but it does seem to have three themes continually woven throughout:

the problems associated with the production of knowledge, culture, and self in postmodernity.

THE DOUBT OF POSTMODERNISM AND THE PROBLEM OF KNOWLEDGE

Modernism posited and relied upon an assumed continuity between physical reality and its expression. In other words, human language was believed to represent accurately the world "out there." This assumption was necessary in order to fulfill the project that modernity had set before itself. Modernism grew out of the de-mystification of the universe. The assurance of divine care and intervention was replaced by the hope that science could discover and use lawlike principles to improve the condition of humanity, not only physically but socially as well. The age of modernity thus began by replacing a fatalistic philosophy with a positivistic approach to life—the universe was controllable and humans could make a difference in their own lives. And undergirding this new hope and determination was the necessary belief that human culture could be used to represent the world accurately. According to this belief, there is a single best language that corresponds to nature as it is and it is possible to discover and use "Nature's Own Language" (Rorty, 1994, p. 50). Therefore, certain languages, like mathematics and science, may be viewed as more objective and real, in this sense of representation.

At the core of postmodernism is a philosophical critique of this notion of representational knowledge. This critique focuses on the problem of representation and denies the assumption that human language can accurately reflect to the individual an image of reality. Signs or words are linguistic objects and not the physical object itself; and because they are constructs that point to something else, the relationship between the sign and its referent may be arbitrary. The complexity of the issue is pointed out by Charles Sanders Peirce (1931–1958). He claims that there are three elements involved in the process of representation: the word, the idea, and the object. None of these elements is equal to the other, nor are there any necessary relationships among them. There are thus potential gaps between the sign and its object, the sign and its meaning, and the meaning and its object. A modernist view assumes that there is a correspondence among these elements and that the sign and its meaning represent the object in the world in a true and clear fashion. This assumption, according to the modernist, is given legitimacy through the scientific method: science through rigorous methodology will close the gaps among the sign elements until there is an exact correspondence. But postmodernists focus on the issue of *assumed* correspondence. Because of the nature of language, it is still a matter of belief that true representation can be achieved and the gaps obliterated.

Richard Rorty (1979) pushes this philosophical critique even further by arguing that "without the notion of mind as mirror, the notion of knowledge as accuracy of representation would not have suggested itself" (p. 12). Thus, from Rorty's point of view, the issue of representational language is founded upon the false assumption that the mind can act as a mirror purely reflecting the world around it.   According to Rorty, it is the job of philosophy to deconstruct this false assumption and its correlate, the ability of language to represent the universe. It is not that Rorty (1979) wants to replace the assumption of representation with another epistemology; rather, it is his hope that "the cultural space left by the demise of epistemology will not be filled—that our culture should become one in which the demand for constraint and confrontation is no longer felt" (p. 315). Rorty espouses a hermeneutic approach to philosophy and knowledge, one that is comfortable with incommensurability. He suggests that the "traditional ideas of 'an absolute ("objective") conception of reality' and of 'scientific method' are neither clear nor useful" (Rorty, 1994, p. 50).

Rorty (1994) further asserts that even if there is a true reality and a true language with which to represent that reality, the moment humans use language it becomes evaluative, "for there is no way to prevent anybody using *any* term 'evaluatively'" (p. 50). The issue then can never be which language is more objective or scientific because the use of language is always directed toward pragmatic ends. Underlying every claim that one language brings a better understanding to a phenomenon than another is the assumption that it is more useful for a particular purpose. Thus epistemology is never a real concern, but, rather, the concern is always directed by the current practical concerns and these concerns are always value based. As Rorty (1994) claims, "vocabularies are useful or useless, good or bad, helpful or misleading, sensitive or coarse, and so on; but they are not 'more objective' or 'less objective' nor more or less 'scientific'" (p. 57). If it is the case that all human knowledge ends up being evaluative or morally infused, then what we are left with as the notion of pure human reality is "our awareness that we are members of a moral community" (Rorty, 1994, p. 56). And, for Rorty, the question of whether this is an objective fact is meaningless.

Charles Lemert (1990; 1995) and Zygmunt Bauman (1991; 1992) also argue that the problem of objective, representational knowledge is not a meaningful one; the problem exists only as an artifact of the legitimizing culture of Western, global domination. According to this position, representational knowledge is a belief that undergirds a cultural system that, in turn, supports a social structure. As with all incorrigible propositions (see Mehan & Wood, 1975, p. 9), it is an empty and senseless endeavor to question the validity of this belief. The issue simply does not exist apart from the culture and social structure for which it provides a basis. As Bauman (1994) explains, the vision of a universal Western culture is no longer practical, if it ever was, and this "impracticality erodes interest" (p. 190) in objective, scientific knowledge.

Lemert (1995) situates the beginning of this "crisis" in 1947 when Gandhi was successful in overthrowing British rule in India, and the crisis continued to build as others who were held under colonial rule fought for and won their independence. Since that time there "has been a continuing state of near global resistance to the idea that one or another Western power ought to rule a well-integrated world" (Lemert, 1995, p. x). Representational, scientific knowledge is thus conceived of as being the cultural support for the structure of a colonizing nation-state. Science provided the moral stance—objectification and manipulation—and the tools—objective knowledge and technology—to use the world and its inhabitants for the "greater good" of progress and world order, without regard for local, subjective experience and knowledge. As Bauman (1991) asserts, the modern state was "born as a crusading, missionary, proselytizing force, bent on subjecting the dominated populations to a thorough once-over in order to transform them into an orderly society, akin to the precepts of reason" (p. 20). Now that the hope of a world-dominating grand narrative is dead, the moral culture of science is held in doubt. And, so, for Lemert and Bauman, the issue of representation and a science of control is perhaps morally wrong, is certainly no longer viable, and has generally fallen out of favor due to the empirical failure of the nationalistic powers to unite the world in peace and safety.

For Jean-François Lyotard (1979/1984) the issue of representational knowledge is not historically specific and linked to changes in the social world, as with Lemert and Bauman. Rather Lyotard claims that the problem is more general: scientific knowledge presents itself as objective and separate from social factors and thus always lacks social legitimation. Building on a concept borrowed from Ludwig Wittgenstein, language as a game, Lyotard argues that the only legitimate use of language is social and thus the language of science is not valid. Wittgenstein (1936–1949/1973) proposes that there is an analogy between the way language works and how games are played. Games are produced and played for their own intrinsic enjoyment; there is no other reason for games to exist but for play, and play is its own reward. And, Wittgenstein claims, it is the same for language: the purpose of human language is to communicate, and the act of communication is both the function and reward of language. The justification for language, then, is not that it might accurately represent some separate reality; the justi-

fication for the existence (or the truth value) of language is simply that
it communicates and produces the social. For Wittgenstein the concept
of language expresses all that is wrapped up in the presentation, reception, and enactment of human expression. It is thus through the performance of "language games" that society exists.

Using Wittgenstein's analogy, Lyotard proposes a distinction between the social-narrative form and the denotative-scientific form of
knowledge. The narrative is a form of expression that is expressed
within a social group for the purpose of producing the social group, but
scientific knowledge is not expressed to produce and edify a social
group. On the contrary, science intends to be divorced from social factors
and simply to discover, represent, and manipulate the universe. From
the point of view of science, social narratives are belittled and seen as
"fables, myths, legends, fit only for women and children" (Lyotard,
1979/1984, p. 27). Science thus exalts itself above the narrative and
proclaims itself as the true form of knowledge, accurately representing
the world as it exists.

Lyotard argues that by bringing into question the legitimacy of
knowledge, science opens the door to having its own legitimation questioned. And because science does not exist to create social bonds, it has
no intrinsic justification for its existence: in its immediate, denotative
discourse concerning a specific phenomenon, science does not exist as a
socially legitimated knowledge system. Lyotard claims that in order
for science to be heard, it must appeal to an external form of narrative
knowledge, in this case a type of grand narrative. Grand narratives are
myths that subjugate local and subjective narratives for the purpose of
unification. The grand narrative that science appeals to is based on the
Enlightenment's promise of discovery and emancipation.   Lyotard
maintains that this need to appeal to a narrative reveals science to be a
language game like any other, simply existing for play and its own reification, and that science thus has no special authority or power to su-
pervise the other languages. Therefore, the authority and knowledge
claims of science are obliterated.   According to Lyotard's vision of
knowledge, dissension must now be emphasized rather than consensus;
heterogeneous claims to knowledge, in which one voice is not privileged
over another, is the only true basis of knowledge.

From the postmodernist position, this critique of representation and
scientific knowledge obviously holds for the social sciences—the social
world by definition does not objectively exist. People subjectively experience the world and express that experience in language. Thus every
attempt by the researcher to articulate the position or experience of
another person or group is simply a text expressing another person's
subjectivity. The problem is compounded in that when someone hears or
reads this expression of the social world, they are interpreting it

through their own subjectivity. Thus every expression of the world is essentially a text, a construction subject to deconstruction in which the factors and ideologies driving the text can be explicated. Each deconstruction of a text becomes itself a text, an object for legitimate analysis; and each subsequent analysis becomes a text, an object for analysis, ad infinitum.

For example, Richard Harvey Brown (1987; 1989; 1990) posits that social and cultural realities, and social science itself, are simply linguistic constructions. Brown (1989, pp. 49–54) advocates an approach to understanding the construction of knowledge that he terms "symbolic realism." Symbolic realism seeks to take the symbolic construction of social reality seriously. The human world cannot exist apart from the use of signs and symbols in communication. And each act of communication is based on prior understandings of the world that are shaped linguistically and symbolically. Symbolic realism critiques social theory and attempts to uncover the ideologies surrounding the premises upon which knowledge, selves, and realities are constructed.

Much like Rorty's pragmatism, Brown argues that the world that is understood as true at any given moment is shaped through normative, practical, epistemological, political, aesthetic, and moral practices which, in turn, are themselves symbolic constructions. Thus, because human reality is nothing more than culture, the search for the first or ultimate world/reality is a fruitless endeavor and the question of representational knowledge is senseless, particularly concerning the social world. Brown (1990) concludes that sociological theories exist as "practices through which things take on meaning and value, and not merely as representations of a reality that is wholly exterior to them" (p. 188). According to Brown, social theorists must recognize that their own theories are rhetorical constructions and simply relativistic texts. This rhetorical approach to social theory will see its discourse as not being *about society*, that is, not a true representation of what society is, but, rather, as being part of what *constitutes society* and completely contained within society and its representations.

Lemert (1995, pp. 17–20) sees a further qualifying factor for social scientific knowledge in that the substance of social science is essentially the product of imagination and talk. He argues that the social sciences are fundamentally concerned with structures and that structures are understood as those elements in reality that account for the most strongly organized and distinct areas within life. Structures thus endure over time and are seen to be important in all human behavior. But, Lemert claims, structures have a unique quality: they are never fully present and therefore depend upon the imaginative and discursive work of individual people for their existence. And social scientific work depends upon data gathered in the sometimes distant past. Therefore the structures that are examined exist, at best, as "virtual realities; at worst, ones dead years before" (Lemert, 1995, p. 19). Thus the world of sociology—or sociologies in Lemert's terms—is a reconstructed world, a world built of theory and story: "The reality of social structures, insofar as it can be grasped, is in what is said about them" (Lemert, 1995, p. 18).

Lemert (1990) indicates that the essential postmodernist position is one that believes that the "philosophical presumption that meaning and reality can be present to consciousness" (p. 236) is wrong and seeks to take language seriously on its own terms. That is, language must be understood not as expressing reality to humans but constituting human reality—language and the texts produced by the use of language are all that exist for human beings. And because this emphasis on language removes any exterior reference point for truth or reality, the texts of language are themselves a reality and are a kind of "play in a forever open and open-ended field which they produce and by which they are produced, and in which they must be interpreted" (Lemert, 1990, p. 239).

THE DYNAMICS OF POSTMODERNISM AND THE PROBLEM OF CULTURE

To take language seriously, as the constitutive feature of human reality, "is to de-center the world, to eviscerate it of grand organizing principles (God, natural law, truth, beauty, subjectivity, Man, etc.) that mask the most fundamental truth of human life, differences" (Lemert, 1990, p. 237). A postmodern understanding of difference demands the decentering of one's own perspective—acknowledging that there is no ultimate or essential truth behind one's perceptions of the world—and accepting the other and the self as equally and inexorably different. One of the grand themes of modernity is equality, but it is an equality achieved at the cost of difference through the production of a mass, unifying culture and a grand society. Ironically, postmodernists point out, it is the pressures inherent within the production of modern mass culture that lead to fragmentation rather than unification. According to this position, the culture of a society may become "schizophrenic" with no central, organizing feature and characterized by shifting and overlapping categories. Subjective experience likewise becomes transitory and uncertain, and the individual becomes the locus of many, perhaps innumerable, social categories, with various permutations of each. According to postmodernists, the culture of a society may become fragmented because of some specific social factors: changes in the capitalist mode of production and accumulation, the move from religion to markets as the central organizing feature of society, and the cultural shift from information to image that is facilitated by the mass media and advertising.

For some postmodernists, the distinction between modernity and postmodernity revolves around the classic Marxian issues of praxis, overaccumulation, and the spatial centralization of capital. But for these Marxists, culture is no longer understood as an epiphenomenon. The culture of a society still originates from the economy and economic relations, but it also, in turn, creates a set of necessary conditions for the economy which may have independent effects. Among the most important of these effects in postmodernity are the loss of national identity and the increased importance of group and personal identities, the loss of a core- or essential-self, the shift from the use of material means of control to symbolic means, the increased saliency and availability of cultural resources for resistance, and a general emotional disengagement of those influenced by postmodern culture.

Drawing on Marx's materialist philosophy of knowledge, Fredric Jameson (1979/1984) uses the concept of praxis to critique the social construction of reality in postmodernity. Marx argues that reality does not exist in concepts, ideas, or reflexive thought but in the material world of production. According to Jameson, praxis, the creation of human reality and consciousness through production, was unproblematically represented by the aesthetic of the machine in earlier phases of capitalism: early market capitalism and steam-driven machinery; mid-monopoly capitalism and a combination of steam and combustion engines. But in multinational capitalism, electronic machines—movie cameras, video, tape recorders, computers—do not have the same capacity for reality construction because they are machines of reproduction and not production.

Because the machines of late capitalism reproduce knowledge rather than produce it, and because the reproduction itself is focused more on the medium than the message, the link from production to signification has broken down. Thus the foundation of thought and knowledge in postmodernity is not simply false, as in classic Marxism, but it is nonexistent. Jameson characterizes this breakdown as the schizophrenia of culture. Based on Saussure's (1916/1966) notion that meaning is a function of the relationship between signifiers, the concept of a break in the signification chain indicates that each sign stands alone, or in a relatively loose association with fragmented groups of other signs, and that meaning is free-floating, not fixed to any external reality. Additionally, the breakdown of the language system and its inability to ground concepts one to another precipitates the disassociation of time and place sequences. The here-and-now is held together with the there-and-then conceptually, and concepts are meaningful only so long as they are related in a sign system; if the sign system is fragmented, meaning is not given nor guaranteed, and the conceptual relationships of time and place break apart. Thus the individual's experience and praxis simply become "a series of pure and unrelated presents in time" (Jameson, 1979/1984, p. 72).

In like manner, David Harvey (1989) posits that capitalism has brought about significant problems associated with the conceptualization of time and place, but, in contrast to Jameson, he argues that the problem is one of overaccumulation and not praxis. Harvey's argument is based on an assumed relationship between the mode of capital accumulation and its mode of regulation, that is, the cultural norms, habits, laws, and regulating networks. Capitalism has used different modes of accumulation, and, due to the capitalist imperatives of growth, exploitation, and technological and organizational innovation, each mode has been subject to the problem of overaccumulation. According to Harvey, this problem may be met through three principal means: devaluation of products, productive capacity, or money; macroeconomic controls; or, the absorption of surplus through temporal and/or spatial displacement. Displacement is the more robust option, but temporal and spatial displacement of capital (e.g., lending speculative or futures capital raised in London to build Latin American infrastructures) must be used together in order to mitigate the problems associated with each.

This kind of "flexible capitalism" combines with other social factors to produce a sense of time/place compression where these two dimensions of human reality tend to lose their significance and become free-floating. Increased communication and transportation technologies, more rationalized distribution processes, faster money circulation, and flexible capitalism all work to move products, people, ideas, and money faster through place with less regard for physical barriers. When these changes occur rapidly, they create a perceived sense of time/place compression wherein people lose their orientation to time and place. Harvey argues that until the mode of regulation, culture, catches up to the changes in the mode of accumulation, a period of disorientation ensues where people are unsure of how to relate to and conceptualize the basic dimensions of time and place. He argues that postmodernity is such a period of time/place compression. Physical place has lost it importance and has been replaced with social space, and the definition of social space is determined by highly differentiated markets and cultural images.

Additionally, Harvey posits, commodity markets have diversified and have become dominated by commodities of service, rather than product, and commodities of identity. The cultural emphasis on image, fashion, and identity, and the shift from product to service consumption, have increased the pace of consumption and the volatility and ephemerality of the products consumed. In the face of a culture that values instant gratification and disposability coupled with the sheer numbers of commodity stimuli, people generally react with sensory block, denial, a blasé attitude, myopic specialization, increased nostalgia, and an increased search for eternal, but simplified truths, and collective or personal identity.

Scott Lash and John Urry (1987; 1994) also argue that shifting conceptualizations of time and place are associated with changes in capitalism and that postmodern culture is influenced by the mass media and advertising, but they add that the "postmodern disposition" is particularly dependent upon the fragmentation of class experience and the rise of the service class. Unlike Harvey, they do not see postmodern culture as necessarily a temporary phase of adjustment, but, rather, a culture to which certain audiences with postmodern dispositions will respond. Postmodern culture is particularly classless and is predicated upon the breakdown of boundaries and "finds an audience when the boundaries which structure our identities breakdown; that is, during personal experiences of 'liminality' during which identity is unstable" (Lash & Urry, 1987, p. 15). Postmodern culture is particularly salient for middle-class youth in late capitalist countries, because of the demands of greater education and the extended period of unstable identity, and for the expressive professions in the service class.

There are three social conditions necessary for the creation of postmodern predispositions: one, the boundary between reality and image must be blurred as the media presents ready-made (as opposed to socially emergent) cultural images; two, a new class must be formed which is created and controlled through the consumption of goods for their symbolic power to produce and proclaim distinctions, that is, the service class; and, three, personal identity must be decentered through the decreasing importance of place for the creation of identity. This loss of place, associated with the spatial deconcentration of capital and labor, leads to an increase in the importance of culture for the formation of subjectivities and identities.

While Lash and Urry are reluctant to speak in terms of causation, it appears that there are at least four lines of deciding factors that bring about these postmodern preconditions. The first line involves the shift from Taylorist to flexible forms of organizing and controlling labor. Like Harvey, this decreased spatial concentration of labor-capital along with increases in communication and transportation technology appear to be Lash and Urry's principal dynamic of change. The second line involves large-scale economic changes: the globalization of a market economy, the expansion of industry and banking across national boundaries, and the spread of capitalism into third world countries. Third, they argue that increases in distributive capacities move the flow of commodities from the local/national to the international level. This increased scope and speed of circulation empties commodities of their symbolic and affective meaning as well as their material content, becoming primarily commodities with either cognitive or aesthetic features. And the fourth line involves cultural changes concerning the commodification of leisure, the decodification of some previously acceptable cultural forms, and the reduction of the importance of time and place into the politics of social space. Together these forces create a spatially fragmented division of labor, a decreased working class and an increased service class in terms of size and resources, increased importance in symbolic rather than material or coercive domination, increased cultural resources for resistance, and increased cultural fragmentation and pluralism with a decreasing ability to create national subjects.

While Jameson, Harvey, and Lash and Urry explicate the social-economic processes involved in postmodernity, they all see the primary effects to be cultural; and these cultural effects reciprocally become causal for the economy, society, and human experience. Postmodernists have placed culture at the center of the social science agenda but for different reasons than did functionalists such as Durkheim and Parsons. Postmodernists argue that it is the fragmenting effects of culture on human experience, subjectivity, and emotional health that make culture a primary concern. As Daniel Bell (1976) argues, the very existence of culture sets in motion a "wheel of questions" concerning existential predicaments such as pain and death. The meanings in back of these issues are ultimately incomprehensible for humans, yet in the case of premodern societies, the endless cycle of questions is stopped by the institutional place of religion. But, modern societies are defined by economic activity, not religious: they are characterized by the boundlessness of capitalism and are therefore ever changing. In capitalism, a tension always exists between the cultural directive of asceticism for capital accumulation and the need of the market for a culture of acquisition. The two can coexist as long as there is a general religious or moral center, as in the case of early Protestantism. But the erosion of the religious center coupled with an increase in discretionary spending has led to a market-driven culture of personality. And because the very nature of fashion trivializes culture, it is no longer morally centered nor able to provide a legitimation for the society beyond a market-oriented, individualistic culture.

Thus, for the postmodernist, culture has become the central feature and dynamic in advanced capitalist societies. Of particular concern for many postmodernists are the effects that the mass media have upon culture. The strongest postmodern statement concerning these effects comes from Jean Baudrillard (1972/1981; 1973/1975; 1981/1994;

1976/1993). In contrast to the postmodern critique of knowledge, Baudrillard's theory is based on the assumption that there is at least potential equivalence between a sign and its physical object. Based on this proposition, Baudrillard posits four phases of the sign. In the first phase, the sign truly represented reality, and there was an exact correlation between the sign and the reality it represented. In the next two phases, signs dissimulated or hid reality in some way: during the second phase signs masked or counterfeited reality, as art elaborating life; and in the third phase, signs masked the absence of any profound social reality. The second phase roughly corresponds to the period of time from the Renaissance to the Industrial Revolution, and the third phase occurred during the Industrial Age, when production became the dominate cultural force creating a commodified sign-value that went beyond the classic Marxian use- or exchange-value.

The fourth stage of the sign is the present postmodern era, and in this time a fundamental break has occurred between the sign and the lived reality of human beings. Baudrillard argues that life in an advanced capitalist society is based largely on images from past lives. People participate in activities that are no longer real in and of themselves but are performed for some other purpose, generally image related. For example, when people in postindustrial societies "work" their bodies, it is usually no longer for the purpose of production, but, rather, as a regimen of exercise designed to alter the body to meet some cultural image. And the method and clothing of this work is not strictly functional but is again concerned mostly with image. Thus when the media and advertising seek to represent this "life," the culture that is produced is pure simulacrum: an image of an image.

Further, Baudrillard argues that the act of presenting information through the media intrinsically destroys information. This destruction occurs because there is a natural entropy within the information process. Any information of an event is a degraded form of the event and is a step removed from the real social world. The media's representation has been removed an infinite number of times from the actual social event and is nothing more than a conglomeration of image bits and signs. The media also destroys information because the bulk of the work that goes into presenting media information is expended on staging. Information is presented in a form whose organization is dictated by the different kinds of information available for delivery—the economic and political concerns of the business, the state of technology, and the current tastes of the consuming public. Mass communication thus comes prepackaged in a meaning form that has no real relationship to the actual events depicted but is intrinsically linked to the medium itself. As a result, the presentation of information through the media is sim-

ply a group of self-referencing images that are nonsystematically related.

Baudrillard additionally posits that the break between reality and
the sign was facilitated by advertising. The act of advertising itself
reduces objects from their use-value to their sign-value: as advertise-
ments become commodities in and of themselves, image rather than information becomes the content of the commodity. According to Marx,
the value of a commodity may be determined by its actual consumption,
its use-value, or by its value in exchange for other commodities. For
Baudrillard, the movement from use-value to exchange-value entails
an abstraction of the former; in other words, the exchange-value of a
commodity is based on a representation of its possible use. This process
of abstraction continues because of the effects of mass media and advertising: the exchange-value of a commodity is replaced with a sign-
value—people purchase commodities more for what they sign than
what they do—and thus the advertised image of the sign-value is
nothing more than a representation of a representation, or, a simulacrum of a simulacrum. Advertising does not seek to convey information
about a product's use-value; rather, advertising places a product in a
field with other unrelated signs in order to enhance its cultural ap-
pearance. For example, the use-value of a car—transportation—is
rarely seen among the advertised images of sex, sport, and status.

Like Baudrillard's media-as-reality approach, Norman K. Denzin
(1986; 1991a; 1992) argues that television and other media forms provide the fundamental reality for people in postmodernity. But, in contrast to Baudrillard, Denzin argues that media images provide a
legitimate reality and function in much the same way as traditional
myth and ritual by integrating individuals into the social fabric by
presenting a set of taken-for-granted identities, in particular, race,
class, and gender. Denzin uses the postmodern critique and emphasis on
media and culture to present a media-based theory of stratification.
Denzin argues that people's lived experience has become the final
commodity in the circulation of capital and that the producers of postmodern culture selectively choose which lived experiences will be
commodified. Hence postmodern culture commodifies only those cultures that present a particular picture of race, class, and gender relations. Through commodification these selected cultures become
objectified and culturally available, and those people that stand outside of these objectified and reified cultural ideals experience alienation.

Yet, Denzin claims, because culture has become of central importance
in postmodernity, this process of commodification may in the long run
have a positive effect, if the lived experience that is commodified is
that of a disenfranchised group. In order to begin this process, Denzin

advocates a method of social activism through hermeneutically and critically reading the texts of media presentations in order to discover the underlying ideologies, discourses, and meanings that the political economy produces. The purpose of these critical readings is to "give a voice to the voiceless, as it deconstructs those popular culture texts which reproduce stereotypes about the powerless" (Denzin, 1991a, p. 153).

THE LOSS OF MEANING: THE PROBLEM OF SELF AND GROUP IDENTITY

For the postmodernist, then, there is a direct relationship between the state of the cultural system and the subjective experience of individuals and social groups. Most of the above theorists arrive at the same critical point: the problems of the individual living in a fragmented culture. As the ready-made meaning structure in religion is deinstitutionalized and systemically available meaning becomes free-floating, the individual subject becomes the locus of meaning construction but is left to flounder in a sea of commodified cultural images produced by the market-driven mass media. For example, Harvey claims that people become blasé and disassociated as culture is unable to keep up with social changes; Lash and Urry agree but add that postmodern culture is most salient for those whose identity is unstable, because of living in liminal space. And Jameson brings the characteristics of late multinational capitalism to bear on the individual subject. Corresponding to his argument concerning the problem of praxis, he argues that the culture of postmodernity has created a fragmented rather than alienated subject; according to Jameson, there is no longer a basis in praxis-knowledge for an alienated subject. Additionally, the decentering of the postmodern self produces a general kind of emotional flatness or depthlessness "since there is no longer any self to do the feeling . . . [emotions] are now free-floating and impersonal" (Jameson, 1979/1984, p. 64). The subject is thus fragmented and dissolved, having no basis in consciousness or narrative.

Like Jameson, Baudrillard sees the end of the core-self identity but bases his pronouncement concerning the death of the subject upon the effects of the mass media and advertising. Because the media present signs, categories, and images that are devoid of any socially based information, and because the media are driven by advertising, itself a commodity concerned with image and not information, the self has only simulacrum with which to be formed and sustained. Baudrillard thus argues that the subject no longer operates as a dramaturgical actor but as simply a mass media terminal with multiple networks filled with empty and disconnected images.

Like Baudrillard, Kenneth Gergen (1991) argues that as a result of postmodern culture the subject has become saturated with images that are simply incoherent and unrelated elements in different languages of the self. And corresponding to Baudrillard's death of the subject, Gergen posits that the category of the self has been erased. Gergen argues that the central psychological problem of living in a postmodern culture is the increased population of the self. That is, due to increases in communication/mass media and transportation technologies—what Gergen refers to as the technologies of social saturation—social encounters have increased in terms of sheer numbers, diversity, frequency of contact, endurance through time, and the level of expressed intensity. People are thus inundated with knowledge concerning different groups, different people, different values, and different modes of expression. Yet this increased social saturation does not stand alone as a problem for subjective experience—social saturation takes place in a cultural milieu of postmodern doubt.

As noted above, postmodernism is based on a philosophical critique of knowledge. This lack of any sure foundation for knowledge, according to Gergen, has been internalized by the general population and has produced a chronic sense of doubt—belief in rationality has been lost as it is now seen as a simple rhetorical device used to justify the position and privilege of certain groups; and authority has been given up to chronic doubt: people have come to view knowledge as transitory and unstable, rather than sure and true as in modernity. The development of this postmodern consciousness has resulted in an increase in the amount of reflexivity in which individuals engage. Gergen seems to indicate that reflexivity becomes almost never-ending for individuals in postmodernity. This increased reflexivity is directed toward the self as people increase their self-monitoring in a culture that is socially saturated and filled with constant change and doubt. And because reflexivity is ever increasing, the individual comes to doubt the objectified-self. The result is what Gergen refers to as multiphernia—vertigo of self-values filled with expressions of inadequacy—and the pastiche personality.

Bauman (1992) argues that as a result of the process of de-institutionalization people live in complex, chaotic systems. Complex systems differ from mechanistic systems in that they are unpredictable and not controlled by statistically significant factors. Thus, in contrast to Denzin's argument, race, class, and gender no longer produce strong or constant effects in the individual's life or self-concept. Within these complex systems, identity formation consists of the nonlinear activity of self-constitution with no reference point for evaluation or monitoring, no life long and consistent project of self-formation. People thus experience a high degree of uncertainty with regard to identity.

Bauman also argues that the absence of any firm and objective evaluative guide tends to create a demand for a substitute. These substitutes are symbolically created. The need for these symbolic group tokens results in what Bauman (1992, pp. 198–199) calls "tribal politics" and defines as self-constructing practices that are collectivized but not socially produced. These neo-tribes function solely as imagined communities and, unlike their premodern namesake, exist only in symbolic form through the commitment of individual "members" to the idea of an identity. But this neo-tribal world functions without an actual group's powers of inclusion and exclusion. They are created through the repetitive, and generally solo or imaginative, performance of symbolic rituals and exist only so long as the rituals are performed. Neo-tribes are thus formed through concepts rather than actual social groups. They exist as imagined communities through a multitude of agent acts of self-identification and exist solely because people use them as vehicles of self-definition: "Neo-tribes are, in other words, the vehicles (and imaginary sediments) of individual self-definition" (Bauman, 1992, p. 137).

Since the persistence of these tribes depends upon the affective allegiance of the members, self-identifying rituals become more extravagant and spectacular. Spectacular displays are necessary because in postmodernity the true scarce resource upon which self and other is based is public attention. In the age of imagined communities, it is the human imagination that is the most sought-after scarce resource. Imagination grants existence, and the imagination is sparked by attention. "To catch the attention, displays must be ever more bizarre, condensed and (yes!) disturbing; perhaps ever more brutal, gory and threatening" (Bauman, 1992, p. xx). It is the symbolic significance of events and displays that matters, not the actual damage that such displays may inflict (e.g., hostages, public poisoning, riots, marches, nudity).

THE REIGNING STRUCTURE AND THE DISABLED AGENT

Postmodernists argue that because there is not a truth or reality that exists for humans apart from language or the ideological interests of humans, discontinuity of knowledge is the norm and a permanent and irreducible pluralism of cultures is the truth that humans must continually face. This postmodern "truth" has been revealed due to specific historical processes, such as the move to flexible or disorganized capitalism, the presence of machines of reproduction rather than production in multinational capitalism, the failure of Western society to dominate the world, increases in communication and transportation technologies, the influence of capitalism and advertising on the mass media, the deinstitutionalization of ultimate meanings, the philosophical critique of knowledge, and so on. Knowledge of this truth produces a pervasive sense of doubt for people living in postmodernity: doubt concerning the hope of grand narratives (e.g., nationalism, religion), doubt concerning the rational process of problem solving, and doubt concerning the possibility of finding stable answers in a shifting culture.

The effect of this doubt on human experience is compounded by the fact that the culture of postmodernity is fragmented and meaning is free-floating. Because religion and the state have receded as the dominant force in society and have been replaced by the market, institutionally legitimated answers are no longer available to people. With the image-dominated market as the central driving impetus in society, culture has become subject to the expansive needs and trivialization of the market. Capitalist markets must continually expand both vertically and horizontally in order to sustain the profit motive. As the market expands, it must continually commodify more and more images. This commodification lifts out from group-specific bounds the subjective experience of its members and thus trivializes that group's culture.

As Mark Gottdiener (1985; 1995) argues, signs in a technologically advanced society may circulate between people's everyday life and the act of commodification, where the symbol is lifted out of the group-specific culture and made available to any with the means to purchase it. Based on Baudrillard's use of sign-value, Gottdiener argues that there are three separate fields of interaction in which cultural signs are given meaning. Within each stage, the actors may "transfunctionalize" the objects (change the functional value) and give them a different kind of meaning. At the first level, economically motivated producers create commodities for their exchange-value. The intent of the people at this level is different than those who buy the commodity. The purchaser is primarily interested, according to Gottdiener, in the product's use-value, not its exchange-value. After purchase, however, the products become involved in the second level where these commodified objects become involved in the everyday life of the social groups that use them. During this stage, users may transfunctionalize the object from its use-value to a sign-value through the process of personalization, in order to connect the object to their subgroup or culture. The third stage occurs if and when the economic producers adopt those now personalized objects and transfunctionalize them into commodities with exchange-value. This third stage involves a "symbolic leveling" or "trivialization" of the signed object and the group's culture (Gottdiener, 1985, p. 996).

According to postmodernists, the outcomes of cultural fragmentation, trivialization, and doubt are automatic: the death of the subject, an emotional flatness or blasé attitude, the loss of unifying narratives, the corresponding rise of neo-tribes and imagined communities, and the decisive break between the sign and reality. Because of the macro-level social and cultural changes in postmodernity, and the effects noted above, the individual is simultaneously seen as the locus of cultural reality and a disabled cultural actor, made such by the fragmented structure of culture and the prevailing doubt concerning the possibility of ever arriving at a place of knowing. As a result of the removal of structural constraints and grand narratives, the subject is saturated with an overabundance of disjointed media images and social encounters and is left with no firm, central orienting image around which to build and reference their own self or reality. Thus individuals experience a high degree of reflexivity, always questioning but never arriving at an answer; they associate primarily with symbolic groups through imaginative rituals and gaudy displays; and, as a result, their ability to invest emotionally in cultural reality is severely diminished. They become disassociated, depressed, and affectively flat.

As a consequence of this line of argument, postmodernists are preoccupied with text. For most postmodernists, reality exists only in texts consisting of free-floating signs. As Baudrillard claims (1981/1994), in the postmodern age the sign "has no relation to any reality whatsoever: it is its own pure simulacrum" (p. 6). Texts are seen as cultural expressions that may be read as linguistic artifacts. Postmodern analysis seeks to "deconstruct" texts and to uncover how they are constructed and given meaning, that is, how signs are related to other signs within the field and to shifting but identifiable ideologies. Thus Gottdiener (1995) deconstructs the linguistic code found in real estate signs to expose their ideological representations; and Denzin (1991b) decodes the "political texts" found in such films as *When Harry Met Sally* and *sex, lies, and videotape*, in order to uncover the postmodern sexual order, or *Rain Man* (1993), to discover the postmodern self.

Yet it is important to note that in one sense the postmodern critique contains no new insights. The critique of absolute or representational knowledge is an accepted part of the philosophy of science and social science (e.g., Kuhn, 1962; Feyerabend, 1975/1988; Dilthey, 1961; Weber, 1904/1949). The reflexive and contingent construction of social/cultural reality is a primary component of ethnomethodology (see Mehan & Wood, 1975). The basic idea that society and self are symbolically constituted has been part of sociology's intellectual heritage since the work of George Herbert Mead (1934/1962). Thus, from the point of view of symbolic interactionism, institutions and identities and social groups have always been principally created through symbolic and imaginative work. That people consume commodities for their symbolic-value and not necessarily their use-value was the central insight of Thorstein

Veblen (1899/1912). Marx and Engels (1848/1961) and Georg Lukács (1922/1971) explained the expansive and devaluing character of commodification. And Simmel (1908/1955; 1950) pointed out the possible complex emotional effects of living in modernity. What is unique about the claims of postmodernism is that a radical schism is hypothesized between the language that humans use and lived reality, a schism that results in a disabled cultural agent. This unique feature is predicated upon emphasizing the macrostructure of culture over the experience of people at the micro-level, a position that has much in common with structuralism.

The intellectual heritage of postmodernism reaches back to French Structuralism and the work of Ferdinand de Saussure (1916/1959) and Claude Lévi-Strauss (1949/1969; 1958/1963). Saussure gave twentieth-century structuralism its basic foundation when he posited a distinction between *langue* (language) and *parole* (speech). This distinction is the core from which Saussure argued that structure is the prime mover of history: Language is immutable in the short term, and it exists as a social fact outside of and a priori to interaction; the structure of language must therefore be the cause of the immediate social phenomenon, that is, speech. Language confronts the speaker as a static state, as having always existed, and it is the static state of language that influences speech, not speech that affects language. Language may change through time (diachrony), but the structuralist approaches it as a closed system at a single point in time (synchrony), just as the individual experiences it.

Further, Saussure argued that the very nature of the sign adds to the constancy, and thus the efficacy, of the language structure. A linguistic sign is a "psychological entity" with two elements: the signified (the concept) and the signifier (the sound image). These two elements are meaningfully connected in that a change in one necessitates a change in the other. Saussure (1916/1959) likens this relationship to a piece of paper in that "one cannot cut the front without cutting the back at the same time" (p. 113). Additionally, the relationship between the two elements is arbitrary, that is, there is nothing inherent within the sound image that links it to the concept. The arbitrary nature of the relation places emphasis on the social origin of the structure: the relationship between signifier and signified is not a function of innate mental categories (à la Kant) nor ultimately a feature of obdurate objects (à la Hume). But the concept also puts the structure of language outside immediate agency. Because the relationship is arbitrary, it has no "reasonable basis" for discussion and thus lacks the necessary foundation for change. For Saussure, then, the immutability of the sign itself and the a priori existence of the language system form the conceptual support for the determinant nature of the structure.

Though Saussure provided its basic tenets, Claude Lévi-Strauss is considered the "father of structuralism" and was the first to adapt Saussure's semiology to the general social sciences (Kurzweil, 1980). He, like Saussure, argued that meaning does not abide in the sign itself but in the relations between signs: "The error of traditional anthropology, like that of traditional linguistics, was to consider the terms, and not the relations between the terms" (Lévi-Strauss, 1958/1963, p. 46). But Lévi-Strauss also extended Saussure's program. In particular, he extended Saussure's linguistic, structuralist approach to include all forms of social phenomenon; he was the first to bring to the forefront the linguistic equivalence model so prominent in postmodernism today. As Kurzweil (1980) notes, Lévi-Strauss's theory of unconscious structures led "to the creation of various new subjects of inquiry such as the relationships between the structures of all signs in language, their function within messages, and their rapport with other sign systems, such as music, gestures, body language" (p. 25).

For the structuralist, the lived experience of groups and individuals is simply an expression of the objectified structure, which, from the perspective of the individual, lies outside the sphere of agency. This emphasis on the structure gave early theorists a fervent hope of emulating the physical sciences: "Structural linguistics will certainly play the same renovating role with respect to the social sciences that nuclear physics, for example, has played for the physical sciences" (Lévi-Strauss, 1958/1963, p. 33). But the failure of this hope is one of the strands that led to the poststructuralist movement. Poststructuralism denies the ability of science to "discover" the structure underlying lived experience, because that structure does not exist. The structure is itself a product of the writing of a text, something Derrida (1967/1976) refers to as "arche-writing," and "although its concept is *invoked* by the themes of 'the arbitrariness of the sign' and of difference, [arche-writing] cannot and can never be recognized as the *object of a science*. It is that very thing which cannot let itself be reduced to the form of *presence*" (pp. 56–57).

Poststructuralism and its methodological counterpart, deconstructionism, reject the notion that there is a universal structure contained within the code of language. Language and its code are themselves linguistic constructions, and every element within the system contains only traces of all the other elements. And since all the linguistic elements exist only by virtue of the other sign elements, there can be no ultimate origin or truth or center to an overarching structure. But, ironically, while poststructuralism has sought to turn structuralism on its head by rejecting the hope of discovering the assumed grand structure and its influence on lived experience, it continues to replicate the basic error inherent within the structuralist approach: the structure of the system continues to be privileged because the subjective experience of the active agent at the micro-level is ignored or is seen as a product of cultural texts. Postmodernism continues to replicate the reductionism of structuralism, as modified through the disillusionment of poststructuralism—text constitutes all that is real. As George Ritzer (1997) states, poststructuralism is "*the* most important theoretical source of postmodern social theory" (p. 32).

The influence of structuralism on postmodern thought also comes through contemporary semiotics (see Nöth, 1995, pp. 295–326). As Mark Gottdiener (1995) states: "An understanding of semiotics is essential for an appreciation of postmodernism. Not only do the arguments of well-known postmodern thinkers, such as Derrida, rely on a knowledge of semiotics, but the entire trajectory of thought that began with poststructuralism draws on the internal critiques of semiotic models" (p. 3). The work of Roland Barthes especially informs the semiotic aspect of postmodernism (see Clarke, 1990, p. 133). Barthes (1964/1972; 1964/1967; 1970/1974) reaffirms Saussure's distinction between language and speech, arguing that language is a social institution and is thus not reducible to action or agency: "the individual cannot by himself either create or modify it. . . . it resists the modifications coming from a single individual, and is consequently a social institution" (Barthes, 1964/1967, p. 14). But, to a greater degree than Saussure, Barthes (1964/1967) explicitly recognizes the dependency of language on speech: "speech phenomena always precede language phenomena (it is speech which makes language evolve)" (p. 16). Additionally, Barthes elaborates Lévi-Strauss's model of linguistic equivalence by arguing that culture is completely reducible to language: "every semiological system has its linguistic admixture. . . . there is no meaning that is not designated, and the world of signifieds is none other than that of language" (Barthes, 1964/1967, p. 10).

Barthes also expands Saussure's concept of the sign; the sign is defined as having both denotative and connotative functions. That is, a primary sign is composed of an expression (signifier) in relation to a content (signified), what Barthes refers to as its denotative meaning. The denotative meaning is the surface or apparent meaning (e.g., Barthes example of a black in a military uniform saluting a national flag). But a primary sign may also form part of a more complex expression: the original sign, its expression and content, can become the signifier of a secondary sign which is linked to a new content; this union forms the connotative meaning (in this example, the state has loyal black citizens indicating that the state is fair and just). Connotation is itself a sign system and becomes increasingly important in modern societies: "the future probably belongs to a linguistics of connotation, for society continually develops, from the first system which human language supplies to it, second-order significant systems" (Barthes, 1964/1967, p. 10). This formulation suggests endless layering of signification systems, each within a larger context, a suggestion that Barthes made explicit in his analysis of myth.

For Barthes, myths are second-order connotative systems, and he moves the analysis of myth from the narrative form (Lévi-Strauss) to an element of everyday life. In Barthes's formulation, myths become instruments of cultural domination: they function primarily through mass media as ideological realities that serve to both oppress and hide the oppression. Thus systems of connotation can link ideological messages to more primary, denotative meanings, making them appear more natural. This perspective of myth and connotation assumes a primary, real level of meaning, the denotative, upon which the connotative is appended. Yet Barthes (1970/1974) came to realize that "denotation is not the first meaning, but pretends to be so; under this illusion, it is ultimately no more than the *last* of the connotations" (p. 9). And this conceptualization implies that there is nothing but language or text and that texts do not have a single structure but are traversed by different codes which are the source of meaning(s), a key perspective for the postmodernist.

Because of the fundamental error of structuralism and the exclusive use of the semiotic linguistic equivalence model, a theoretical gap exists in the postmodern critique. Like the structuralist, the postmodernist places almost exclusive emphasis on the culture of a society; and whether influenced by economic, societal, or media forces, the culture is seen as fragmented. From this fragmented structure of culture, it is postulated that the subject's experience of meaning and reality is shattered as well, but this assumption is made with little theoretical basis. Because of their intellectual heritage, postmodernists, in general, have not been sensitive to the theoretical ramifications of reality construction. According to the general theory of meaning and reality construction presented in this book, in the face of a fragmented culture, it is not necessarily the case that the experience of individuals and groups will become emotionally flat and significantly divorced from reality. Yet because of the conceptual core inherited from structuralism and semiotics, postmodernism has neglected the general ramifications of reality production on the individual, overestimated the emotional effects of fragmentation, and in the main neglected the action of agents at the micro-level that allows them to produce a sufficiently reified and stable reality.

More importantly this same theoretical gap exists in many of the major, contemporary sociological perspectives of culture. As will be demonstrated in the following chapters, the culture-as-language approach as first proposed by linguistic structuralism and modified by

semiotics has become the reigning paradigm in cultural analysis. Mac-
Cannell and MacCannell (1982) refer to this cross-disciplinary influence of structuralism as "the semiotic revolution" and argue that the
revolution occurred because "central human concerns were coming to be
understood as problems of *language*" (p. 4). However, as Eugene Halton
(1992) eloquently points out: "Such theories claim to do justice to the
systematic nature of human signification, but in reality they grossly
exaggerate those aspects of signification concerning conceptual systems—as though culture were a domain of knowledge instead of a way
of living—while ignoring or distorting those aspects of signification
that reside outside the boundaries of rationality and systems" (p. 33).
In the final analysis, the structuralist, linguistic equivalence approach
tends to produce consistent theoretical and analytical problems: agency
is disabled, and meaning is understood simply in terms of sense-
meaning. If the social dynamics proposed by postmodernism are correct,
as I believe they are, then the paramount sociological problem of this
time concerns the production and stabilization of cultural reality at the
micro-level, a problem which contemporary theory has neglected.

2

The Subjective View and the Social Construction of Sense-Meaning

> All animals are confronted with the challenge of material sub-
> sistence, but only humans are straddled with the vexing ques-
> tion of its meaning.
>
> —Snow and Anderson (1993, p. 229)

Culture is principally concerned with the production and reproduction
of meaning. There are two analytically distinct attributes of meaning
when used with reference to culture and reality construction. The concept of meaning may be used to refer to sense-meaning: the meaning that
is attributed to a sign or symbol as the result of the structured qualities
of language. For example, Saussure (1916/1959) argued that "language
is a system of interdependent terms in which the value of each term
results *solely* [italics added] from the simultaneous presence of the others" (p. 114). In other words, the meaning of a sign is constructed
through its relationship to other signs.

According to Saussure, there are two specific types of relationships
between linguistic terms. Within a sentence, whether in a written text
or a conversation, combinations of elements are supported and given
meaning by linearity. That is, the combinations of words that can appear together in a sentence are limited. These limited combinations
define the meaning of any one word that stands within a combination
through opposition to every other element that comes before or after it.
Saussure (1916/1959) termed this relationship "syntagmatic" (p. 123).

The other specific relationship that a sign may have is more conceptual and lies outside the immediate sentence. These are associative
relations and, because the concept behind the sign suggests other like
concepts, they constitute relations of equivalence. Saussure offered the
example of an architectural column. The column has a certain relationship with the rest of the building that it supports; this arrangement of
physical elements in space illustrates the syntagmatic relation. But if
the column is known to be Doric, it might also suggest a mental comparison with other styles even though none of the other styles is present in
physical space.

But, whether the relationships are syntagmatic or associative, the
meaning that is derived is based upon the structured relationships
among the signs. This kind of meaning is what I intend by the term
"sense-meaning"—the meaning that makes sense. Yet there is another
kind of meaning that is associated with culture and reality, affect-
meaning. With affect-meaning I am trying to capture the emotional
impact that a sign or discourse may have upon human beings. The concept does not denote the emotional, subjective experience that may be
associated with any given cultural item. That kind of emotion tends to
be individualistic and refers to the specific content of the experience;
for example, my dislike for artichokes is subjective and refers to the
content of my feelings about the vegetable. Affect-meaning refers to the
level of emotional energy (see Collins, 1988, pp. 361–362) that any specific part of culture can elicit from individuals or collectives and thus
the symbol's degree of impact.

The concept of affect-meaning is important for cultural analysis because it draws attention to the emotional component of culture that produces the general motivation that people feel, that creates group
boundaries, and produces a sense of "facticity" about culture. Much of
the culture that humans use is formulated through a set of arbitrary
relations. Peirce's (1867/1991, p. 30) distinction between the sign and
symbol will help clarify what I mean. Peirce's concept of the symbol
has a corresponding relationship to the physical universe. For example, the e-mail symbol of :-), a smile, has a corresponding relationship
to an actual, physical smile. On the other hand, a sign's relationship
to the physical universe is completely arbitrary—there is no correspondence between the words used in these sentences and a physical reality. This arbitrary nature of signs makes their meaning ultimately
contingent upon human interaction and agreement. Signs thus intrinsically have a certain amount of uncertainty about them, they are by
definition one step removed from obdurate reality. Thus, when culture
is perceived as being factual, that sense of facticity is a social product,
even in the case of science. One important way in which this facticity
is achieved is through investing culture with affect-meaning. Cultural

reality must be felt-to-be-real; and, as Durkheim (1912/1995) argued, social facts are created by swaddling culture in emotion.

But the issue of affect-meaning has generally been ignored by cultural theorists. There are at least three reasons for this neglect. First, because of its association with Durkheim and Parsons, issues of emotion and culture are generally regulated to the realm of values. As Ann Swidler (1986) comments, although sociologists may talk about values and culture, it "is not because sociologists really believe in the values paradigm. Indeed, it has been thoroughly criticized" (p. 273). Second, the concept of emotion and meaning seems to indicate an investigation into the subjective realm of personal experience. For example, Robert Wuthnow (1987) argues that the subjective experience of actors is inaccessible to sociologists, and, as such, he wants to move the analysis of culture beyond "local knowledge" and "the ultimate phenomenological quest to probe and describe subjective meanings in all their rich detail" (p. 64). The third reason for the neglect of affect-meaning is cultural theory's overemphasis on the internal structure of culture.

As noted previously, this stress on the structure of culture is one of the problems associated with the postmodern approach. It is not the case that the structural relations of culture are not important. The structure of culture provides both a resource and a constraint for social interactants, it stabilizes meaning and renders social encounters repeatable and predictable across time and place, it provides the scaffolding that reciprocally reproduces social structure, and it lends a quality of objectified reality to culture. But an emphasis on the structured qualities of culture that neglects the more micro-level processes is only half the picture. A myopic focus on the structural components of culture neglects affect-meaning and generally conceives of the human agent in some enfeebled form, as can be seen from the postmodern analysis of culture. More important, this concern also misses the reality function of culture. Human reality is primarily a cultural reality, and that reality must be felt-to-be-real. And it is the affective component of culture that produces that reality feature. Unfortunately, this focus on the internal structure is one that dominates much of contemporary cultural theory in the social sciences.

As it is used in this chapter, subjectivity here refers to culture as the knowledge-producing systems—the world is subjectively ordered and experienced by the individual through culture. From this perspective, primal experience is a continuous stream without borders and without meaning. The quintessential human act is the separation of experiential elements and the designation of some as meaningful and others as essentially nonexistent (Weber, 1904/1949, p. 81; Geertz, 1973, p. 434). The human universe is constructed and comes to make sense and constitutes reality as it is categorized and typified (Berger, 1967, p. 6). Primal experience is thus replaced with cultural experience in which the concrete is replaced with the symbolic. According to the subjective school, the sense-meaning component of culture is not created through the internal structure of language, as in the linguistic-structuralist view, but through the process of typification, a social process that emerges from repeated interactions. Thus, while both the linguistic-structuralist and subjective points of view are concerned with sense-making, the subjective school has a socially based theory concerning how sense-meaning is produced. This perspective, therefore, is more sociological and dynamic than the structural school.

The subjective perspective is defined by three characteristics. First and foremost, the human world without culture is understood to be a chaotic, continuous flow of inane experience. The function of culture, then, is socially to render experience subjectively meaningful, to create sense-meaning. Second, the subjectivist approach understands culture as based on the primary experiences and perceptions of individuals. Cultural reality is therefore viewed as precarious and unstable, and this assumption leads to a search for the stabilizing factors of subjective meaning and to an interpretive methodology, the third defining feature.

Max Weber's (1904/1949; 1968) emphasis on subjective meaning, social action and his statements on methodology form the initial conceptualization for the subjective school. But it is the work of Alfred Schutz (1932/1967; 1962) that first brought Weber's seminal ideas of meaning, *verstehen*, and social action into the realm of cultural theory. Schutz grounded his elaboration on the philosophical work of Edmond Husserl (1913/1931) and his notions of intentionality and phenomenological reduction. Peter Berger (1967), Thomas Luckmann (1967; 1991; and Berger & Luckmann 1966), and Clifford Geertz (1966; 1973; 1983) are contemporary examples of this perspective's orientation.

WEBER AND SCHUTZ: THE PRODUCTION AND STABILITY OF SENSE-MEANING

For Weber (1904/1949), culture is the process of singling out from the plethora of activities and events "the meaningless infinity of the world process" (p. 81), a finite portion that is in turn infused with meaning and significance. The process of selecting out is accomplished through the formation of typical expectations of meaning and behavior in interaction. As people interact with the same individuals in repeated situations, behavior tends to become patterned; patterned behavior and their situations tend to be interpreted by the participants in a homologous manner. These patterned behaviors and their corresponding meanings are formulated in terms of typical expectations. It is important to note the difference between Weber and Durkheim at this point. Whereas Durkheim saw the result of patterned and repeated interaction to be moral sentiment, Weber understood the result to be a categorical schema through which sense could be made of the universe and a distinctly human reality produced. The importance of this distinction lies in the fact that both sense-meaning and affect-meaning are created in the same manner, through the focus of either mental or emotional energy.

According to Weber (1968), if the subjective meaning of a social relation remains "relatively constant," the meaning will tend to be formulated in terms of "maxims which the parties concerned expect to be adhered to by their partners on the average and approximately" (p. 28). Additionally, Weber (1904/1949) argued that consistent meaning and action tend to create value orientations to the world: "The concept of culture is a *value-concept*. Empirical reality becomes 'culture' to us because and insofar as we relate it to value ideas. It includes those segments and only those segments of reality which have become significant to us because of this value-relevance" (p. 76). Thus, in situations where repeated social action takes place, cultural categories tend to be expressed to others and experienced by self as normative and ethical.

According to Weber, action is social action if and only if it is meaningfully oriented to the action of others. That is, action becomes social "insofar as its subjective meaning takes account of the behavior of others and is thereby oriented in its course" (Weber, 1968, p. 4). There is also an element of future-oriented intentionality about Weber's definition of social action. Weber (1968) argued that action is without meaning unless it can "be related to an intended purpose" (p. 7). Thus, of his four ideal types of social action—instrumental-rational, value-rational, affectual action, and traditional action—only instrumental- and value-rational behavior are considered meaningful by Weber, because they are the only ones that are explicitly formulated in terms of means/ends. For Weber, then, culture functions as a set of typified actions and orientations that categorizes the world and provides individuals with sense-meaning and goal-oriented behavior in social action.

Weber (1968) argued that cultural reality ultimately depends upon the action of individual actors, and stated that all "social collectives, such as states, associations, business corporations, foundations, . . . must be treated as *solely* the resultants and modes of organization of the particular acts of individual persons, since these alone can be treated as agents in the course of subjectively understandable action" (p. 13). Implicit within this understanding of where society "exists" is the notion that culture depends upon human activity. It must constantly be produced and reproduced. Culture is, therefore, inherently unstable, precarious, and susceptible to change. Thus the very nature of culture contains within it an imperative to create stability. That is, the production of cultural stability is a fundamental problem facing humanity on an ongoing basis.

Weber argued that subjective meaning is initially stabilized in social relations through maxims and values, that is, customs. Mutual agreements and legitimated systems also increase the stability of social relations and associations and hence the sense-meaning of culture. As an agreement is reached concerning a given social relationship, actors orient their behaviors and expectations based on the agreement. In back of this type of agreement is value-rationality or a sense of duty. Nevertheless it is the stability derived from a legitimated system that provides the greatest solidity to culture. Yet, Weber notes, the transition from stability based on custom or mutual agreement to a legitimated order is empirically gradual and requires the possibility of sanctions. The sanctions may take the form of coercion, generally expressed by law, or convention, "the expression of approval or disapproval on the part of those persons who constitute the environment of the actor" (Weber, 1968, p. 319). And these sanctions will ultimately be guaranteed by subjective means, that is, the presence of internalized ethical and religious norms. But a legitimated order does not imply uniform behavior or sense-meaning. Partial deviations from the system are normal, although when noticed they require justification as legitimate. And a plurality of interpretations may exist within any group, but in defining a social relation as having a mutual orientation, what is important is the assumption on the part of one or more of the actors of a shared meaning and the subsequent orientation of action.

Because society is produced at the level of individual interaction, Weber argued that it is imperative that culture be understood from the point of view of the individual actor, not from a system or societal level. For Weber this quest entailed the use of *verstehen*. There are two types of *verstehen*: intellectual and empathetic understanding. The intellectual grasp of action elements surrounding the action "consists in placing the act in a intelligible and more inclusive context of meaning" (Weber, 1968, p. 8). This *verstehen* is the logical and rational understanding of the general motives behind the action; it is a case of direct observation. The second type of *verstehen* is the grasp of the emotional context. This understanding is an empathetic, intuitive comprehension of the emotional motives and meanings of an action to the involved actors, the intended meaning. But because even the conscious motive of the individual may conceal ulterior motives, Weber (1968) advocated the use of ideal types: "it is convenient to treat all irrational, affectually determined elements of behavior as factors of deviation from a conceptually pure type of rational action" (p. 6). The

Weberian perspective of culture, then, stresses the place of agency in producing sense-meaning, understood generally in terms of categorical distinctions and evaluative hierarchies, but devalues the emotional component.

Schutz (1932/1967) criticized Weber for leaving "the problem of meaning" (p. 12) unchallenged—Weber accepted the construction of motives and meanings as unproblematic. Of particular concern for Schutz (1932/1967) was the way in which Weber defined meaningful behavior: "when Weber talks about meaningful behavior, he is thinking about rational behavior and, what is more, 'behavior oriented to a system of discrete individual ends' (*zweckrational*). This kind of behavior he thinks of as the archetype of action" (p. 18). For Schutz, this conceptualization of teleologically meaningful action is based on an incorrect view of what meaning is and how it is created. Schutz argued that the meaning of an act is something that is constructed after the fact, and thus Weber's meaning is like a predicate that can be attached to action. For Schutz, meaning is a constant construction that can only be understood by analyzing the tension between consciousness and lived experience.

To understand and explain this tension, Schutz employed Husserl's concept of intentionality (see Husserl, 1913/1931, pp. 112–125). For Schutz, lived experience occurs as a never ending stream without borders and without beginning or end. Meaning occurs through the conscious act of an individual picking out from the stream of experience a particular object as the focus of attention. This conscious act is a "turning of the attention to an already elapsed experience" (Schutz, 1932/1967, p. 215) and constitutes the meaning-endowing experience of consciousness: "Only that experience which is reflexively perceived . . . has meaning" (Schutz, 1932/1967, p. 57). Thus, while Weber saw meaning as something that could be determined antecedent to the experience, Schutz argued that meaning is an act of intentionality occurring only after the experience, whether in terms of milliseconds or decades.

Further, Schutz argued that social action, a series of discrete behaviors, becomes meaningful through the same backward glance. Because action is a set of behavioral objects, the meaning of action is an act of synthesis that creates a context of meaning into which separate acts may be placed, and thus it provides a unity to experience. Each synthesis can be added to other syntheses, and the meaning-context grows larger with every new experience. Schutz (1932/1967) argued that "this constitution is carried out, layer by layer, at lower levels of consciousness no longer penetrated by the ray of attention" (p. 77). These different meaning-contexts form a reserve stock of knowledge, are always taken-for-granted in terms of their existence, and provide an ever-expanding context for experience. This context becomes, in the eye

of the actor, motivation for action. But, according to Schutz, this motivation is always attributed to behavior after the fact in the backward
glance of meaning construction.

Schutz saw the order of the everyday lifeworld of people as an ongoing construction. These fabrications are given stability through the
transmission and unquestioned acceptance and use of shared stocks of
knowledge. The most important element found in a collective's stock of
knowledge is a typification. Typifications are much like Weber's average expectations: they are built up from past experiences, create a
general type upon which future anticipations can be based, and they
ignore individual and unique characteristics. For Schutz, language is
the medium par excellence of guaranteeing social order and intersubjectivity. Language as an object in the lifeworld preexists and was created
outside of all individual, private worlds. Thus language is a taken-for-
granted objective reality that is held to be common to "everyone who
belongs to us" (Schutz, 1962, p. 75).

But Schutz, like Weber, recognized that the methods of stabilizing
sense-meaning do not warrant uniformity. Typifications are commonly
held, but they are not homogeneously applied. For example, the use of
typifications varies by social distance. Schutz categorized social relations as either close ("we") or distant ("they"). We associations are
defined by immediate face-to-face interaction where both parties are
mutually aware of the other. In We relations, participants are faced
with the possibility that they may have to modify their typifications
of the other. But, Schutz argued, even in face-to-face relations individuals usually do not have to seriously reflect on and challenge their
stock of knowledge. And when changes are made, modifications are
slight and the other is still understood in terms of a type.

Additionally, Schutz recognized that uniform subjective meaning
may be threatened in problematic situations. Problematic conditions
are defined as situations in which an individual's current stocks of
knowledge cannot embrace or explain every relevant object. In nonproblematic situations, people operate through the use of typifications
"automatically." But when a match cannot be made between an already constructed meaning-context and an observed phenomenon, the
individual becomes "motivationally conscious" and begins the "process
of explication." The process continues until the problem is solved and a
new type is constructed: "Through every 'problem's solution' something
'new' becomes consequently something 'old' . . . a type is constructed
('dog': four-footed, wags its tail, barks, bites)" (Schutz & Luckmann,
1973, p. 231). They relations take place in the indirectly experienced,
not face-to-face, lifeworld. These associations are stratified and occur
in a "series of ever increasing anonymization" (Schutz, 1932/1967, p.
291). Because of this increasing distance from immediate experience, an

individual's understanding of who "they" are becomes increasingly typified, the greater is the social distance, the stronger will be the typification, to the point where others are not regarded as free agents. According to Schutz, this locked-in typing cannot be overcome unless they become part of the directly experienced lifeworld. Schutz's theory of meaning construction is much more flexible and emergent than is Weber's. Schutz clearly stresses the on-going construction of meaning at the micro-level, though he acknowledges the place of language in producing a taken-for-grantedness about meaning and reality. Yet he, like Weber, focuses on sense-meaning and appears to completely neglect affect-meaning.

SENSE-MEANING, REALITY, AND SIGN SYSTEMS: BERGER, LUCKMANN, AND GEERTZ

Schutz principally developed Weber's explanation of the process whereby sense-meaning is created; Berger and Luckmann assume this development and explicate its individual internalization and social institutionalization. Though Berger and Luckmann both collaborated and worked independently, for the purpose at hand, I consider their corpus as a single whole—the phenomenology of culture. Berger and Luckmann's theory of culture is posited on the premise that humans are born incomplete; they are underdeveloped in the sense that they have no, or very little, instinctual abilities. The process of becoming human is a construction accomplished while standing in relation to an environment that is hostile and chaotic to an instinctually impotent being. Thus the project of being human involves the enterprise of world building: "Biologically deprived of a man-world, he constructs a human world. This world, of course, is culture" (Berger, 1967, p. 6).

Berger and Luckmann argue that the act of cultural world building involves three movements: externalization, objectification, internalization. Externalization is the "ongoing outpouring" of human essence into the environment. Animals are born with an interior set of instinctual devices that help them survive in their world. Humans, on the other hand, must create "instinctual knowledge" outside of themselves in the form of cultural tools. Externalization "is an anthropological necessity. Human being is impossible in a closed sphere of quiescent interiority. Human being must ongoingly externalize itself in activity" (Berger & Luckmann, 1966, p. 52). Culture is therefore a necessary correlate to human nature, but it stands outside of the species. The tools that humans create to survive come to be understood as real objects existing within the environment—this perception is created as culture is institutionalized and thus objectified, the second phase in world building. Institutionalized culture presents itself to humanity as having a facticity, a reality, external to, and other than, its creators. As such, culture has a determining quality. Once a cultural object has come into an objectified existence, it tends to compel users to arrange their activities "in a way that conforms to *its* own logic . . . that may have been neither intended nor foreseen by those who originally devised it" (Berger, 1967, p. 9).

The third movement in the act of world building is the process of internalization. The formation of a human-self is accomplished in relationship with the cultural environment. A self is created as individuals fit the meaning of discrete moments of personal experience into a consistent biographical framework. But this construction of self is not accomplished in a purely individualistic manner. It is performed vis-à-vis the institutional culture: "the individual's own biography is objectively real only insofar as it may be comprehended within the significant structures of the social world" (Berger, 1967, p. 13). Thus consistency of a biographical-self is accomplished in relation to a culture that is available to all and internalized in the individual through socialization.

Berger and Luckmann argue for the primacy of early childhood socialization over later, or secondary, socialization. Primary socialization occurs in childhood "under circumstances that are highly charged emotionally" (Berger & Luckmann, 1966, p. 131). Because of a child's emotional attachment to significant others, the child identifies her own self and world with the reality presented by the significant others. All other subsequent worlds are internalized with reference to the primary world received from initial, significant others, as most secondary internalization does not take place with the same intense identification with others as does early socialization. Berger and Luckmann argued that without a traumatic shock to an individual's life, each subsequent act of internalization must be perceived as being congruent with the primary reality, for only thus will it have an "accent of reality."

Through primary socialization the child accepts and internalizes the world of the parent with an absolute, never-to-be-repeated certainty. This process of internalization is the genesis of human reality for the individual. "Primary socialization accomplishes what . . . may be seen as the most important confidence trick that society plays on the individual—to make appear as necessity what is in fact a bundle of contingencies, and thus to make meaningful the accident of his birth" (Berger & Luckmann, 1966, p. 135). What is important for Berger and Luckmann is that the world of significant others is a world constructed out of collectively available typifications and stocks of knowledge. Thus the self that is internally constructed is a typified self—it is consistent with the typifications of the human world and receives its orderliness and its sense of history with reference to the shared stocks of knowledge. It is not the case that a unique, subjective experience that may be termed a self does not exist. But "whatever these self-interpretations may be, there will remain the objective interpretation of the individual's biography that locates the latter in a collectively recognized frame of reference" (Berger, 1967, p. 13).

Berger and Luckmann add to Schutz's solution to the problem of culture-contingency by conceptualizing a process of institutionalization and legitimation. Institutionalization occurs when a shared history is built up between typified actors. Individuals accept this institutional history and its legitimation. Thus institutions, (for example, religion) bring order by "setting up predefined patterns of conduct" (Berger & Luckmann, 1966, p. 55). Social order is achieved by the very nature of an institution, and order is generally achieved apart from the use of sanctions, conceived of as secondary control measures. Because institutions have a history, involve large numbers of people, and are external to the individual, they appear as unalterable and self-evident: The individual "cannot wish them away. They resist his attempts to change or evade them. They have coercive power over him, both in themselves, by the sheer force of their facticity, and through the control mechanisms that are usually attached to the most important of them" (Berger & Luckmann, 1966, p. 60).

Additionally, institutions cannot be understood by introspection. Because institutions are, by definition, a product of history, people do not have direct access to the historical, original meaning. It is not part of their biographical memory. Therefore, institutions have an ontological status outside the individual, and they must be interpreted for the individual by various legitimating formulas, for example, maxims and mythological constructions. And legitimation has one further foundation: significant themes within a collectivity that span institutions and different spheres of reality tend to be expressed in a special sign system, or symbolic language. Symbolic objects, symbolic actions, and symbolic roles (living symbols) function as memory aids so that members of a society will not forget the maxims and myths that surround an institution. Berger and Luckmann conceptualize rituals as a kind of memory aid, dramatic enactments that reaffirm the meaning of symbols. They are an indispensable tool for reminding people of institutional legitimation: "Religious ritual has been a crucial instrument of this process of 'reminding.' Again and again it 'makes present' to those who participate in it the fundamental reality-definitions and their appropriate legitimations" (Berger, 1967, p. 40). Berger and Luckmann thus add the structure of institutions to Schutz's on-going meaning production through accounting; subjective sense-meaning is stabilized through association with objectifying structures. However, from this perspective, when these structures begin to differentiate and become unstable—much like the postmodern model—a problem with sense-meaning ensues, as Luckmann points out.

Luckmann (1967) argues that the basic function of any institution is to provide a set of predetermined meanings for the perceived world and simultaneously provide legitimation for those meanings. Religion in particular provides a shield of solidarity against the questions of ultimate meaning through giving and legitimating an ultimate meaning set that protects against the "terror of anomy . . . the nightmare threats of chaos" (Berger, 1967, p. 26). But, Luckmann (1991) argues, modern structural differentiation and specialization have made the ultimate meanings of religion institutionally unstable. This structural instability coupled with the mass media's exaltation of subjectivity and individuality has resulted in the privatization of religion. As a consequence, the social constructions designed to cope with the various levels of transcendence are extremely heterogeneous and the individual consciousness has become one of immediate sensations and emotion. This consciousness is unstable and offers resistance to general legitimating myths, symbols, and dogmas, producing Lyotard's incredulity toward grand narratives.

Luckmann argues that capitalist markets have taken up this challenge and turned it to profitable business. The individual is faced with a de-monopolized market of ultimate meanings created by mass media, churches and sects, residual nineteenth-century secular ideologies, and substitute religious communities. The products of this market form a more or less systematically arranged meaning set that refers to minimal, intermediate, but rarely ultimate meanings. Under these conditions, a meaning set may be taken up by an individual for a long or short period of time and may be combined with elements from other meaning sets. These meaning sets may also be used by periphery groups and converted into a sectarian model, but, according to Luckmann, the chances of firm institutionalization are slight. Some members of modern or modernizing countries have reacted to this privatization of ultimate meaning by trying to revive "traditional models of wholeness" (Luckmann, 1991, p. 178). The chances of success of these revivals are low due to the lack of fit with the structures of modern society.

The above argument is the point of Luckmann's theory that is most strongly influenced by postmodernism. Severe structural differentiation, mass media, commodification, heterogeneous social constructions and the resultant instability or fragmentation of the institutional grand narratives and the individual self are all major concepts in the postmodern literature. But Luckmann does not cite the literature, and one would be hard-pressed to classify Luckmann as a postmodernist. He, like so many others, has simply been influenced by the diffusion of these concepts and the contemporary flight from meaning at the micro-level.

The Schutz/Berger/Luckmann model of discovering subjective meaning is substantially different from Weber's. Their phenomenology of culture is a search for the ultimate foundations of the lifeworld through the process of "transcendental reduction, i.e., attending to phenomena as they 'present' themselves" (Luckmann, 1973, p. 183). Husserl (1962/1970) initially argued, and Luckmann (1973) later affirmed, that the "life-world does have, in all its relative features, a *general structure*. This general structure, to which everything that exists relatively is bound, is not itself relative" (Husserl, 1970, p. 139). The method espoused by Schutz and Berger and Luckmann to discover this structure is based on Husserl's phenomenological epoché, or transcendental phenomenological reduction. This reduction is to the level of pure consciousness through "bracketing" the cultural tools with which the lifeworld is recognized, organized, and understood as meaningful. In the epoché a researcher suspends belief in the reality of this world and directs her attention exclusively to her own consciousness of the stream of experience. This reduction is performed in order to prove the relativity of the world of culture to the transcendental subjectivity which alone has the ontological sense of absolute being, and, in doing so, to render intelligible the intentionalities (i.e., the intentional focus of psychic energy) that have constructed the reality and indubitableness of the lifeworld.

Schutz avoided claiming that the intersubjectivity of knowledge could be derived from the transcendental features of a single consciousness. He took the "natural attitude" as a given and attempted to discern the structural features of the natural attitude of the everyday lifeworld. Thus, in performing phenomenological social research, the investigator posits the experience of others as the null point of reference. This point of reference, by necessity, becomes an "ideal type" that is derived from the segment of the lifeworld identified for analysis. In this typology a danger exists in that the types may be considered as reality by the researcher rather than method. Luckmann (1973) argues that the ultimate product of this type of analysis is the formation of a metalanguage into which the phenomenologically discovered meanings and the ordinary historical languages of others may be translated, but this metalanguage must meet the criterion of subjective adequacy. That is, the translation must be "plausible in principle if not in immediate fact to the speakers-actors who produced the [original] statements" (Luckmann, 1973, p. 181). For the purpose at hand, it is important to note that this methodology assumes a general structure and has as its concern the sense-meaning processes of meaning-endowment.

Geertz takes Berger and Luckmann's proposition of humanity's cultural dependence one step further; he posits a dual scheme of human evolution. He presents a model of evolution where culture and biology form a symbiotic system: "Between the cultural pattern, the body, and the brain, a positive feedback system was created in which each shaped the progress of the other" (Geertz, 1973, p. 48). Geertz argues that the defining difference between the Australopithecine and their immediate predecessors is not physical structure but cranial capacity, and the prime mover of that capacity difference is the use of significant symbols. But Geertz parts company with Schutz, Berger and Luckmann, and Weber in his conceptualization of the mechanism whereby culture creates subjective meaning. He is in agreement with the notion "that man is an animal suspended in webs of significance he himself has spun" (Geertz, 1973, p. 5), and that "the imposition of meaning on life is the major end and primary condition of human existence" (Geertz, 1973, p. 434). He also agrees that subjective meaning emerges through "the conceptual structures individuals use to construe experience" (Geertz, 1973, p. 313). But, for Geertz, the method whereby meaningful concepts are formed is the process of symbolic exhibition, not the process of typification based on chains of similar behaviors and actions. Thus Geertz's notion of ritual as collective memory is somewhat different than Berger and Luckmann's.

Geertz argues that in any society there are a multitude of cultural meanings. These meanings are so varied and complex that they are virtually unknowable even to the inhabitants within a culture. In order for the complexity of human meaning to become comprehensible to the individual, it must be selectively organized into what amounts to a public morality play. Public enactments (rituals) order the themes of a culture into an "encompassing structure" and render them "meaningful— visible, tangible, graspable—'real,' in an ideational sense" (Geertz, 1973, pp. 443–444); "*subjectivity does not properly exist until it is thus organized* [italics added], [public enactments] generate and regenerate the very subjectivity they pretend only to display" (Geertz, 1973, p. 451). Thus Geertz's work is phenomenological in its perspective and blends different elements that may by see in Schutz and Berger and Luckmann.

For Geertz, the stability of social order and meaning is produced in the repetition of public enactment. Through public performances, culture and meaning are historically transmitted. Geertz is not unaware of the function of language as a system of signs in perpetuating and stabilizing meaning, but he lays primary importance upon cultural acts— "the construction, apprehension, and utilization of symbolic forms" (Geertz, 1973, p. 91)—as the means of transmitting and preserving subjective meaning. It appears that Geertz also views culture as being organized into different arenas that may help to stabilize meaning. He mentions six: politics, religion, science, the aesthetic, common sense, and ideology, but he places the greatest emphasis on religion. Geertz's conceptualization of the function of religion is very much in keeping with Berger and Luckmann, as well as Durkheim and Parsons. Religion exists to control humanity's chronic anxiety that the world and humanity's "life in the world, has no genuine order at all" (Geertz, 1973, p. 108). Chaos threatens at three points: the limits of our analytic capacities (the problem of ultimate meaning), the limits of our powers of endurance (the problem of suffering), and the limits of our moral insight (the problem of evil). As with others in this perspective, Geertz's emphasis remains on sense-meaning and the production and limits of human understanding.

Geertz proposes a hermeneutic method of analyzing subjective culture through the use of "thick descriptions." In talking about thick description, Geertz eclectically borrows tools and concepts from diverse sources—at times he even uses a semiotic approach and investigates the invariant relations among the elements in public rituals. Geertz also makes use of Schutz's concept of typification; in particular, how the process of categorization varies by social distance. But the use of analogy is probably his chief device for illuminating a culture to those outside: "What the level did for physics, the chess move promises to do for sociology" (Geertz, 1983, p. 22). Analogies may be borrowed from theater, art, literature, law, or play—almost any human enterprise. The function of analogy or any analytic tool is to allow the researcher to provide a thick description of a cultural event.

Geertz borrows the term thick "description" from Gilbert Ryle (1971). Ryle presents the problem of the twitch verses the wink. The difference between the two cannot be photographed, but it is vast. Further, the twitch or the wink may be parodied, in which the physical action is neither a wink nor a twitch. Further still, the parody may be practiced; it is then not a wink or twitch or parody but an act of theater. In order to understand the difference, Ryle and Geertz advocate the use of thick description—an ethnography that describes the many layers of meaning that occur in a setting. Geertz (1973) refers to the layers of meaning as "piled-up structures of inference and implication" (p. 7). Thick descriptions do not require the researcher to empathize or sympathize with the natives, as Weber's *verstehen* does, but it is required that the descriptions be microscopic in detail.

LOOMING STRUCTURES AND NEVER-ENDING STORIES

The subjective approach to culture repeats the structuralist error found in postmodernism in a number of ways. The fundamental problem that the subjectivists face is the stabilization of culture. Because culture is produced by humans and is not moored in the objective, physical world but in the subjective, social world, cultural meaning is susceptible to change and fluctuation. There is a logical thread that ties together Weber's categorical types, Schutz's typifications and language, and Berger and Luckmann's institutionalization. Each maintains a focus on cognitive types and the perception of reality, but each also represents a progressive step toward greater structuration. And the agency of the individual and small groups tends to get lost under the structures of typification and institutions.

All but Weber posit an impending chaos against which individuals must be shielded. For Schutz, the shield against this terror is the creation of common stocks of knowledge based on typifications. These typifications are so deeply embedded in our consciousness that even in face-to-face interaction they are rarely modified. Berger and Luckmann posit a process of institutionalization that in the end the individual is helpless against: the institution preexists the individual and thus has an ontological status outside the individual. And the cognitive, objective reality of an individual is one that is apparently set in early childhood; like Schutz's typifications, the reality schemes acquired in youth tend to reject all but that which resonates with the existing structures. Additionally, Berger and Luckmann's theory of the process of self is "structuralist" in the sense that the self is objectively real only insofar as it reflects the institutional order. They do not consider the construction of self through micro-interaction and the objective reification of that self through affect-meaning.

And this progression toward structured culture ends up with the same problem as postmodernism: in the face of a fragmented culture, the subjective experience, of necessity, becomes fragmented. All the theorists covered in this review posit a strong role for religion in the preservation of meaning. And with the removal of religion as a cohesive, institutional force, meaning falls victim to the fragmenting nature of the market. Thus Luckmann argues that cultural meanings and the individual consciousness are unstable as there is a posited one-to-one relationship between the individual's self and the institutional structure.

Additionally, much of the work in this perspective is informed by a phenomenological approach to culture. Generally, phenomenology posits an underlying structure, an objective reality apart from human perception that may be discovered. But this approach ends up in the same kind of endless regression as does postmodernism and poststructuralism. The work of phenomenology is to reveal and analyze the assumptions and foundations of everyday life. But, as Psathas (1989) correctly notes, "the effort to provide a full explication of such assumptions proves to be a task impossible of completion because as meanings are revealed, the assumptions being made in the analysis must also be explicated, and this further explication, involving additional assumptions would also need to be explicated, and so on, *ad infinitum*" (p. 11).

Luckmann also recognizes this problem of never-ending reflexivity. In his discussion of the contribution that phenomenology can make to the social sciences, the same discussion in which he defends the existence of invariant structures, Luckmann (1973) maintains that in the process of articulating the structures, it is possible that some of the metalinguistic expressions will find correlations in the descriptive results of "naïve" empirical sciences. With the discovery of these correlations, there is an implicit invitation to "embrace the pretheoretical immediacy of the *Lebenswelt* or to join the traditional cosmological enterprise of 'naïve' science" (Luckmann, 1973, p. 184). And Luckmann (1973) sees no reason to decline the invitation so long as the "differences in cognitive style, method, universe of discourse, and purpose" (p. 184) are kept distinct. But here another round of reflexivity begins. If the first round of reflexivity was based on the preinterpretation of social scientific data and the historical specificity and "ordinariness" in which the preinterpretation is expressed, then the second round may be based on further nonproblematic assumptions of science, for example, the unity of experience and the givenness of communication. In the end, Luckmann's (1973) purpose in engaging in unending epistemological reflexivity is to be "satisfied, more or less plausibly, more or less effectively, and perhaps *less* naïvely, by science" (p. 185).

While it does not appear that Geertz posits an underlying structure, he nonetheless conceptualizes his approach as a phenomenology of culture (Geertz, 1966, p. 7) concerned with the internal relationships within culture, as his use of semiology demonstrates (Geertz, 1973, p. 29). And his methodology is one that produces the same kind of endless regressions as postmodernism and concludes with no other legitimation for its existence than that of a language game. Geertz recognizes that thick descriptions of an event are, of necessity, interpretations and that interpretations are removed from the reality of the culture: only a native experiences his/her culture firsthand. Thick descriptions are often based on perspectives gathered from informants, and sometimes on information gathered from other ethnographers. "They are, thus, fictions; fictions, in the sense that they are 'something made' . . . not that they are false, unfactual, or merely 'as if' thought experiments" (Geertz, 1973, p. 15).

Geertz thus sees cultural analysis as intrinsically incomplete, as itself producing a kind of text. While general themes may be uncovered, it is not the job of the researcher to generalize across cases but only within them. Geertz (1973) argues that cultural theory can never get far from the ground: "In ethnography, the office of theory is to provide

a vocabulary in which what symbolic action has to say about itself—
that is, about the role of culture in human life—can be expressed" (p.
27). Neither is the cultural knowledge gained cumulative: "progress is
marked less by a perfection of consensus than by a refinement of debate.
What gets better is the precision with which we vex each other"
(Geertz, 1973, p. 29). The aim of Geertz's (1973) semiotic, interpretive
approach, then, is to gain "access to the conceptual world in which our
subjects live so that we can, in some extended sense of the term, converse
with them" (p. 24).

Additionally, this perspective does not contain a consideration of affect-meaning. Meaning in the subjective school is the process whereby
the infinity of experience is divided into sense-making categories—the
emphasis is on cognition, not emotion. Weber denies significant status
to two of his categories of social action because they are not rational,
they do not contain the elements of self-conscious formulation and consistently planned orientation. When Weber (1968, p. 6) did consider
emotion, it was in terms of its content and not as a component in reality
construction. Schutz and Berger and Luckmann follow Weber in his conceptualization of types as cognitive categories and Husserl in his emphasis on the individual consciousness. Thus the typified categories
that actors use are emotionally sterile. But humans are not simply rational minds; they are emotional beings as well. These typifications
have affect-meaning for the interactants, sometimes volatile meaning;
and as Goffman (1963, p. 2) points out, the use of these categorical expectations in interaction involves righteously presented demands. The
failure to meet these demands also involves emotion, from simple dis-
appointment to righteous indignation, depending on the intensity of the
interaction. Further, the level of affect-meaning associated with any
modicum of culture helps to determine its felt reality.

The production of affect-meaning is explicitly associated with ritual
enactment. But when ritual is considered in this perspective, it is conceptualized as a dramatic act. Ritual is seen to function as a memory
aid to make present to the participants some social event from the past.
Or, as with Geertz, public ritual selectively chooses out from the endless array of cultural meanings some portion to bring to the attention of
the public, and thus to produce the immediate and perceivable reality
of the collective. But how this ritual performance is organized and
what motivates its construction and selection are not clear. Perhaps
given Geertz's propensity to use structural analysis, it might be driven
by a deep structure similar to Lévi-Strauss's conceptualization (see
Geertz, 1973, pp. 345–359).

THE REALITY-VOICE OF CULTURE

Yet there is much here to be gleaned in forming a general theory of cultural meaning: the dependency of human reality upon culture, the contingency and instability of culture, and the production of sense-meaning. As this perspective argues, human reality is constituted by culture. That is not to say that the physical universe apart from culture does not exist for people, but, rather, because the human animal's evolutionary advantage is the manipulation of the environment, a behavior that is accomplished through culture, and because humans apparently require a meaningful relationship to life, it is difficult for humans actually to experience or relate to the physical environment apart from culture, once they have acquired language. As Ernst Cassirer puts it:

No longer can man confront reality immediately; he cannot see it, as it were, face to face. Physical reality seems to recede in proportion as man's symbolic activity advances. Instead of dealing with the things themselves man is in a sense constantly conversing with himself. He has so enveloped himself in linguistic forms, in artistic images, in mythical symbols or religious rite that he cannot see or know anything except by the interposition of this artificial medium. (Cassirer, 1944, p. 25)

And because culture is an exclusively human production, it is not tied to any objective reality other than its own, and it is thus unstable and contingent upon human action. Weber had a tendency to conceptualize this stability at the micro-level, but his successors have moved the process up to more macro-levels. This movement away from the interactional level has created problems for this perspective similar to those experienced in postmodernism, with its overemphasis on the structure of culture. But the point that culture is dependent upon human action is a good one and one that has been explicated by contemporary ethnomethodologists.

Mehan and Wood (1975) argue that cultural reality is essentially a reflexive project. As Weber argued, all cultural elements are part of larger culture systems and achieve their legitimacy as members of those systems. Mehan and Wood explain that this legitimacy is a function of two particular elements: incorrigible propositions and secondary elaborations of belief. Incorrigible assumptions are those beliefs that undergird every cultural system and are never seriously questioned, such as the existence of a personal god for Christians and the object consistency assumption for scientists. But no cultural system ever completely lives up to all of its assumptions and predictions; there are times that the experience of those living within the systems does not match up to what the culture indicates as reality. Therefore, a set of legitimate

explanations must exist that will, in a taken-for-granted manner, preserve the integrity of the incorrigible assumptions. Those explanations
are what Mehan and Wood term secondary elaborations of belief.
These secondary elaborations function to deflect criticism when God
does not answer prayer (e.g., there was hidden sin) or when the experiment does not work (e.g., the method was incorrect). Each cultural system also provides its own set of confirmatory methods. In other words,
the kind of knowledge that is considered worthy and valid, and the
methods whereby that knowledge is produced, are provided by the culture itself. Thus the religious notions of faith and theocracy and the
scientific ideas of empiricism and positivism determine what will be
selectively seen as confirmation for the culture. Mehan and Wood's
point is that culture is a cultural product, it is a reflexive enterprise,
and as such it is dependent upon continual human action and interaction
at the micro-level for its survival.

In the following chapters, the dynamics involved at the micro-level
for the production and preservation of cultural reality and meaning
will be explicated. But at this point it is important to recognize the
contribution that the subjective perspective can make to a theory of reality at the macro-level. The nature of reality is commonly held to be
an issue of philosophy. But from the perspective of real people in real
lives, reality is experienced and it is felt at different levels—some concepts and things seem more real than others. From a sociological position, then, reality may be conceived of as a variable. Because humans
create reality, they can also deny it. So, for example, for those in technically advanced societies it is comparatively easy to deny the
shamanic reality of the *hekura* spirits:

> Novices attempt to attract particular *hekura* into their chests, a process that takes
> a long time and much patience, for the *hekura* are somewhat coy and fickle, apt to
> leave and abandon their human host. The interior of the shaman's body is a veri-
> table cosmos of rivers, streams, mountains, and forests where the *hekura* can dwell
> in comfort and happiness. Only the more accomplished shamans have many *hekura*
> inside their bodies, and even then they must strive to keep them happy and con-
> tented. (Chagnon, 1992, p. 117)

One way to conceptualize the issue is to say that the variability of
reality is determined by the ease with which the influence of an object
may be denied and/or the meaning of an object may be changed.
Throughout their course in the lifeworld, people are able to "tune out"
some intrusions from their conscious life, while other stimuli prove to be
irresistible. The stronger the demand for attention, the more real is the
experience of the symbolic object. Again, from an empirical point of
view, it is not the case that biological, physical, and coercive realities
do not exist independently from culture. But each of these areas is cul-

turally informed and at times will present competing reality-voices demanding attention. The intent in this book is to understand the reality-voice of culture.

Berger and Luckmann present a good beginning toward that understanding in their conceptualization of institutions. Institutions have a reality and meaning that is difficult for people to deny. Berger and Luckmann reason that this difficulty exists because institutions have history and involve large numbers of people. They are thus perceived to be external and objective to the individual. Berger and Luckmann's formulation has common ground with Collins's (1988) more general statement of the "three irreducible macro factors" (p. 394). Collins argues that the "macro-ness" of any phenomena may be determined by the extent of the geographic space involved, the number of people or situations implicated, and by the length of time the phenomena exist. Collins's formulation adds the dimension of space to Berger and Luckmann's, and I think it is applicable to culture. The size of the geographic space that is embraced by a concept influences the macro-level, or perceived magnitude, of the concept independently of time and people. But because culture inherently needs carriers, people, the effect of space is probably not as great as that of time (history) or the number of people.

From Collins's formulation of the elements contained in this perspective, I propose that the perceived reality of any cultural item to people in an interaction will generally vary by its level of perceived magnitude (macro-ness), a positive, additive function of time, the number of people accepting, believing and using a cultural element, and the amount of geographic space embraced by the culture. Generally, the greater the perceived magnitude of a cultural element, the less likely is an individual in interaction to resist its influence or change its character. Because these macro-elements are based on a person's perception, and ultimately on their imaginative ability, the macro effects on culture are probably curvilinear. That is, there is probably a threshold beyond which additional time, space, or people have little influence.

The subjective perspective also adds to our understanding of how meaning is created in two ways. First, sense-meaning is a function of *the intentional focus of attention on an object*. It is important to note this departure from the structuralist school that conceives of meaning as the function of the relations among sign elements at the system level. The structure of culture certainly informs the production of meaning, but, unless and until a sign becomes the focus of attention by agents at the micro-level, the sign will remain meaningless to actors in social situations—the potential of the structure must be realized by people in interaction. The focus of attention, intentionality, brings to bear the mental energy of the individual upon an object. This intentionality works in a manner similar to the focus of emotional energy. The focus of emotional energy tends to define an object as having emotional boundaries that create a distinction between it and other objects. Objects with levels of emotional energy that are alike tend to be understood in like affect-meaning terms, e.g., sacred or profane. The focus of mental energy tends to create categorical distinctions among objects with like objects being categorized together. This focus of psychic energy functions to slice the stream of experience into meaningful bits that are categorically or typically related one to another.

The second way in which this perspective increases our knowledge of meaning construction is related to the concept of categorical knowledge. As Schutz argues, people and situations are experienced as typical of some non-unique category. It is not the case that anything or anyone can be uniquely known—Goffman (1963) offers the example of a man's wife: all her unique characteristics and behaviors are understood by the man as a peculiar incident of a general type, wife. Each object then is understood as an incident of a broader category, each category is understood in relation to other categories, and each object is known as an element in a series of objects, either sequentially through time or spatially in the physical environment. Thus when an object is given meaning through the focus of emotional and/or psychic energy, its meaning is concurrently understood in its relation to other objects and categories. And by extension we can argue that meaning can be, to a certain degree, transferred to like objects or categories apart from the intentional focus of attention or emotional energy simply through their association. The more similar objects and/or categories appear to be, the more likely it is that the meaning of one object will be associated with the other object. Further, the more two symbols with dissimilar meanings are repeatedly perceived together in a single meaning-context, a kind of category, the more likely the meaning of the two symbols will tend to be linked together, with the more specific or salient meaning being transferred.

This second process of meaning production is similar to the structuralist's argument—meaning is produced through the relationship among the elements in a sign system—in that meaning is a function of categorical relationships. Yet it is distinct in that the focus is on human agency and not on an artifact of interaction. Much semiotic and postmodern analysis seems to focus on what Barthes (1964/1967) refers to as connotative meaning, or secondary signs. This level of meaning is assumed to be taken-for-granted, from the viewpoint of the agent, and thus capable of influencing the actor in a non-conscious manner. While this perspective may offer insights into the way which culture influences people and helps to provide a certain kind of meaning, it is my position that a more fruitful way to understand meaning is to begin with the actor rather than the sign structure.

This second method is also distinct from the focus of energy in that meaning production tends to be more passive because it occurs through association. It is my position that this process of association is a secondary dynamic of meaning production and cannot in and of itself produce the same levels of meaningfulness as focused attention or emotional energy. And this process of association has limitations. First, it is not the case that any two cultural items can be brought together in the same context and be associated. The association cannot be overly problematic for people otherwise the cultural items will not be defined as part of the same meaning context. Second, under normal circumstances, associative meanings can never have the same depth or reality that meaning created though focused interaction can have. The process of association is the process through which a kind of tertiary culture becomes meaningful for an individual or a group. I am making a distinction among three different levels of meaning and culture: primary, secondary, and tertiary. Each of these types indicates a particular group or individual's significant relationship to the culture. Primary meaning is produced by and controlled within identifiable groups at the micro-level; secondary culture is legitimated by meso-level organizations and professional groups; and tertiary culture is created outside an immediate group's interaction but becomes meaningfully available to the group or individual through association (for example, the postmodern media images produced by advertisers). For an element of culture to be available to a group for use, it must have some type of sense- and affect-meaning. But association is a *passive* process unless focused energy is involved. Thus, from the position of the agent, cultural meaning that is created through association tends to be emotionally flat, that is, unable to elicit high levels of emotional energy in interaction, and lacking in a specific sense-meaning definition. At the micro-level of agency, then, it is principally through association that the typical postmodern culture comes to exist and have its influence.

3

The Moral Perspective and the Social Construction of Affect-Meaning

> The very act of congregating is an exceptionally powerful stimulant. Once the individuals are gathered together, a sort of electricity is generated from their closeness and quickly launches them to an extraordinary height of exaltation. Every emotion expressed resonates without interference in consciousnesses that are wide open to external impressions, each one echoing the others. The initial impulse is thereby amplified each time it is echoed, like an avalanche that grows as it goes along.
>
> —Émile Durkheim (1912/1995, pp. 217–218)

The central issue of this book is the felt reality of culture. In the last chapter, I argued, with Berger and Luckmann, that cultural reality varies according to its level of objectification through perceived magnitude: as the number of people, length of time, and size of geographic space increase, so does the perceived objective existence of any culture. It is precisely at this point that postmodernism can argue that people's experience of reality is fragmented, schizophrenic, and emotionally flat: in postmodernity each of the objectification elements are decreasing—culture is localized with few people adhering to it for short durations of time.

But it is not necessarily the case that the lived experience of reality decreases. There are certain social and social-psychological effects of living in a culturally produced world that tend to create pressures a t the micro-level that mitigate the postmodern problem. I argue, with Durkheim, that one of the ways an element of culture may appear to be real to people is though the level of emotion it can generate, its degree of sacredness or affect-meaning. And, as Durkheim argues, the level of sacredness attached to any symbol is a function of interactional processes at the micro-level. Historically, the moral perspective of culture has explicitly incorporated a concept of affect-meaning through the work of Durkheim and Parsons. But in the wake of the justifiable critique of cultural cohesion and coherency, an explicit consideration of affect-meaning has fallen out of the contemporary expressions of this perspective. This deficit is amplified by the inclusion of elements from the structuralist position by contemporary theorists.

There are three main features that distinctively define this perspective of culture: culture is understood as a system of morals and values; society is assumed to have some functional need for moral culture; and cultural change is generally theorized in evolutionary terms. The work of Émile Durkheim (1887/1993; 1912/1995; 1957) as elaborated by Talcott Parsons (1951; 1961; 1966) forms the conceptual core of this perspective. In addition to Durkheim, Parsons used the work of Max Weber and Sigmund Freud to formulate his theory. Parsons took Durkheim's concern with social solidarity and moral sentiments and integrated them with Weber's emphasis on rational action and legitimacy. He also provided a micro/macro link through his conceptualization of the cybernetic system and the process of internalization, using Freud's concept of cathexis and the super-ego.

Major contemporary examples of this perspective are Robert Bellah (1970; 1980; and Bellah, Madsen, Sullivan, Swidler, & Tipton 1985; 1991) and Robert Wuthnow (1987; 1989).[1] Both Bellah and Wuthnow are decidedly different from Durkheim and Parsons in one crucial aspect: they generally focus on discourse analysis, an emphasis inherited from linguistic-structuralism. A focus on public discourse understands society as held together by "conscious discussion and activities aimed explicitly at shaping public debate" (Wuthnow, 1992, p. 10), not by implicit consensus or by a set of taken-for-granted assumptions. And, because a public discourse is an intentional construction, it will clearly exemplify, indeed it will be restricted by, the accepted rules, devices, and strategies that make discourse meaningful. Implicit within this focus is an assumption that "symbolism is itself a reality that can be subjected to systematic investigation" (Wuthnow, 1992, p. 10), and the thrust of this type of investigation is "analyzing the internal structure of texts that make up public discourse" (Wuthnow, 1992, p. 12). Wuthnow thus explicitly adds the structuralist influence by his concern with the internal structure of the discourse. Bellah's incorporation is a bit more subtle, as he is occupied with the loss of public discourse over moral issues and the use of specific languages in moral discourse.

DURKHEIM AND PARSONS: MORALITY AND THE PRODUCTION OF AFFECT-MEANING

The moral-culture perspective is grounded primarily in the work of Durkheim, for whom the creation of a moral culture is almost an automatic consequence of people gathering together. Moral culture is created through group interaction, and its authority is rooted in group identity. Individuals are drawn together through an initial attraction based on similitude; and, if repeated interaction occurs, it will lead to the formation of a "limited group" and a sense of group identity. Group identity is a collective sentiment that takes on the ideals and moral attitudes necessary for the group to survive: "Once a group is formed, nothing can hinder an appropriate moral life from evolving" (Durkheim, 1887/1993, pp. 23–24). The more an identifiable group interacts over time, the greater will be its moral culture, in terms of the number of normative rules, amount of symbolic culture, and authority of the group.

Durkheim claims that culture is a type of social fact, and he argues that the defining feature of social/moral facts is the external nature of their authority: "[Social facts] are ways of acting, thinking, and feeling that present the noteworthy property of existing outside the individual consciousness. These types of conduct or thought are not only external to the individual but are, moreover, endowed with coercive power, by virtue of which they impose themselves upon him, independent of his individual will" (Durkheim, 1895/1938, p. 2). This external authority is based upon the group sentiment, affect-meaning, a feeling of something superior to the individual that brings the entire being into subjection: "Whence, then, the feeling of obligation? It is because in fact we are not purely rational beings; we are also emotional creatures" (Durkheim, 1925/1961, p. 112). This emotional base is objectified by the group in sacred symbols and produced and reinforced through ritual enactment. From a Durkheimian point of view, the primary function of ritual is to produce emotion, affect-meaning, and a sense of factness about culture. This moral reality forms the central core of society, according to Durkheim.

Parsons also argues that society's core is constituted by moral culture and he ties moral culture to emotion. But he moves beyond Durkheim by formulating a multileveled morality with orientations and preferences at the basic level and ultimate meanings at the highest level. Following Weber, Parsons argues that all social action is understood in terms of some form of relation between means and ends; and, for Parsons (1990), "this appears to be one of the ultimate facts of human life we cannot get behind or think away" (p. 320). The evaluative aspect of culture is particularly important in this respect because it defines the patterns of role-expectations and -sanctions, and the standards of cognitive as well as appreciative judgments. Thus Parsons understands the basic function of culture as setting a scale of priorities that contains the fundamental alternatives of selective orientations.

Both Durkheim and Parsons argue that it is the practical function of moral culture to make an integrated society possible. According to Durkheim, the need for moral discipline is based on two problems: human nature and the limits of rationality. By nature, humans are self-satisfying animals with boundless and insatiable appetites. People are motivated to form group culture/morals because anarchy is painful and destructive: "[The individual] suffers from the everlasting wranglings and endless friction that occur when relations between an individual and his fellows are not subject to any regulative influence. It is not a good thing for a man to live like this on a war footing" (Durkheim, 1957, p. 24). Durkheim, like Parsons, sees that a set of value orientations is necessary for human interaction but linked that need to an explicit concept of human nature. Moral, normative culture is also necessary because of the limits of human rationality. Durkheim (1925/1961) argues that if it were necessary in an encounter to "grope *de novo* for an appropriate response to every stimulus from the environing situation, threats to its integrity from many sources would promptly effect its disorganization. . . . To this end, it is altogether necessary that the person be free from an incessant search for appropriate conduct" (p. 37).

But, according to the moral perspective, prioritizing goals and means cannot by itself integrate a society; integration requires commitment. Action can be stabilized through a common measure of meaning and a system of priorities, but for a system to be integrated, people need to be committed to paying the costs necessary to preserve the system. Commitment is a function of the affect-meaning component of morality. People are compelled to sacrifice when the collective *means* something to them, that is, when they have a significant level of emotional investment in the group; the more meaningful the collective in terms of affect-meaning, the more willing people will be to make sacrifices. There are some modes of evaluative interest that imply only acceptance, for example, scientific facts to those outside the scientific community. But this type of evaluative interest does not lead to integration, according to Parsons. Integration requires the degree of commitment that not only believes that something is true but will also lead one to make the sacrifices necessary to preserve it. As Durkheim argues, this affective component of meaning is the result of repeated, focused group interaction.

Parsons's notions of how meaning is created and how it influences action are generally drawn from Weber and Freud, not Durkheim, although the conceptualizations are complementary. From Weber, Parsons incorporated the idea that at the most basic level, culture arises out of the repeated and patterned actions of individuals. These typical actions become symbolized and part of a generalized symbol system, and they are taken into account and treated as situational objects during interaction. This generalized symbol system is what Parsons (1951, p. 11) terms a "cultural tradition" and argues that it becomes meaningful to and part of the "need" disposition of individuals through cathexis, the Freudian notion of focused psychic energy—this conceptualization captures the same general process as the phenomenological idea of intentionality. So, for Parsons, subjectively felt need may be produced culturally and the motivation to conform comes principally from within the individual through Freudian internalization patterns of value orientation and meaning. Thus, while Durkheim emphasizes the dynamic whereby nonmaterial social facts are created, Parsons explicates the mechanism through which social facts are internalized. As the same set of value patterns and role expectations is internalized by a collective of people, that cultural standard is said to be, from the point of view of the individual, institutionalized.

Institutions, defined by Parsons as sets of status positions and role expectations, are hierarchically related one to another and are derived from the ultimate value orientations of the collectivity. People conform to institutionalized value patterns and role expectations because they hold them to be intrinsically valuable; thus, institutions are "in a strict sense, *moral* phenomena" (Parsons, 1990, p. 326). As an institutionalized system, culture is part of Parsons's hierarchy of control: each element of the system is embedded in the other and eventually "defaults" back to the highest level, culture. Culture is paramount because the links between the systems—cultural, social, personality, and behavioral organism—are ultimately symbolic. Because the culture system ultimately functions to guide action through the choice of means and ends, the most important types of cultural components are evaluative symbols, a symbolic system that allows people to place similar values on objects and concepts. The value system is at the superordinate level and contains ultimate meanings and sources of legitimacy. The institutional form that best encompasses these kinds of meanings and legitimacy is religion.

Both Durkheim and Parsons recognize a basic human need for ultimate meanings. Durkheim (1887/1993) argues that meanings that transcend place and time must have a solid base in the emotion of morality:

"Morality is the result of efforts people make to find a lasting object to which to attach themselves and to experience a pleasure which will not be transitory. . . . The fact is that we have a need to believe that our actions do not exhaust all their consequences in an instant . . . but that their consequences are extended for some distance in duration and scope. Otherwise they amount to very little . . . and they would hold no interest at all for us" (pp. 118–119). Thus Durkheim sees an intimate connection between the production of meaning that extends beyond the subjective moment and affective culture. And morality and the fundamental categories of time and place are connected to the religious life, at least in their origin.

Parsons's argument concerning the need for ultimate meaning is tied to group identification and Weber's concern with legitimacy. Parsons argues that interaction requires that individual actions have meanings that are definable with reference to a common set of normative conceptions. By its very nature, normative specificity and conceptualizations are a collective endeavor and thus presuppose a sense of collective identity. Group identity always carries with it some sense of legitimacy, and legitimacy, according to Parsons (1966, p. 11), is always "meaningfully dependent" upon issues of ultimate meaning, and thus is always in some sense religious. Of all institutional forms, religion produces the strongest sense of collective identity, and thus, for Parsons, religious organizations and feelings play key roles in the collective integration of society.

In keeping with an emphasis on integration, Durkheim and Parsons both posit that cultural change is generally slow and gradual with a tendency toward integrated equilibrium; however Parsons also has a notion of cultural change that goes beyond the usual concept of equilibrated change. Durkheim sees cultural change as slow and evolutionary in the Darwinian sense. In general, moral evolution follows the Law of the Three Stages, which posits that early human society was marked by natural affinity and homogeneity. As the population size grows and the division of labor increases, people begin to have differentiated social networks. Durkheim argues that the second stage of moral evolution is characterized by social/structural differentiation and the resultant particularized culture. The presence of particularized culture creates pressures that move society toward the third and final stage—integration through an abstract and universal moral system. In addition to population size, the division of labor, and social/structural differentiation, moral evolution is also driven by increases in communication and transportation technology, which tend to increase the rate of symbol circulation and, in turn, make morals less particularized and increasingly independent of time and place. Because improved communication and transportation technology can cross national boundaries, Durkheim (1887/1993, pp. 101–103) argues that the general culture will eventually embrace the "sole ideal of human-ity" and that differences among people will disappear.

Thus, for Durkheim, culture does not shift radically and equilibrium is the normal state for society. Durkheim bases this position upon his understanding of the need for consistency and the way in which culture functions to produce objective meaning. Durkheim argues that equilib-rium is a function of the individual's need for consistency in meaning. Because human reality is a cultural reality, it is important that mean-ing not shift abruptly nor "capriciously" (Durkheim, 1887/1993, p. 67). In order to stabilize culture, humans invest their meaning systems with morality. Even during times of change, times during which the imagi-native forces of the conscience are active, there is still a need for the individual to have "some object to which one can commit himself, an ideal to which he can dedicate himself—in a word, the spirit of sacri-fice and devotion—that becomes the province, par excellence, of moral-ity" (Durkheim, 1925/1961, p. 101). Thus, whether in agreement or flux, Durkheim argues, humans have a psychological need for consis-tency and equilibrium that can only be met through collective moral symbols.

Another reason that Durkheim sees cultural change as slow is the need for human beings to have stability in sense-meaning. The posses-sion of meaning, the attribution of import beyond the thing-in-itself and the ability to communicate to others through universal signs, is one of the most salient and distinctive features of the human species: "A man who did not think with concepts would not be a man, for he would not be a social being. Limited to individual perceptions alone, he would not be distinct from an animal" (Durkheim, 1912/1995, p. 440). And in-dividual "sense representations are in perpetual flux; they come and go like the ripples of a stream, not staying the same even as long as they last" (Durkheim, 1912/1995, p. 434). So to stabilize meaning across time and place, people use universal concepts or categories to signify and understand the world around them. These categories are collective representations that are contained in language and provide the indi-vidual with an objective framework that forms the basis of all rational thought and "embraces all known reality" (Durkheim, 1912/1995, p. 445). This objectivity coupled with the need for stable meaning across time and place makes culture slow to change.

According to Durkheim, the objectivity of sense-meaning has two bases. First, cultural representations, because they are collective, do not originate in the experience of the individual and are therefore ob-jective, having their genesis outside of subjectivity. The second basis for the objectivity of sense-meaning is much more important, from Durkheim's perspective. He argues that the traditional philosophical approaches to understanding knowledge have not solved the problem of epistemology, that is, the origin of categories. Classic empiricism posited that categories are constructed out of bits and pieces of the empirical world and that individuals are the producers of these categories. This position thus denies that the categories of knowledge are universal or necessary. On the other hand, apriorism generally affirms the universality categories. Because representations are meaningfully used and understood among different individuals, categories cannot be derived from individual experience; they must in some way be logically prior to human experience. For this logical source, apriorism postulated a mystical or supernatural beginning for categories. This postulate is based on a need to find something prior to all individual experience, something objective that could stop the endless regression of subjective experience.

Durkheim argues for a third approach that would ground categories of thought in an empirical reality and yet maintain their universal characteristic: that empirical reality is society—a reality *sui generis*. Socially generated categories do not simply belong to society and not to nature; if that were the case, then human categories of thought could only be applied in a metaphorical manner to nature, hence the problem of representation. But Durkheim (1912/1995) argues that society is a part of nature and "nature's highest expression" (p. 17). Thus these collective representations are a part of the natural world, for "it is impossible that nature, in that which is most fundamental in itself, should be radically different between one part and another of itself" (Durkheim, 1912/1995, p. 17). The problem with other approaches to epistemology is that they have taken the individual to be the culmination of nature; but, in fact, it is society in which nature finds its fullest expression. Thus there is an affinity between collective representations and nature.

But these categories and their objective nature are not simply a function of sense-meaning. Durkheim is primarily concerned with "preeminent concepts," those concepts that direct all other thought and concept formation. There are six of these categories of understanding: time, space, classification, force, causality, and totality. These are pure concepts of understanding, concepts that are used to organize and make sense of sensations. And, according to Durkheim, these categories are a product of religion and religious activity, namely, ritual. Much of Durkheim's argument found in *The Elementary Forms of the Religious Life* is concerned with explicating the relationship between an essential category and the ritual activity that generated that category. Durkheim finds a correspondence between the ritual and the category: the ritual is the real basis, the empirical fact behind the category. This approach is the essence of Durkheim's social morphology: the form of society is basically the ritualized distribution of people in time

and place. Thus there is not only an empirical basis for these categories, but these essential thoughts also have a moral force about them, a
high level of affect-meaning. These categories not only function as pure
categories of understanding, ordering our sense perceptions, but they
also function to "govern and contain the other concepts. They form the
permanent framework of mental life" (Durkheim, 1912/1995, p. 441).

Thus, for Durkheim, culture tends toward equilibrium for specific
reasons, but Parsons simply assumes systems to be in a state of equilibrium. He felt that every social system would have a fair degree of
permanence, and thus there must be a tendency to maintenance of order
except under exceptional circumstances (Parsons & Shils, 1951, p. 107).
Parsons (1951) calls this tendency to equilibrium the "first law of social
process" (p. 205) and the "law of inertia" (p. 482).   Like Durkheim,
Parsons argues that the principal dynamic of evolutionary change is
differentiation. Structural differentiation brings problems of integration and coordination.[2] These problems create pressures for the production of integrative, generalized value-culture and a generalized media
of interchange. But the process of generalization, Parsons (1966) notes,
may also bring about severe conflicts: "To the fundamentalist, the demand for greater generality in evaluative standards appears to be a
demand to abandon the 'real' commitments" (p. 23). Thus Parsons sees
the true believer or oversocialized actor to be a hindrance to functional
cultural and social change. Societies that are able to resolve the conflicts brought about by fundamentalists move ahead to new levels of
adaptive capacity through innovation. Others may "be so beset with
internal conflicts or other handicaps that they can barely maintain
themselves, or will even deteriorate" (Parsons, 1966, p. 23).

Parsons (1951) also has a theory that posited a dynamically changing social system in which the conceptualization of the conflict of interests is more in line with a revolutionary model of change than a
model concerned with preserving equilibrium. Parsons argues that the
basis of any change is strain between a system and its environment, and,
in this sense, the strain experienced is a disturbance of the expectation
system. Strain always sets up reequilibrating processes, but these processes may take a long time to reach equilibrium, and the system may be
substantially different as a result. Structural strain may be dealt with
through institutional processes and a kind of cultural lag. Because all
structures are systemically related, a change in one will eventually
bring about a change in all through the production of more generalized
media of exchange. But structural strain may also form the occasion for
revolutionary change. Change due to revolution occurs in two phases:
the ascendancy of the movement; and the adoption of the movement as
"setting the tone" for the society, the reequilibrating process.

There are four conditions that must be met for the rise and success of a revolutionary movement. First, there must exist cultural potential for change, what Parsons refers to as alienative motivational elements. People become motivated to change the system as the result of value-inconsistencies. These inconsistencies are inevitable and continually present in every empirical cultural system. While there are systemic tendencies to produce generalized culture in the face of structural and social differentiation, elements of particularized culture inevitably make their way into the whole, as when a social movement is co-opted. Thus the general culture will contain elements within it that are not logically consistent with one another. These inconsistent elements constitute alienative motivational elements that not only provide the cultural space and opportunity for change but also may psychologically motivate people to push for social change. But dissatisfaction with the system is not enough to begin a revolutionary movement; the subgroup must also become organized. The organization of a group around a subculture enables members to evade sanctions of the main group, create solidarity, and create an alternative set of normative expectations and sanctions; it also enables expressive leadership to arise.

Parsons's third element indicates that the organized group must develop an ideology that incorporates symbols of wide appeal and can successfully put forward a claim to legitimacy. The ability to develop an alternative claim to legitimacy is facilitated by two factors. One, the central value system of large societies is often very general and is therefore susceptible to appropriation by deviant movements. And, two, serious strains and inconsistencies in the implementation of societal values create legitimacy gaps that can be exploited by the revolutionary group.

The fourth condition that must be met indicates that a revolutionary subgroup must eventually become connected to the social system. It is this connection that institutionalizes the movement and brings back a state of equilibrium to society. There are three processes involved in this phase. One, the utopian ideology that was necessary to create group solidarity must bend in order to make concessions to the adaptive structures of society (e.g., kinship and education)—the revolutionary group must meet the reality of governing a social system. Two, the unstructured motivational component of the movement must be structured toward its central values. In order for the new social order to function smoothly, the movement must institutionalize its values in terms of both organizations and individuals. Three, outgroups must be disciplined vis-à-vis the revolutionary values that are now the new values of society.

BELLAH AND WUTHNOW: MORALITY AND THE INTRUSION OF STRUCTURAL CODES

In contemporary expressions of the moral-culture perspective, there has been a move away from considerations of ultimate meaning systems and dominant values, and a cohesive and coherent culture. Unfortunately, there has also been a move toward a general emphasis on the structure of culture and a move away from affect-meaning. Of contemporary, cultural theorists, Robert Bellah's work most closely follows the Parsonian model. Bellah posits that all interaction, whether between social individuals, individuals and nature, or between individuals and their social commitments, is mediated by institutions. Institutions embody and transmit definitions of right and wrong behavior, normative expectations of proper means and ends, and general contextual expectations. Institutions "themselves are premised on moral (and religious) understanding, what sociologists call ultimate values" (Bellah, Madsen, Sullivan, Swidler, & Tipton, 1991, p. 288). Bellah, like Parsons, argues that all social action is embedded in a hierarchy of value systems with the sacred system forming the final strata of reference.

But Bellah also wants to distance his project from Parsons. He asserts that his theory does not assume a central, unified value system, though societies do require "some degree of shared values" (Bellah et al., 1991, p. 290). The theme of Bellah's (1975) work is a call to re/create a civil religion because "only a new imaginative, religious, moral, and social context for science and technology will make it possible to weather the storms that seem to be closing in on us in the late 20th century" (p. xiv). Neither does Bellah, in contrast to Parsons, assume that existing institutions are functional; he thus avoids the criticism of tautology to which Parsons's theory is subject. Bellah posits that moral debates over the dysfunctions of institutions are an intrinsic element of the culture of any society and argues that these debates constitute culture; culture, then, is a dynamic conversation or moral argument. He thus envisions cultural and institutional changes as having a quality of conflict and agency about them.

Yet Bellah follows Durkheim and Parsons by arguing that religion contains the highest order of symbolization and values. Religion is defined as "a set of symbolic forms and acts that related man to the ultimate conditions of his existence" (Bellah, 1970, p. 21). The function of religion is to solve two problems. First, the problem of identity: in order to control the environment, humans must create a symbolic border between themselves and nature—humans must identify themselves as separate and the environment amenable to manipulation. Bellah (1970) argues that "prereligious men could only 'passively endure' suffering or other limitations imposed by the conditions of their existence, but religious man can to some extent 'transcend and dominate' them through his capacity for symbolization" (p. 25). This need for symbolic identification is particularly acute during times of stress and disturbance. In other words, part of the reason that people form groups with a high degree of solidarity during times of threat is that high collective identification allows for greater manipulation of the physical environment, an entity seen as separate from human society.

The second function of religion is to solve the problem of motivation control. Humans have motivations, genetic or Freudian, that are outside the immediate control of conscious, decision-making processes. These asocial motivations also become most acute and problematic during times of threat, uncertainty, or breakdown. Thus, in times of social stress, "the emotional investment in the maintenance of such superordinate systems is extremely great and may take the form of irrational attachment and hostile reaction to any threat. When this occurs one is apt to say that the superordinate system has become in some sense 'sacred'" (Bellah, 1970, p. 261).

Though a less clear statement of functional need, two of Bellah's recent books, *Habits of the Heart* and *The Good Society*, form a "voice in the wilderness" that decries the results of capitalistic exploitation and the "colonization" of everyday life and the public sphere by institutions that have failed to live up to their moral obligation. What we need is to "move away from a concern for maximizing private interests" and to move toward "justice in the broadest sense—that is, giving what is due to both persons and the natural environment" (Bellah et al., 1991, p. 143). This can be accomplished through the cultivation of face-to-face communities where people are "involved in the creation of regional cultures in some degree of harmony with the natural environment, where individuals, families, and local communities could grow in moral and cultural complexity" (Bellah et al., 1991, p. 265). This argument echoes Durkheim's concern with the creation of intermediate moral groups and the need to interact in face-to-face situations to produce moral culture, and the postmodern interest in local cultures.

I must admit that I have pieced together Bellah's "communitarian" argument, and he is careful to try to distance himself from being defined as strictly a communitarian. Indeed, he lays emphasis on individual citizen involvement in a variety of institutional environments. But the argument throughout his work is one that is based on the loss of a "moral ecology" and a "vigorous public sphere" (Bellah et al., 1991, p. 265). Although Bellah does advocate individual involvement in various settings, it is predicated on "more substantive ethical identities" created in the context of stable relationships, in terms of geographic space. Additionally, Ann Swidler (1986, p. 276), one of Bellah's co-authors, refers to their approach as communitarian. I thus feel the communitarian framework is justified.

For Bellah (1970), societal evolution is defined as a "process of increasing differentiation and complexity of organization that endows the organism, social system, or whatever the unit in question may be with greater capacity to adapt to its environment" (p. 21). The evolution of religion, as the main institutional storehouse of humanity's ultimate symbols and values, is of particular concern for Bellah. He outlines a five-stage evolutionary scheme of religion: primitive, archaic, historic, early modern, and modern. But increasing institutional differentiation, size, and complexity have created a problem. Bellah argues that the central feature of the modern stage is the collapse of the dualism between the sacred and profane that was crucial to past religions and morals. The collapse of the sacred is due to the loss of an institutional sphere where collective morals are self-consciously formed—institutional differentiation and size have grown to the point where individuals have lost the ability to collectively inform moral culture and have become passive recipients of institutional control. Additionally, capitalism has created institutions whose central values are exploitation and individualism. Thus the institutional control that is exercised over individuals is oppressive, in terms of moral values.

Further, Bellah argues that in post-traditional societies there may be more than one type of moral discourse. These "languages" may be selectively used at different times and for different ends, much like Swidler's (1986) notion of culture as a tool kit. Moral languages contain and are expressed through representative characters. Representative characters are a type of symbols, a way in which people define what is good and legitimate in a social environment. As with the discourse language as a whole, representative characters compete for legitimation through collective, moral rhetoric. In the case where moral debate has ceased (Bellah identifies contemporary America as such a case), legitimation is established through large-scale organizations and institutions by default. Thus Bellah privileges the micro-level for the production of affect-meaning but sees this era in contemporary America as a time when institutional legitimation has overshadowed interaction as the source of moral culture.

Robert Wuthnow moves his program even further from Parsons's approach to morals, with its emphasis on the circumscription of action by subjectively meaningful values. Wuthnow (1987, pp. 18–65) refers to the emphasis of Durkheim and Parsons as "the problem of meaning" and embraces a program that has as its central concern the analysis of the textual structure of culture. For Wuthnow, the internal structure of the text is the most objective social form available: he argues that social scientists make a "leap of faith" when they accept the product of research as truly indicative of any reality in the world of others. What these products represent, in Wuthnow's estimation, are a discourse about meanings, a text—in this understanding of social, scientific analysis, Wuthnow most resembles the postmodern critique. Thus Wuthnow's analytic concern with moral culture is its internal structure, its moral code, not its affective value.

In explicating the structure of moral codes, Wuthnow is interested in outlining the symbolic distinctions that comprise the code. The manner in which structural distance is maintained between discourses constitutes a type of moral logic. Three symbolic distinctions make up the moral code—though he allows that there may be other elements to the structure, his use of these three suggests that he considers them to be general properties of the moral code—and each distinction within the code is constituted by two concepts that are set in a type of binary opposition, à Lévi-Strauss. The first symbolic distinction is between the moral object (the object of commitment) and the real program (how people are culturally expected to act). The second distinction is between the true inner-self and the roles an individual plays. And the third distinction is comprised of "some particularly powerful symbols . . . [that] have powerful symbolic value because they happen infrequently, are unusual or divine, and sometimes influence circumstances or represent changes in one's life" (Wuthnow, 1987, p. 73). This last distinction is between the inevitable and the intentional.

The essential difference between all pairs of symbols is that one may be empirically known and the other is not amenable to empirical investigation. Thus the moral object of commitment, for example, god, is unknowable through one's senses, but the action that is connected to the moral object, for example, Bible reading, may be known. An important point for Wuthnow (1987) is that the concepts are loosely bound together in a relationship that he terms "connected-but-separate" (p. 75). This close but distant relationship is needed to negotiate the discrepancy that always exists between the ideal and the real, and it is needed to maintain one's commitment in the face of the discrepancy. But if the boundary between the two is blurred and the individual ceases to be able to distinguish between the ideal and the real, then either cynicism or loss of justification for action will result.

One of the problems that has been associated with the moral approach is that culture is presumed to be cohesive with a high degree of commitment. Wuthnow attempts to mitigate these issues by arguing that moral codes contain a built-in distance between the ideal and the real. His point is that this structural distance allows people to maintain somewhat low levels of commitment, in terms of actual behavior, and still cleave to the moral culture. The ideal value becomes a symbolic object in and of itself that can be maintained in the face of disparate behavior. This distant-but-close relationship conceptually lessens the influence of moral culture on behavior, but it still preserves the cultural, symbolic value of morals. Commitment is maintained, uncertainty is controlled, and moral values still have some effect on behavior.

Unfortunately, Wuthnow does not fully explain his concepts and their operationalization, and, as a result, much of how this structural separation works must be inferred. It appears that Wuthnow posits that the three symbolic areas—moral object, self, and inevitability— are the general features of any moral code, and that the distinction between them and their empirical counterparts does not vary. That is, there is never a time when the actions of people and their moral ideals have greater concordance than at other times. What changes culturally in response to history, according to Wuthnow, is the meaning-content of the symbolic area, that is, the meaning of god and self, and the arena in which the moral codes are played out. Thus it seems that in Wuthnow's scheme the moral structure never varies.

Wuthnow argues that the function of moral codes is to reduce the level of uncertainty.[3] Uncertainty may arise with regard to "social positions, commitments to shared values, or behavioral options likely to influence other actors" (Wuthnow, 1987, p. 120). It is most likely to occur when there is a large number of available options of behavior, when the culture system experiences an external shock, or when the meaning of a situated, symbolic object is ambiguous. In addition to moral codes, it is the function of rituals to reduce uncertainty: when uncertainty is high, ritual enactment will be high as well. The function of a ritual is to reduce uncertainty by dramatizing, and thus maintaining, the moral order.

According to Wuthnow, a ritual is any set of behaviors that has meaning beyond instrumental purposes; it is a set of symbolic acts that communicate meanings about social relations rather than being purely practical. He argues that rituals are not a special category of action but are found everywhere and anytime, can occur sporadically, and can be communicated through any means—it does not require face-to-face interaction. Rituals may also contain intentional and nonintentional messages and thus may have various levels of interpretation. And the expressiveness of a ritual "may have to do with emotions, but it may also be strictly intellectual" (Wuthnow, 1987, p. 100). Wuthnow (1987) is careful to note that this need to alleviate uncertainty is not predicated on an individual psychological requirement to relieve anxiety, but "it posits a requirement strictly at the social level for communication about the nature of moral expectations" (p. 156).

Thus, like Berger and Luckmann, Wuthnow sees rituals as dramatic realizations that, in their most powerful form, are illustrations of the moral code. Rituals are signs that point to some other meaning; his most basic definition of ritual is expressiveness, "simply that communication is taking place" (Wuthnow, 1987, p. 100). As an example he offers the ritual of changing a tire—"the activity may communicate one's value to friends or family" (Wuthnow, 1987, p. 101). Thus any type of communication that is more than utilitarian qualifies as a ritual. His examples of rituals range from tidying one's desk to a wedding, from brushing one's teeth to a television program. Interpretations of rituals, according to Wuthnow, can fall on a wide spectrum due to the possibility of nonintentional messages. A televised program concerning the holocaust may mean different things to different people.

Wuthnow thus distances himself from Durkheim's concept of ritual and the one espoused in this book. Durkheim claimed that culture is a type of social fact, and he argued that the defining feature of social facts is their objectivity. Affect-meaning produces objectivity through ritual enactment and the investment of emotional energy (see Durkheim, 1912/1995, pp. 208–216; Collins, 1988, pp. 192–197). From a Durkheimian point of view, then, the primary function of ritual is to produce emotion, affect-meaning, a point from which Wuthnow wants to distance himself.

Wuthnow's theory of cultural change is an evolutionary model, albeit a different type than that espoused by Durkheim and Parsons, and probably by Bellah. He decidedly wants to distance himself from "theoretical formulations [which] are concerned primarily with broad evolutionary tendencies" (Wuthnow, 1989, p. 533). But since his overarching model is derived from population ecology, and he understands cultural change in terms of "relatively abrupt periods of cultural upheaval" (Wuthnow, 1989, p. 530), it is difficult not to categorize his scheme as a type of cultural evolution. Durkheim's and Parsons's evolutionary model is one that has affinity with Darwinian evolution, gradualism. Biological gradualism posits slow and gradual change with a species tracking the environment at all times, thus staying in functional equilibrium. Biology's alternative evolutionary model is punctuated equilibrium. In this model, the species is not assumed to be tracking the environment. Thus, at different points in time, a species may not be in equilibrium with its environment. Abrupt changes in either the species itself or in its environment will produce a plethora of alternative life forms. Survival is a function of how well the species performs in the competition for resources. Wuthnow's model follows the latter evolutionary scheme.

Wuthnow's model of evolutionary change revolves around the concept of ideology—his use of the term "ideology" is value-neutral and noncritical, distinctly different from the Marxian notion—and a model of population ecology. Ideology, according to Wuthnow (1987), is a subset of moral culture; it may be a set of written or verbal utterances, visual images, or events that propose how "social relations should be conducted" (p. 154). There are two qualities that set ideology off from the rest of moral culture: it has a high degree of cognitive manipulation, ideology attempts to persuade; and it is produced in response to ambiguities or disturbances in the moral order—here again Wuthnow's move away from affect-meaning to sense-meaning or cognition is evident. Ideologies create alternative models of moral order that may be symbolically experimented with as possible ways of reconstructing social relations.

Wuthnow proposes a three-phase model of cultural change that has great affinity with population ecology. Phase one concerns the production of ideologies. Generally, a disturbance in the environment— defined as the general social, cultural, political, and economic contours of the society—produces uncertainty, which, in turn, gives rise to the production of various ideologies. In a very loose manner, Wuthnow identifies these disturbances as being associated with changes in the size of the population and economic expansion. Economic expansion leads to changes in the institutional arrangements of the society. In particular, expansion influences the organizational setting in which cultural production takes place: he posits that there will be a decrease in centralized, restrictive cultural authority, an increase in the number and diversity of elites willing to support alternative ideologies, an increase in conceptual opportunities for culture producers, and an increase in the population that has access to the institutional arrangements of culture production. These open niches create pressures that produce sets of contending ideologies that seek to bring certainty and "equilibrium" back to the institutional arrangements.[4]

Another issue in the production of ideology is the "problem of articulation" (Wuthnow, 1989, pp. 1–22)—the influence of linguistic-structuralism is quite clear at this point. Ideology must be formulated and stated in a balance between creativity and conservatism. The public discourse around ideology must stay close to the social settings and structure of the existing moral code and simultaneously distance itself from the standard in order to offer a viable solution. Within an ideology a "discursive field" is formed, that is, the incorporation of social conflicts in general, symbolic, and abstract terms. This symbolic space is fundamentally defined by a set of binary opposites, but more complex structures are also possible. Binary opposition applies not only to categories but also to the forms of ideological discourse to which symbols become attached. Binary opposition defines separated ends of a continuum, and the incorporation of various continuums defines the fundamental categories of the ideology, the range of problems the ideology addresses, and the parameters of the discourse.

A special feature of a discursive field is its representative action and actors. Within a field, binary opposition defines the problems to be addressed, and "figural action" presents possible solutions. Figural action prescribes courses of action that "make sense" given the identified problems (Wuthnow, 1989, p. 14). Also included in the discursive field are "figural characters." These characters constitute a "'model for' a new kind of social actor" (Wuthnow, 1989, p. 332). These figural characters are different from Bellah's representative characters in that the former depicts a proposed solution to a perceived problem, whereas the latter are icons of legitimation.

The second process in Wuthnow's ecology model is selection—ideologies compete for the available niches in the structure of the moral code. Both local and regional contexts create pressures that select for or against certain ideologies. Success in competition for niche space is predicated on a carrier movement's ability to access resources: for example, power, money, personnel, communication networks, and technology. This access is a function of the group's ability to influence power elites. Additionally, the success of an ideology is a function of local conditions. Local selective pressures depend on preexisting ideological diversity, conditions affecting the ease of ideological diffusion (communication and transportation technology, the degree of ecological integration, and the level of value and interest consensus), the presence of heterogeneous moral niches, and the state's perception of locally enacted ideology as constituting a threat or an enhancement to the mission of the state.

The third process in Wuthnow's model of cultural change is institutionalization, much like Parsons. Once an ideology is selected, the carrier movement must routinize the "mechanisms for the production and dissemination of particular modes of discourse" (Wuthnow, 1989, p. 10). But, unlike Parsons, Wuthnow's emphasis in institutionalization is on linguistic-structural concerns. His mechanisms of institutionalization involve the prescription of responsibilities, parameters of discourse, ritual enactments, festivals, and gatherings that will increase the likelihood that producers and audiences will stay in contact and acquire a tangible identity. Institutionalization of an ideology is a function of the routinization of the means of access to resources, the level of internal communication, and the ability to set the standards by which it will be evaluated. It also implies the embedding of ideology in concrete communities of discourse and the regular production of social organization. The ideology must become accepted as legitimate and become the regular product of social organizations dedicated to its fabrication and diffusion.

AGENCY AND AFFECT-MEANING LOST

In general, there is a tendency for analysts who view culture as a set of moral imperatives to assume that society is integrated through cultural consensus and identity. While it is unequivocal that some type of cultural consensus is necessary for a society to function, the degree of consensus for each type of culture must be formulated as a variable with a threshold level. Too much moral consensus can result in a rigid society unable to respond to internal or external changes, a situation Parsons recognized when he referred to value-fundamentalists. Too little moral consensus and identity can result in a society unable to muster the level of commitment needed to complete large-scale projects, for example, building a space station, eliminating poverty, or participating in a long-term or costly war—as Durkheim and Parsons note, commitment is a function of group identity and group identifying symbols. It is self-evident that a society needs a certain level of identity in order to protect its borders or to accomplish large-scale, costly projects; and, as Bellah points out, cultural identity enables humans to control their environment. Thus identity, sacrifice, control, and commitment are all tied up together. The high levels of commitment that are necessary for individuals and groups to pay extreme costs are a function of general symbols that have the capacity to elicit high levels of emotional response.

I should note that my saying that this need for some level of consensus and identity is self-evident is based on an assumption that may not be shared by everyone. I assume that some form of the nation-state, and thus large-scale projects, are necessary entities for organizing and mobilizing resources for large populations. But there are those who disagree, postmodernists among them, arguing that unified collective action and identity are no longer necessary or desirable. However, I have yet to be convinced that any other mechanism exists for meeting the needs or countering the problems of large populations. As the postmodern project now stands, society is conceived of as devolving into smaller and smaller localized, symbolic groups. As Bauman (1992) recognizes, bereft of some generalized culture these groups will fall into various levels of conflict. Postmodernists are thus left having to put forward some kind of value orientation, much like Durkheim felt constrained to do: "Tolerance reaches its full potential only when it offers more than the acceptance of diversity and coexistence; when it calls for the emphatic admission of the *equivalence* of knowledge-producing discourses; when it calls for a *dialogue*, vigilantly protected against monologistic temptations; when it acknowledges not just the *otherness* of the other, but the legitimacy of the other's interests and the other's right to have such interests respected and, if possible, gratified" (Bauman, 1992, pp. xxi–xxii).

But to be "functional" a society does not have to maintain a high level of consensus or identity at all times. This assumed need is based on a perspective that privileges culture as a separate entity wherein moral culture exists in a kind of static state. However, from a point of view that is oriented more towards agency, what is necessary, if a society has occasion to need high levels of commitment and sacrifice, is that there be a common stock of generalized, identifying symbols around which the collective can interact and re/create affect-meaning and the felt reality of the group. It is not necessary that these symbols be "active," that is, continually be the focus of interaction, nor is it necessary for these symbols to be occasionally "reinvested" with emotion in order to maintain a certain level of meaningfulness and solidarity. On the contrary, one of the advantages of a focus on interaction rather than structure in the study of culture is the recognition that sacredness is not a simple function of the sign. Ultimately meaning resides at the micro-level of the encounter and may collectively be produced or re-created in a relatively short period of time. Because meaning is functionally dependent upon people in interaction, the emotional energy necessary to create an intense sense of identity and commitment does not reside in the symbol but in the interaction. Cultural symbols are triggers or reminders that are used to recall past emotions and experiences and to facilitate their reenactment. Thus what is necessary for a society to produce identity is not a high level of moral solidarity but a stock of symbols with the *potential* to exclusively identify and emotionally border a large collective.

Nor is it the case that a functional, that is, operational, level of societal integration is simply a result of cultural consensus and/or identity. A society can be functionally integrated through means other than cultural—a point neo-functionalists expand.[5] Durkheim (1893/1984) himself considered the division of labor and the idea of dependent opposites as an integrating force, but he later backed down from the notion and argued that intermediate moral-producing groups were needed in a highly differentiated society. Wuthnow attempts to mitigate this issue of high-level commitment by arguing that moral codes contain a built-in distance between the ideal and the real. His point is that this structural distinction allows people to maintain somewhat low levels of commitment, in terms of actual behavior, and still cleave to the moral value. The ideal value becomes a symbolic object that can be maintained in the face of disparate behavior, and, I would argue, that can become the focus of group interaction. This distant-but-close relationship conceptually lessens the influence of moral culture on behavior, but it still preserves the cultural, symbolic value of morals. Commitment is maintained, uncertainty is controlled, and moral values still have some effect on behavior. On the whole, Wuthnow's notion of separate-but-connected is an illuminating concept. It could be used to explicate the methods by which people maintain commitments and morality in the face of disparate behavior, much in the same way the concept of "accounts" has been used (see Scott & Lyman, 1968). But I think Wuthnow has weakened the concept by not conceiving of the distance between the real and ideal as variable, a structuralist's error. It seems reasonable to posit that under conditions of traditionalism the distinction between the two binary oppositions would be less than under conditions of modernity.

The moral approach to culture also disables agency at the micro-level, generally speaking. In both Durkheim's and Parsons's conceptualization, actors appear but only in delineated boxes. For Durkheim, moral culture is an external force to which an individual feels obligated to conform; Parsons has the actor not only constrained by the environmental conditions of the action system but also internally restrained by both the super-ego and the ego since they share a common system of emotional symbolization. While there are certainly reasons why an actor will abide within the perceived boundaries of cultural significance—vested interests, power/authority, conflict/exchange, reciprocity, reality construction, and so on—it is always the actor that acts, and acts selectively, using culture to negotiate her or his way through interaction and strategic-action; it is not culture that acts or even acts upon the actor.

Culture is the source from which we must draw in order to interact with others and thus does set certain parameters. Ann Swidler (1986) argues that culture is better understood with reference to general strategies of action rather than morally driven discrete acts. Within these general strategies, people act based on their cultural style and skills, not on their values or morals, according to Swidler. Culture, then, is like a "tool kit" from which people draw to organize their overall behavior with a circumscribed set of tools. While Swidler does devalue affect-meaning and neglects considerations of reality construction, her understanding of culture as a resource from which actors strategically and creatively draw rather than a determinative structure is correct. From the perspective of reality construction, to view the interplay between the actor and culture as essentially nonproblematic, as the moral perspective does, minimizes the importance of the actor and restricts inquiry into the most interesting and dynamic facet of the culture-interaction process: people creating and recreating affect-meaning in social encounters.

Although Bellah talks about individuals and the importance of individual involvement and agency, his recent work is little more than a clarion call to arms, with vague illusions to Durkheimian group interaction and the creation of moral communities. Bellah is most like postmodernism in his emphasis on the ramifications of the de-institutionalization of religion. As the institutional space provided by religion for moral discourse decreases, through increases in institutional size and complexity, the distinction between the sacred and profane breaks down. In the stead of religion, capitalist markets arise and become the moral foundation for society. One of the primary results of this process, according to Bellah, is the production of many languages of discourse, a distinctly postmodern/structural emphasis (see Gottdiener's [1995] explanation of postmodern semiotics). Bellah's actor is as equally disabled as the postmodern subject, being oppressed under a disassociated institutional system, though Bellah holds out greater possibilities for the subject through moral discourse.

Wuthnow has done away with individual agency and emotion on at least three counts. First, he explicitly moves from the "subjective features of culture" to the objective structure of moral codes. This structuralist turn inherently leaves the subject behind. Second, Wuthnow's understanding of ritual as dramatic enactments explicates the cognitive, sense-meaning aspects of ritual, rather than the affect-meaning, reality construction aspects. And thus his theory misses a sociological understanding of the emotional experience of the subject and the production of a reified reality. Third, Wuthnow's theory is centrally concerned with the social-structural conditions surrounding the production and reception of a discourse, and, like Bellah, loses the agent under large-scale processes.

The relationships among economic expansion, the rearrangement of organizational/institutional elements, the production and selection of ideologies within those changes, and their relationship to culture producers (elites) and resources are enlightening aspects of Wuthnow's approach. But his theory is focused on high-level culture producers, generally organizations (Wuthnow, 1989, p. 539), and he ignores the ultimate dependency of the producers upon, and the potentially creative contributions of, individuals and small groups in interaction. He conceptualizes the culture-consuming public at the mercy of the producers, with producers circumscribed only by the structure of discourse: "We may be at the mercy of wordmongers who deliberately construct the realities in which we must live, but the wordmongers themselves depend on the rules of symbolic use of which culture consists, if only to violate them" (Wuthnow, 1992, p. 2).

Because Wuthnow has set aside a consideration of the subjective experience of both sense- and affect-meaning, he fails to take into account the dependency of the producers on the "consumers." He either conceptualizes the individual as a passive recipient or so locked into the structures of a produced discourse that she cannot freely act.[6] But, regardless of what the elite or the "wordmongers" produce, it is meaningless to the majority of people in a society unless and until individuals or small groups in encounters create and recreate meaning. Meaning is ultimately dependent upon local production. As Randall Collins (1986) states: "meaning does not emerge automatically; it requires a certain kind of social activity, the inputs of ceremonial labor and front-stage props that bring about ritual" (p. 254).

And, finally, this perspective on culture inaccurately depicts the need for ultimate, religious meaning. The production of meaning is intimately tied to issues of time and place. Meaning for humans is always something other than the pure experience of the thing-in-itself in the present here and now. As Durkheim (1887/1993) notes, humans have a need to believe that "actions do not exhaust all their consequences in an instant . . . but that their consequences are extended for some distance in duration and scope" (p. 119). This sense of meaningfulness is inherently unstable and requires a certain degree of organization and human action and interaction in order to survive, and religion is an ideal social form for these processes. But the moral perspective tends to focus on the *content* of the meaning—ultimate religious or sacred meanings—rather than the processes that create a given level of meaningfulness or emotional energy.

Durkheim misses the mark when he explains the existence of god as the symbolic expression of collective "effervescence" and identity. The sacred is not simply an overinflated sense of group. While the presence of the sacred, in either Durkheim's or Bellah's terms, does provide a strong sense of legitimated identity, it is not the principal function of the sacred to provide a collective identity. The primary function of high levels of affect-meaning, sacredness, is to mitigate the tenuous nature of reality and the problems of ontology and facticity associated with the production of a meaningful universe. As a whole, the function of culture is to produce a meaningful object-universe for humanity. This insight is not new; Weber explicitly based his theory upon that assumption. Culture also imparts the ability to symbolically and imaginatively manipulate and be reflexive about the object-universe; again, this is not a new insight (see Mead, 1934/1962). But the existence of a symbolic object-universe, and the ability to be reflexive about that universe, imply that everything in the universe has meaning and that meaning tends to be layered, or self-referential, and may be critically examined.

Human meaning is possible because of the reflexive act. Meaning is essentially a human creation and not an inherent characteristic of any object. Thus the meaning of a sign or symbol can change through history or across cultures. For example, the swastika has appeared in ancient Rome, Greece, China, Egypt, and India, and has been associated with as diverse groups as early Christians, Native Americans, and mid-

twentieth-century Nazis. The definition of the swastika has also varied from a mystical symbol of peace to the racist superiority of white
supremacy. Meaning, then, does not reside in the sign but must always
be imputed and interpreted. Generally speaking, the imputation of
meaning is an effect of collective action and has a certain taken-for-
grantedness about it. Meaning thus appears to the observer as having
an objective existence and ontology of its own. But meaning must also be
read; it must be interpreted and applied to and by an individual situated in real circumstances and interactions. This act of interpretation
and application is a reflexive act.

For a symbol to be a symbol it must have meaning other than the direct experience of an object; culture separates an object from its experience and demands the act of interpretation, that is, reflexivity (see
Mead 1934/1962, p. 67). And, by extension, reflexivity implies the
question or problem of meaning. For the sake of argument, let us assume
that nonhuman animals experience the world as it is, in its pure, unin-
terpreted form. If that is the case, then the animal's experience of the
world is essential: the meaning of the world is a sensual meaning, the
world as it is directly experienced through the senses. But for humans,
the experience of the world is different. Because of culture, the thing-
in-itself is no longer available to humans. As Ernst Cassirer (1944, p.
44) puts it, "No longer can man confront reality immediately; he cannot
see it, as it were, face to face. Physical reality seems to recede in proportion as man's symbolic activity advances." It is thus that Mead
(1934/1962, p. 78) could argue that physical objects can only exist for
humans as they are symbolized; it is the symbol that constitutes human
reality.

The symbolic act at once exalts and empties the object. For humans,
the object is emptied of its essential character (sex can never again be a
simple biological act for humanity) and invested with a meaning that
far exceeds its intrinsic nature. This meaning must be interpreted and
directly applied to the actor for the object to become subjectively real.
This interpretation and application constitute a first-order reflexivity.
In nonproblematic situations, objects are culturally and situationally
read and the meaning apprehended by the actor. Thus, when walking
in a forest, a tree may become the object of consideration due to its unusual beauty. The walker may be drawn to it and experience its ele-
gance in comparison to the trees around it. A meaning is applied to the
tree—beautiful—and experienced by the actor as an aesthetically
pleasing encounter. And as long as the object is nonproblematically read
in its immediate context with all of the potential meanings intuitively
and discursively, but not consciously, available, then reflexivity remains at this basic level and meaning is simply applied and experienced.

But, if our walker comes closer to the tree and notices peculiar signs engraved upon its surface, and notices a circle of stones surrounding the tree with four corners marked in recognition of the four elements or powers of the world, then the meaning that had been ascribed to the tree becomes an object itself for consideration. The tree is no longer read simply as a beautiful, aesthetic experience, but it now must be seen as something more. A new meaning is ascribed and reflexively read as a result of this second-order reflexivity. Thus, in the case where the contextual reading of an object has somehow been rendered problematic and the imputed meaning itself becomes an object of consideration, reflexivity moves up another level. Unless there are problems reinterpreting the object, this process usually does not represent a problem for humans. In the case where the reassignment of meaning becomes problematic, that is, a new meaning is not forthcoming in view of the new information, then people will cycle through this second-order reflexivity until a new meaning is achieved, or, if it is determined that no new meaning is possible in this situation—with these cues, using this particular cultural "tool-kit"—people will tend to leave the situation.

Yet a third-order of reflexivity is possible. It is in this level of reflexivity that the problem of meaning resides. In this level there is no objective referent, no tree in the forest to consider, but there is simply a philosophical inquiry into the pure symbol: what is the meaning of meaning? This kind of inquiry may come about as the result of continued problems at the second level of reflexivity (and will thus tend to become more pronounced under conditions of rapid cultural and social change) or as part of an abstracted academic pursuit. At this level, the entire meaning structure becomes problematic and subject to doubt. Because there is no ultimate truth or reality in back of culture, third-order reflexivity will tend to make people become ontologically and existentially insecure, and facticity will tend to become a vaporous phantom. The important issue for this argument is that *this order of reflexivity is inherently implied in the first order.* The problem of meaning and third-order reflexivity has always been at least a potential problem for humanity. As Luhmann (1985) argues, the problem of meaning originates from a paradox: culture both creates and makes contingent meaning and reality. The self-referential character of culture and humanity's essential reflexivity inexorably create a sense of uncertainty and insecurity about reality and meaning. And, as I will argue, the "necessity of contingency" (Luhmann, 1985, p. 210) pushes people toward certain types of interactions.

In order to be effective, humans must accept cultural reality in a taken-for-granted manner. Reflexivity must be avoided, and the incorrigible assumptions underlying culture and its self-referential nature must be left intact (see Mehan & Wood, 1975). This taken-for-grantedness of cultural reality is produced in one of two ways: through massification/institutionalization or sacredization. Of the two processes, sacredization, as produced through ritual activity, provides the more effective block to reflexivity. Rituals have the peculiar property of being able to "fuse" reflexivity. Though Mead was not referring directly to rituals, he nonetheless explained their ability to stop reflexivity. According to Mead, reflexive thought occurs between the "I" and the "Me" of the self. Mead (1934/1962, p. 273) posited that in some social activities, like rituals, the individual can become engrossed in a "common effort in which one is stimulated by the others to do the same thing they are doing." In such cases, people get caughtup in the moment, and reflexivity is inhibited. "It is where the 'I' and the 'me' can in some sense fuse that there arises the peculiar sense of exaltation which belongs to the religious and patriotic" (Mead, 1934/1962, p. 273). When reflexivity is fused, people perceive their experience as an essential one, one that is directly related to the thing-in-itself and one that appears to possess its own inherent reality. This kind of experience carries its own ontology and facticity. Thus it is the primary function of ritual to dampen reflexivity and prevent the collapse of social reality. It is interesting to note that this sense of internal at-one-ment is the goal of much religious meditation. In the Judaeo-Christian scriptures this state is spoken of as an inner stillness: "meditate in your heart upon your bed, and be still" (Psalm 4:4, New American Standard Version). In eastern religions this "eternal bliss" is generally expressed as a diffusion of the self with the true nature of the universe—emptiness. For example, Prajna is the Hindu expression for intuitive insight into emptiness or the true nature of reality.

On the whole, then, this perspective of culture has placed an undue emphasis on the content of religion and the place of religion in society. Ultimately, it does not matter what religion is present, that is, its content. What is important are the kinds of behaviors for which religion has historically created space. Society does not need organized religion to function, and neither do individuals. What is needed is the process of creating high levels of meaning that render important areas of culture less contingent. Some of these important areas have to do with ultimate questions—the meaning of life, death, suffering, tragedy—but the content of the answers is superfluous, and they do not need to be contained in a holistic system. Thus, in a postmodern society, the "answers" may be found and created in diverse situations and symbolic cultures that have relatively little connection one to another and do not constitute an integrated, complete whole, and those answers may be experienced as real as the ones produced in more traditional societies. It is the interaction around these questions and their answers that is paramount.

Additionally, it may be the case that these existential questions do not need to be asked in postmodernity. Questions such as these are the product of a certain kind of reflexivity: thinking about lived issues concerning life and death. It is theoretically possible that in a postmodern society these questions will be less pressing than in the past. Anthony Giddens (1990; 1991) argues that one of the defining features of modernity is the presence of disembedding mechanisms. There are two types of mechanisms: abstract systems—generalized media of exchange, systems of abstracting time and place, and communication systems—and expert systems of knowledge. These disembedding processes tend to remove from daily life considerations of death and certain dynamic issues of life. Thus the "insane," the seriously ill, and the criminal are all hidden away, as is the process of dying; issues concerning family and children and sexuality are given over to knowledge systems controlled by experts and are thus cloistered away from vital interaction. The result is that people have little exposure to situations that would engage them morally about existential or important questions, this is Bellah's lament. The removal of these "problems" from daily consideration indicates that people will tend to be less reflexive about them and that these existential questions are, for all practical purposes, set aside.

Thus the "need" for organized and reified answers to life's great transcendent questions would diminish. The reflexivity concerning suffering and death would be institutionally dampened and the need to stop that particular reflexivity by producing a reified reality through ritual performance would tend to lessen. Nonetheless, in a more general fashion, cultural reality must still be reified, reflexivity must be held in check, if not from transcendental questions, then simply from the terror of meaninglessness, and rituals must produce high levels of affect-meaning, regardless of the content. And while the moralists may mourn the passing of the religious content, as they have in every era, the dense rituals surrounding football, soccer, basketball, rock concerts, and extreme sports can theoretically provide a strong enough sense of reality and identity to prevent problematic levels of reflexivity and the postmodern loss of meaning and death of the subject.

Additionally, in the moral perspective, religion and the need for religious meaning are understood explicitly in terms of the societal level rather than the individual or group level. But the need to relieve uncertainty and reflexivity, and the need for some level of meaning and reality, are best understood at the level of the interaction and in terms of the individual as a socially produced entity, particularly in a postmodern society. Because signification culture is paramount for human life, there is a tendency to maintain a level of cultural stability at the highest possible level of society. But because of the problems that postmodernism has identified, it has become increasingly difficult to stabilize culture and its meaning at the system level. Thus it is the micro-level dynamics of culture that provide and stabilize meaning and reality for people in a postmodern society.

In many aspects the social system is ultimately dependent upon symbolic and, by implication, imaginative activity.[7] Cultural meaning has always had at its core "agreement reality," people collectively agreeing upon a specified and restricted meaning. This agreement, and the need to maintain a sense of continuous reality, are what Goffman had in mind when he argued that every encounter represents an opportunity for an individual to

> derive a firm sense of reality. . . . When an incident occurs and spontaneous involvement is threatened, then reality is threatened. Unless the disturbance is checked, unless the interactants regain their proper involvement, *the illusion of reality* [italics added] will be shattered, the minute social system that is brought into being with each encounter will be disorganized, and the participants will feel unruled, unreal, and anomic. Aside from the sense of reality it offers, a particular encounter may be of little consequence. (Goffman, 1967, p. 135)

And because meaning has always had a dependency upon the micro-level, and because culture inherently produces reflexivity, culture has always produced certain needs felt at the individual and interactional level, and these needs have driven the production of ritualized affect-meaning.

One such need is a sense of facticity, the assurance of living in a shared intelligibility in a cultural and historical context. Jonathan Turner (1988, pp. 49–51) uses the term facticity to conceptualize the ethnomethodological concern with the construction of social order: actors use folk methods in encounters—for example, accounting, waiting, indexicality—to construct, sustain, or repair a sense of shared external and internal worlds. This sense of shared social and subjective worlds produces a perception of these created worlds as being factual, as having a sense of facticity about socially constructed reality. At a more nonconscious level, this need is expressed as a need for what Giddens (1984) terms "ontological security" (p. 50), a concept derived from the work of Martin Heidegger. Heidegger (1926/1962, pp. 228–235) points out that there is a certain anxiety that accompanies the human being in the world. This anxiety is intimately tied to living in a meaningful universe, to existing in time. Every attribution of meaning involves a move from the particular to something more general, or from individual things to the properties which they have. This move inherently calls into question the existence of the general properties: Do these properties truly exist? Do they have a separate being apart from the particulars? These are the questions of ontology.[8] Social categories fall prey to this question of ontology as do identities and the ultimate identity of the self. From the point of view of meaning endowment, every experience is a particular, it exists in a single moment without reference to any past or future, and it is thus without meaning, it simply is/was. In order for the experience to mean something, it must become the object of consideration by a self-aware being, and it is that intentionality that lifts the experience out of its simple and essential reality and situates it in time and biographic history, as the subjective perspective points out. But the entire process of intentionality presupposes an already existing property called the self, for the experience must be understood with reference to something that already exists out of the moment. The self is a property that has been generalized out of the particulars; the self is an object to the individual. And, as such, it, and the reality that it experiences, are subject to ontological questions and problems.

Giddens links ontological security with trust and routine and autonomy of bodily control. However my emphasis in considering ontological security is a bit different than Giddens's; I argue that ontological security and facticity become issues for humanity because culture intrinsically produces reflexivity. While I certainly agree with Giddens's position, the issue of sign-uncertainty (Do symbolic objects have an ontological existence?)—the inevitable effect of cultural meaning and reflexivity—must be considered as well; an issue that I think is more in keeping with Heidegger's concerns. While Giddens argues that people deal with the anxiety that ontological insecurity produces on a daily basis through the use of routine, my argument emphasizes the use of ritual and emotion to handle ontological anxiety. Because of the *emotional impact* that the meaning produced during intense interactions carries, it presents itself, and the symbols and general categories that are involved, as facts carrying their own ontology: reflexivity is thus dampened and the problem of meaning and the resulting ontological insecurities are resolved.

THE MICRODYNAMICS OF CULTURE AND THE PRODUCTION OF AFFECT-MEANING

I have made a distinction between sense- and affect-meaning. Structuralists are correct in that most sense-meaning is derived from the way in which signs and symbols are organized and presented. What they have missed is the mechanism though which sense-meaning is originally created and subsequently experienced by humans: the focus of psychic energy (Parsons) or intentionality (Schutz). On the other hand, affect-meaning is primarily produced by humans as they focus their emotional energy on an object, singling it out from the plethora of experience in which people are involved. The level of affect-meaning is directly associated with the experience of reality a person may have with a cultural entity: the higher the affect-meaning, the greater is the reality associated with any culture system or part thereof. This reification function of affect-meaning generally works in tandem with the process of massification: greater numbers of people, length of time, and geographic space. Thus the level of objectification, or felt reality, associated with culture is a positive function of affect-meaning and massification. Although these two processes generally work together, they are analytically and empirically distinct. For example, the affective reality of radical and religious groups is preferred by them over the massified reality of society at large. And, in the case of postmodernity, reality that has become fragmented at the structured level, due to the processes that lead to demassification, may become reified at the micro-level through ritualized activity.

Durkheim argued that groups in interaction confer emotional significance on symbolic objects. Thus, as humans focus their attention on objects in their environment, these objects become significant and "infused" with a certain degree of emotional energy. I use the term "infused" metaphorically. It is not the case that signs can contain meaning in and of themselves: sense-meaning is experienced through the focus of psychic energy and affect-meaning through the focus of emotional energy. Thus symbols are used as points of mutual reference around which participants may interact and create and recreate different kinds of meanings. Affective symbols are used in interaction, which in turn triggers an emotional response in the people who have in the past focused their attention upon the object.

Randall Collins (1988, pp. 193–201) has explicated the Durkheimian process of interaction. Collins uses the concepts of physical co-presence, common focus of attention, mutual awareness, and common emotional mood to define an interaction ritual. While I agree with Collins that these elements are necessary conditions for a ritual, they are not sufficient. Collins's four elements can occur during any interaction, thus facilitating the buildup of emotional energy, but never be repeated again in the same way with the same people. A ritual, on the other hand, while it contains these four elements, also has the quality of patterned and repeated interaction that is indigenous to a specific group or individual. I thus use Collins's concepts to explain the variability of interaction intensity, and I see ritual as an added dimension. I further modify Collins's conceptualization by assuming mutual awareness in the presence of physical proximity and common focus of attention; I do not conceive of awareness varying independently of co-presence and mutual focus.

Generally, then, interactions vary by their level of intensity, intensity being a positive, multiplicative function of mutual presence, com-

mon focus of attention, and common emotional mood. Each of these interactional elements may vary independently. Because it is the focus of
attention that links for the interactants the emotional experience and
the symbolic object, mutual focus of attention is the most important of
the interactional dimensions. An ideal type of mutual focus can be conceptualized as a single focus of attention where everybody in the group
is focused on the same object and the same time. As a group moves away
from this ideal type, the amount of available energy lessens. Thus the
more the interests of interactants are diverse and/or crosscutting, the
lower will be the available collective energy for any one item. Additionally, the greater are the diversity and/or crosscutting interests of
members in an encounter, the greater is the possibility of conflict, and
the less likely is the possibility of mutual focus.

Mutual focus of attention and common emotional mood tend to be
jointly reinforcing. As Collins (1988) argues, a common focus of attention "cumulatively interacts" with a common emotional mood, such
that "the spread of a common emotion enhances the pressure for a common focus of attention" (p. 194). Although the subjective experience of
each participant need not be identical, the more similar is the emotional mood of the interactants, the more likely they are to focus on the
same object, and the more similar will be the affect-meaning associated
with a symbolic object. Mutual presence is defined by proximity: the
closer individuals are in physical space, the more likely is the interaction to be intense. There are three reasons mutual presence is important.
First, a mutual focus of attention is encouraged through monitoring, and
monitoring is a function of co-presence. Second, interaction consists of
physically enacted cues as well as speech. The more discernible are
these cues, the more the interaction will tend to be meaningful. Because
many of these cues are minute gestures, proximity aids in perception and
interpretation. And, third, the level of emotional energy that is
achieved is a function of the pace or time-sequencing of the interaction.

There are two elements that define the pace of interaction: rate and
rhythmic synchronization. The level of emotional energy developed in
an interaction is a function of the rate of interaction. If we employ
Mead's (1934/1962) definition of meaningful interaction—the presentation of a significant symbol, a response to the significant symbol, and a
response to the response—then the speed at which this "loop" can be
repeated influences the level of emotional energy. Each "read and response" entails an emotional response, and these emotional responses
cumulatively reinforce and add to one another. The rate of the interaction has a curvilinear effect: initial increases in the rate of interaction
will tend to increase the level of emotional energy, but if the interaction loop occurs at too rapid a pace, then the interaction and its emotional energy will tend to break down. There also tends to be an ebb and

flow to the rate of interaction; people move in and out of rapid interaction sequences. The second element to the pace of an interaction is the rhythm of the interaction. The rhythm of an interaction and rhythmic entrainment tend to be ritualized elements of an interaction, and so I will defer consideration of the place of rhythm in interaction until the section on rituals.

To recapitulate so far, the level of emotional energy experienced in an interaction, and thus the culturally available affect-meaning, is a positive function of the level of interaction intensity. Interaction intensity is a positive and multiplicative function of mutual presence, common focus, and common emotional mood. Thus the higher the proportion of individuals in group interaction that share a common focus of attention and common emotional mood, and the closer their proximity one to another, the greater is the tendency for the group to experience a high level of affect-meaning and emotional energy. And, as Durkheim points out, the higher the level of emotional energy in an interaction, the greater is the tendency for the interactants to associate that emotion with an object or sign, thus creating a trigger to help elicit the same interaction pattern and resultant affect-meaning in later interactions and reproducing a meaningful reality.

The probability that intense interactions will occur and be repeated is a general function of network density and uncertainty. Uncertainty is a sporadic dynamic and was mentioned by both Bellah and Wuthnow. Uncertainty is sporadic in the sense that the experience of acute uncertainty generally occurs only occasionally. But as I have stated, diffuse anxiety or uncertainty over the reality of culture is almost a constant but nonconscious pressure for human beings, as Garfinkel's (1967) breeching experiments demonstrate. Bellah argues that the level of uncertainty will rise as the result of the presence of perceived threat or system breakdown, which, in turn, will tend to create pressures for people to produce greater emotional investment in the superstructure, to the degree that it will take on a sacred quality. Wuthnow argues that uncertainty arises as the result of an external shock (external to the culture system), an increase in available behavioral or definitional options, and/or the ambiguity of the meaning of a situation. In response to uncertainty, Wuthnow argues, ritualized behavior will increase in order to dramatize the qualities of the society that will reinstate equilibrium. Generalizing Bellah's and Wuthnow's concepts, uncertainty tends to increase in the presence of a perceived threat and/or sudden or rapid change. Rapid change tends to increase the number and complexity of culturally available options for behavior and simultaneously to decrease taken-for-granted definitions of the situation.

Both threat and change negatively influence facticity and ontological security. Facticity is based on the need for a taken-for-granted sense of shared external and internal worlds; threat and change challenge that taken-for-grantedness. Ontological security is founded on trust in the predictability and continuity of the symbolic-object world. Again, threat and change render predictability and continuity uncertain. Driven by the needs of facticity and ontological security, individuals will, in the face of threat and/or change, seek to alleviate uncertainty. One of the ways uncertainty is addressed at the micro-level is through the construction and reinforcement of symbolic meaning. This assertion is like Bellah's but on the micro-level of interaction, where meaning "abides." Thus, when there is an increase in the level of experienced uncertainty, interactions will tend to occur more frequently and become more intense.

The second element that increases the probability that intense interaction will occur is network density. Network density refers to the degree to which an individual's encounters are repetitious in terms of people, time, and situations. Low network density is in keeping with Collins's (1975, p. 75) concept of cosmopolitanism and refers to an interaction pattern that tends to have diversity of communication occurring with diverse groups in various places—individuals constantly interacting with different people in different situations for different reasons. In a dense network, individuals primarily interact with a relatively small group of people over extended periods of time in similar circumstances. Due to the social network structure, ease of interaction, and the presence of a stock of particularized symbols, dense interaction networks tend to facilitate repeated and intense interactions. And because symbols that are highly particular are subject to repeated, patterned interaction, they tend to take on the characteristics of Durkheim's sacred symbols with clear boundaries and high amounts of affect-meaning. That is, the sacred is perceived and experienced as having emotional boundaries separating it from other objects. These sacred symbols thus appear to the interactants as having a different reality than nonsacred symbols. Therefore, the greater the density of an interaction network, the larger is the stock of particularized symbols, both in terms of absolute numbers and affect-meaning, and the greater is the tendency for intense interaction. The presence of particularized symbols and repeated, intense interactions are mutually reinforcing.

One of the important points that postmodernism tries to make is that the boundaries between categories have broken down and people are subject to ambivalence. Ambivalence is the possibility of assigning an object to more than one category—it is a failure of categorization. It is through the classificatory function of language that humans are able to impose an order upon a seemingly chaotic world; the endless stream of the physical world is broken up into discrete chunks that in turn impart meaning to (from a human point of view) a meaningless universe

(Zerubavel, 1991). The success of categories to provide and maintain meaning is dependent upon the strength of their borders; as the boundaries between classified objects breaks down, ambiguity increases. Postmodernists claim that as a result of the fragmentation of culture and social structure, the borders between categories, and thus the experience of meaningful reality, have broken down. Bauman (1991) characterizes ambivalence as the waste of modernity, the failure of modernism to sufficiently and obdurately categorize the world: "the other of the modern intellect is polysemy, cognitive dissonance, polyvalent definitions, contingency" (p. 9). But the conclusions of postmodernism are based on a myopic view of reality construction, seeing only the macro-level, sense-meaning properties. Yet boundaries between categories are not simply creating and maintained through cognitive and structural processes but are also emotionally produced and reified. Thus people in their networks of interaction may preserve and creatively produce the boundaries that make up the meaningful world even under conditions of postmodernity; in fact, as I have argued, people are pushed by the twin needs of facticity and ontological security to produce an affectively meaningful universe at the micro-level in a postmodern era.

Because affect-meaning is a characteristic of interaction and not the symbol, it is important that the interaction be repeatable. The existence of a symbol facilitates the initial affective response, but it is the process of ritual that renders the level of emotional energy associated with the symbol repeatable and a stable feature of interaction. As we have seen, ritual is typically defined as a reflection or dramatic display of social-structural relations and history that functions as a collective memory or a metalanguage in which society talks about itself. Yet, from a social constructionist point of view, it is important to emphasize that rituals consist of "stereotyped sequences of behavior that symbolically denote and *emotionally infuse* [italics added] the ongoing flow of interaction" (Turner, 1988, p. 161). This emotional energy, in turn, functions to meet the individual's needs for group inclusion, trust, ontological security, symbolic gratification, self-confirmation, and facticity. Thus rituals are best conceived of as the patterned and stereotypical gestures, both verbal and nonverbal, that have come to be associated with explicit symbols and/or portions of an action or interaction *that facilitate the dynamics of intensified interaction.* In this definition, the presence of the elements determining interaction intensity is vital; not including these elements has led to conceptualizations of rituals as being lifeless or empty (see Halle, 1984). But if I am correct in my assertion that the primary function of a ritual is to keep reflexivity at a manageable level, then it is imperative to understand rituals in terms of interaction intensity and affect-meaning.

One element of interaction that is particularly amenable to rituali-zation is rhythm, due, in part, to the fact that many of the rhythmic elements in interaction occur faster than the conscious mind can register. Rhythm refers to recurrent patterns in the use of personal-interactional space and nonverbal cues during interaction. People of similar groups have the ability to pace an interaction in terms of conversation, ges-tures, and cues in a like manner. Part of the success or intensity of an interaction is a function of rhythm or timing. Commenting on the life-style of monks, Eviatar Zerubavel (1981) argues that "temporal symme-try, which involves synchronizing the activities of different individuals, is actually one of the fundamental principles of social or-ganization" (p. 65). Zerubavel asserts that synchronization helps to form a sense of togetherness, a kind of Durkheimian mechanical soli-darity. On a more minute level, in a study of body motion and speech using 16 mm film, Condon and Ogston (1971) discovered that in interac-tion "a hearer's body was found to 'dance' in precise harmony with the speaker" (p. 158). Based on these and similar empirical studies, Col-lins (1988) proposes that individuals in interaction may reach a "rhythmic synchronization" in which "people become 'locked into' the ritual and engrossed by the reality it creates" (p. 202). In like manner, I am arguing that the level of affect-meaning created in an interaction is a function of the pace of the interaction, its rate and rhythm.

Rhythm has two general qualities: stress and alacrity. Stress refers to the degree of punctuation a rhythm has. There tends to be a concor-dance between the rhythm of speech and the rhythmic expressions of the body (see McNeill, 1992). Thus an interaction may be highly punc-tuated with large movements and strong voice inflection or it may be very subtle with small movements and more monotone voice inflection. Alacrity refers to how quickly the different cues follow one another. Alacrity in interactions may occur quickly with cues following on the heels of one another, or overlapping. Generally, the faster the rate of alacrity and the greater the stress in an interaction, the greater is the intensity of the interaction and the subsequent level of emotional en-ergy. Again, the effect is curvilinear.

While rituals are most powerful and are generally found in group in-teractions, rituals may be performed in private. I use the term "ritual" guardedly here. Individual rituals are not interactions per se, but they do seem to be able to produce the same type of emotional responses with regard to reality construction as the group-based rituals. Yet, for most people, there is a felt necessity to experience their realities as objective and to be accepted by the collective as a normal and unthreatening member; thus there will be a general tendency to link private rituals in some fashion with a social group, but these private rituals do stand as a distinct form of human behavior. The most important elements for individual rituals are the presence of a single focus of attention, a strong, consistent emotional reaction, and patterned, rhythmic behaviors. People must experience both the cognitive and emotional focus of attention for an individual ritual to occur. But this focus is obviously not sufficient to produce ritual effects; the individual must also perform patterned behaviors around this emotional and psychic focus. The greater the level of emotional and psychic focus and the more rhythmic the patterned behaviors, the more likely is it that the individual will produce a ritual that will be performed for the experience of affect-meaning-reality construction, and the greater will be the level of emotional energy. A music fan who produces for a given song a particular set of sequenced actions that are repeatedly performed in a similar manner with a similar focus, for example, a dance, is an example of a private ritual. Oftentimes these kinds of rituals incorporate certain patterned behaviors, like lighting candles and burning incense, that aid in the focus of attention and recreating the proper emotional mood. Again, this person will have the tendency to try and translate this private experience into a group ritual by performing it at a concert, preferably with other fans. This link will objectify the individual's reality, confirm their membership in a social collective, and add to the level of affect-meaning experienced.

NOTES

1. My summary of Bellah's ideas includes work from sources he co-authored with others: Richard Madsen, William M. Sullivan, Ann Swidler, and Steven M. Tipton. For ease of discussion, I generally refer to this corpus as simply "Bellah." The corporate work is distinctly defined by Bellah, as a comparison with Swidler's (1986) work will testify, and represents a continuation of his earlier theorizing.

2. The association between differentiation and problems of coordination and control was first discovered by Herbert Spencer (1873). Also see Jonathan H. Turner (1985; 1995) for an elaboration.

3. It is interesting to note that many of Wuthnow's central concepts— uncertainty, decoupling, and systemic shock—have a great affinity with the literature on organizations. Uncertainty is a central dynamic in DiMaggio and Powell's account of institutional isomorphism (Paul J. DiMaggio and Walter W. Powell, "The Iron Cage Revisited: Institutional Isomorphism and Collective Rationality in Organizational Fields," *American Sociological Review*, 1983, 48:147-160). Meyer and Rowan argue that conflicts between the ceremonial rules of an organization and the demands of efficiency are resolved by decoupling formal structure from actual work activities (John W. Meyer and Brian Rowan, "Institutionalized Organizations: Formal Structure as Myth and Ceremony," *American Journal of Sociology*, 1977, 83 [2]:340-363). And the concept of institutional shock is explicitly used by Neil Fligstein. He argues that a shock to an institutional field will provide a "turbulence" in the field which in turn will create a gap in the normative,

accounting, and cognitive structures of the social actors within the field (Neil Fligstein, "The Structural Transformation of American Industry: An Institutional Account of the Causes of Diversification in the Largest Firms, 1919-1979," in *The New Institutionalism in Organizational Analysis*, edited by Walter W. Powell and Paul J. DiMaggio, 1991, Chicago: University of Chicago Press). And, of course, Wuthnow's use of the environment and population ecology is foreshadowed in the work of Amos H. Hawley and Julian H. Steward ("Ecology," in *International Encyclopedia of the Social Sciences*, edited by David L. Sills, 1968, New York: Macmillan and Free Press), and Michael T. Hannan and John Freeman ("The Population Ecology of Organizations," *American Journal of Sociology*, 1977, 82 [5]:929-964).

4. Although Wuthnow never uses the term "equilibrium," his entire population ecology model is premised on a disturbed moral environment. To state the obvious, disruption presupposes some state of equilibrium.

5. For example, see Niklas Luhmann, *The Differentiation of Society* (New York: Columbia University Press, 1982). For a more generalized approach, please see Jonathan H. Turner (1995, chapter 8).

6. It is important to note that this particular kind of passivity is for Wuthnow a characteristic of modern communities. He does have a concept of Catholic rituals as local community interaction in a more historical or traditional setting.

7. I recognize the inherent danger of cultural reductionism in my position. I am not arguing against the reality or independent causal force of structural or material processes. But I am arguing that undergirding these forces is a cultural reality. For example, Turner (1995) effectively argues for a number of macrodynamics, among them population, production, and power. But these dynamics assume a cultural base. The initial force in Turner's theory is population: as a population increases in size, so does the need for production and for coordination and control, power. But the concept of population assumes identity. If the number of unconnected individuals in a geographic space increases without the benefit of a cultural identity, the ensuing dynamics will be very different form those proposed by Turner. Power and production both assume an institutional framework: the economy and the state. Again, both are upheld by culture. I am not denying ontological status to any of these macro-forces, nor am I denying them independent causal force. But I am arguing that their ontology and causality are predicated upon a culturally defined reality, and that reality varies.

8. "Ontology [refers to] that theoretical inquiry which is explicitly devoted to the meaning of entities" (Heidegger, 1926/1962, p. 32) and seeks to uncover the essential characteristics of existing in the world (Grossman, 1992).

4

The Ideological Perspective and the Challenge to Meaning and Reality

> The demons can be exorcised, but only by seeing them for what they are. Those who claim that the demons can be exorcised only by action in the world, not by theorizing about them, seem to be possessed by demons of their own, especially the demon of asceticism; one senses here the communal hostility of the ascetic to the individual luxury of intellectual contemplation. And here is the danger. Those who deny everything for the self deny it as well for others; our altruism, taken too exclusively, is an infinite regress, passing a bucket from hand to hand that never reaches the fire. When we act, we call out the demons to meet us. Be careful; they are ourselves.
>
> —Randall Collins (1974, p. 440)

My general argument is premised on the assumption that most human experience is constructed through culture and that cultural production tends to create pressures for equilibrating behaviors. Culture produces sense- and affect-meaning and reality for people. Because it is symbolic, the stability of culture is intrinsically precarious and contingent upon human agency for its existence, and this contingency pressures humans to stabilize meaning and reality through producing social-order and equilibrium. Recognizing this effect on the micro-level, Goffman (1967) states that in encounters "the ritual order seems to be organized basically on accommodative lines" (p. 42), so that people may be able "to maintain a specified and obligatory kind of ritual equilibrium" (p. 45). But culture is also based in the practice of exclusion. In order for meaning to be significant, it is not the case that it can mean everything. By their very nature, categories exclude and obtain meaning as they are defined in contrast to something else; the most powerful categories are set in binary opposition, an extreme case of exclusion. This process of exclusion not only influences elements of culture but groups of people as well, since meaningful groups exist culturally and socially only through exclusion. But this process is at times oppressive, and, because of culture's relationship to real people, the perspective of culture-as-ideology presents a challenge to the process of meaning and reality production.

GENERAL INTRODUCTION TO THE IDEOLOGICAL PERSPECTIVE

There are two defining features of this perspective: culture functions as an ideology that produces or is based upon a type of false consciousness and works to oppress a group of people; and, there is generally an imperative for change that is accomplished, to one degree or another, through the formation of a critical and/or class consciousness. The contours of this perspective were initially drawn up by Karl Marx and Frederick Engels (Marx, 1888/1978; Marx & Engels, 1844/1978; 1848/1961; 1932/1978), and later elaborated by Georg Lukács (1922/1971) and Antonio Gramsci (1971). My contemporary examples of this perspective of culture are the Birmingham School of Cultural Studies (Hoggart, 1957; Williams, 1958, 1961, 1976, 1993; Hall & Jefferson, 1976; Hall, 1980, 1982) and Pierre Bourdieu (1971, 1979/1984, 1983/1986, 1989, 1991).

Because of his polemic against idealism, Marx was unable to take into account the importance of culture to human meaning and reality. This failing led to an overemphasis on the material-economic structure. Additionally, he did not see the implications in his concepts of commodification and exchange-value for culture. These elements were left for later theorists to stress and develop. Conceptually, from Marx to Bourdieu, there is a marked progression, from a focus on class-material relations and coercive oppression to an emphasis on symbolic relations and "cooperative oppression."

Marx, and to a lesser degree Engels, posit a material-class base for culture, ideology, and false consciousness. Lukács maintains Marx's class-material base, in the sense that he argues that commodification is the force behind false consciousness, but he also grants culture a force of its own through a conceptualization of the process of reification. But Lukács was not the first to posit culture in a nonreductionist manner. Though Marx clearly argues for economic determinism, Engels maintains that ideology, once formed, does not stand isolated and impotent with reference to the economy. Rather, there is a reflexive element: "once an historic element has been brought into the world by other, ultimately economic causes, it reacts, can react on its environment and even on the causes that have given rise to it" (Engels, 1893/1968, p. 710; see also, Marx & Engels, 1932/1978, p. 164).

In terms of institutions, this process of feedback begins with the state as "the first ideological power over man" (Engels, 1885/1968, p. 627). A state is brought into existence through the whole of society's desire to protect its interests against threat. Eventually and inexorably the state becomes the tool of a given class. "But once the state has become an independent power *vis-à-vis* society, it produces forthwith a further ideology" (Engels, 1885/1968, p. 627). In a sense, the state becomes occupied with itself as a perceived independent entity, albeit from a pure Marxian point of view through a false consciousness, and produces for itself a reified ideology. Engels argues that this process occurs with all ideologies and institutions, with the result that a developed ideology becomes subject to its own laws and reacts back on the ultimate cause, the material relations of the economy. The concept of an independent culture system becomes progressively more pronounced with later theorists.

Gramsci's work represents a major turning point in viewing culture as ideology. He asserts, in contradiction to Marx, that possessing the material means of production does not necessarily equate to controlling the mental means of production. In order to dominate culture and society, an elite class must control the ideational institutions as certainly as they control the economic organizations. This control is won through the process of hegemony with the participation of the oppressed. The contemporary school of Cultural Studies expands Gramsci's analysis of hegemonic processes and explicitly adds elements from the linguistic-structuralist school. The general rubric of Cultural Studies refers to an analytic tradition that began and continues to be defined by the Birmingham Centre for Contemporary Cultural Studies. Stuart Hall, the Centre's director from 1969 to 1979, characterizes the ongoing work as having a certain theoretical pluralism, drawing from diverse sources and never arriving at an orthodoxy. In his account of the Centre's theoretical roots, Hall (1980) lists such diverse sources as Marx, Weber, Mead, Becker, Barthes, Lukács, Althusser, Foucault, and feminisms.[1] But although change and debate are seemingly central to the project, the originating texts by Hoggart, Williams, and Thompson, and Gramsci's concept of hegemony have dominated the discourse from its inception to the present; it is Cultural Studies' concern with hegemony, ideology, and class that justify the Centre's inclusion in this perspective. The Birmingham School tends to define culture in pluralistic terms and finds the process of hegemony in the act of communication, particularly mass communication. Within this emphasis, there has been an acknowledged shift to reading culture as a text through semiotic analysis.

My inclusion of Bourdieu requires justification and comment. On some level, Bourdieu's work defies categorization. He has been variously labeled Functionalist, Marxist, Post-Marxist, Structuralist, Post-Structuralist, and Weberian. I think one of the reasons behind this problem of categorization is hinted at by Mahar, Harker, and Wilkes (1990), though I do not think that they would agree with my conclusion. They characterize Bourdieu as working in a "spiral" manner moving between theory, empirical substance, and different levels of theory; his conceptualizations are written and rewritten in a dialectic fashion. But this approach has resulted in a body of work that is, at best, mystifying. As van den Berg (1995) notes: "Perhaps the persistent 'misunderstandings' of his work are at least in part due to his own impenetrable prose" (p. 277). Mahar, Harker, and Wilkes also argue that to truly understand Bourdieu, one must trace his theory through its entire thirty-year development. That is, later formulations are not necessarily built upon nor do they include his earlier work—Bourdieu's theory does not progress in linear fashion, and it is nowhere succinctly stated. Regardless, given Bourdieu's theoretical link between reality and symbolic recognition, it is both understandable and ironic that his work defies and he actively fights attempts at categorization. Bids at typing his work have been met with disdain from Bourdieu himself; he generally feels "mis-recognized" by his American readers (see Calhoun, LiPuma, & Postone 1993).

Bourdieu (1989) refers to his own work as "structuralist constructivism" (p. 14).[2] He uses the term "structuralist" to describe his basic approach: he posits the existence of structures that order the social world and that lie outside the consciousness or efficacy of the individual or social group. Put another way, "interactions . . . mask the structures that are realized in them" (Bourdieu, 1989, p. 16). For Bourdieu, "the real" is not to be found with individuals or groups—substances—but with relations among objective elements within a structure. His conceptualization of the interplay between the structure and the social world is gathered together under the term "constructivism," and his social construction is carried out by habitus.

My reason for placing Bourdieu under the general rubric of culture-as-ideology is the centrality of the process of misrecognition to his theory, a concept that is in back of Marx's notion of false consciousness—reality is misrecognized for its true nature, and misrecognition is a necessary condition for symbolic violence and oppression. It must be noted that this misrecognition does not necessarily occur at the level of the individual. Bourdieu works hard at distancing himself from the subjective consciousness, as will be seen in his intent behind the use of habitus. Misrecognition is to some extent dependent upon the power of symbolic definition, and this power lies squarely in institutionally accredited sources.

MARX, ENGELS, LUKÁCS, AND GRAMSCI: IDEOLOGY AND SOCIAL CHANGE

In general, the concept of ideology is descriptive of an entire set of false ideas, categories, and understandings through which an individual or group is aware of the world. As Engels (1893/1968) notes: "Ideology is a process accomplished by the so-called thinker consciously . . . but with a false consciousness. The real motive forces impelling him remain unknown to him" (p. 700). The term "ideology" appears very little in the bulk of Marx's writings, but his conceptualization of ideology is an unmistakable thread running throughout his corpus. Larrain (1979, p. 15) argues that it was Marx who first fused the term "ideology" with a critical meaning.

Marx's formulation is founded on Hegel's concepts of inversion and dialectic. Hegel argues that reality is ideational and that the meaning behind empirical objects is best understood in terms of dialectical relations of determinate negation. According to Hegel, the material world is an illusion, and ultimate reality is to be found in the Idea. Throughout history the Idea is presented to humans in the form of a thesis, a kind of proposal for life. But, of necessity, every thesis implies its antithesis. These two elements of the Idea are in a sort of conflictual dialogue, warring with each other for supremacy. Out of this conflictual state eventually arises a synthesis, a creative blending of the thesis and its antagonist. And, according to Hegel, each new synthesis is a closer approximation of Truth: human history is thus the irresistible evolution of ideas toward complete knowledge. But Truth and the dialectic process are not generally perceived by humanity. True Reason is alienated because reason has taken the material world to be real; reality has been inverted from ideal to material. Hegel's notion of the dialectic is evolutionary and utopian: the final stage occurs when Reason recognizes itself as reality and the reified perception of the material world as ultimately a mistake.

Marx (1888/1978) accepts the process of the dialectic and concealment, but he argues that reality does not exist in concepts, ideas, or reflexive thought but rather in the material world of "human sensuous activity, practice" (p. 143). For Marx, the practice that is the basic defining feature of humanity is production: "They themselves begin to distinguish themselves from animals as soon as they begin to *produce* their means of subsistence" (Marx & Engels, 1932/1978, p. 150). Thus, in contrast to Hegel, Marx argues that it is material praxis, the means and relations of production, that constitute reality. Marx employed the concept of praxis to emphasize actual human experience and to solve the dilemma between the passivity of materialism and the speculation of idealism. Reality for Marx is created out of the things that humans do, out of their experience of production. But the perception of reality has been inverted since the time of primitive communism—the contradictions and oppression within the different economic systems have been successively hidden through different ideologies. In the capitalist system, the market is a prime mechanism through which the inversion takes place and ideology is created. The ideology of the market is individuality, equality, and freedom; the reality of the capitalist system is class, inequality, and oppression.

Marx ties the notions of ideology and false consciousness to the concept of class and the production of specific ideas, that is, culture. False consciousness is most clearly understood through a comparison to "species-consciousness," the concept of humanity as self-knowing, creatively producing beings (Marx & Engels, 1844/1978, p. 76). For Marx, the particular quality of being human is defined through the self-aware, free, and creative production of goods. These goods stand as a mirror by which humanity can know itself and its own reality. But when the productive movement and externalization of "species-being" is controlled by others, people are alienated from their labor as humans and produce a false consciousness of reality. Along with this separation comes the division of material from mental labor, and thus the ideology that forms the working class's understanding of reality comes from outside itself: "The ideas of the ruling class are in every epoch the ruling ideas. . . . The class which has the means of material production at its disposal, has control at the same time over the means of mental production, so that thereby, generally speaking, the ideas of those who lack the means of mental production are subject to it" (Marx & Engels, 1932/1978, pp. 172–173). These ideas of the ruling class to which the nonelite are subject constitute the essence of ideology.

Marx thus posits a dual process of ideology. On the one hand, false consciousness is produced individually through alienated praxis; and on the other hand, false consciousness is the result of not owning the means of ideational production. The first proposition identifies the location of the process of ideology within the experience of the individual and their conscious reflection on that experience; the second posits that the process is located in the superstructure of society. But neither of these themes is played out to their fullest potential in Marx's writings; that task remained for subsequent theorists.

Marx's commitment to economic determinism limited his view of the dynamic behind social change to the material dialectic and overt conflict. There are two dialectic processes at work in capitalism. First, the capitalist's drive for profit and expanding markets creates an ever-widening business cycle of overproduction and capital-centralization. The second dialectic concerns culture and involves the praxis of the proletariat: Marx argues that along with the crises of the business-profitability cycle, the class consciousness of the proletariat would eventually replace false consciousness. Class consciousness is the result of the ecological concentration of workers under conditions of mass production and the emergence of trade unions. As the oppressed are gathered together by the capitalists in ever larger factories, communication is facilitated and they can become aware of their collective interests. This beginning awareness leads them to question the legitimacy of the existing system and to form a distinct, unifying counter-ideology. The formation of this unifying culture is facilitated by the emergence of leadership, increasing levels of education, and more sophisticated means of communication and travel. Marx posits that these two elements, the business cycle and the production of class consciousness, will work together to create overt conflict and revolution.

Lukács reaffirms Marx's emphasis on the material class conditions underlying ideology, but at the same time he enlarges the role of consciousness "as the ascribed world-view of the class to a point in which it may appear as a substitute for the concrete practice of the class" (Larrain, 1979, p. 79). This class consciousness "consists in fact of the appropriate and rational reactions 'imputed' to a particular typical position in the process of production" (Lukács, 1922/1971, p. 51). Thus the construction of reality through conscious reflection begins to take on more importance in the formulation of ideology.

Lukács focuses on one aspect of Marx's critique of capitalism, commodification, to explain false consciousness. For Marx, commodification is the process through which the products of labor become reified and appear as independent and uncontrolled entities. Lukács (1922/1971) expands Marx's conceptualization and argues that the process of commodification affects every sphere of human existence and is the "central, structural problem of capitalist society in all its aspects" (p. 83). Commodification translates human activity and relations into objects that can be bought or sold. Value is determined not by any intrinsic feature of the activity or the relations, but by the impersonal forces of markets, over which individuals have no control. The objects and relations that will truly gratify human needs are hidden, and the commodified object is internalized and accepted as reality. Thus commodification results in a consciousness based on reified, false objects. This Lukácsian "reified mind" does not attempt to transcend its false foundation but through rationalization and calculation "progressively sinks more deeply, more fatefully and more definitively into the consciousness of man" (Lukács, 1922/1971, p. 93).

According to Lukács, class consciousness is difficult to achieve in precapitalistic societies: social status categories are too entwined with the economy for the ultimate economic determinants to be clearly seen. It is not until the dawn of capitalism, where the economic base is brazenly displayed, that "class consciousness arrived at the point where *it could become conscious.* From then on social conflict was reflected in an ideological struggle for consciousness and for the veiling or the exposure of the class character of society" (Lukács, 1922/1971, p. 59). Thus Lukács linked social and cultural conflict more explicitly than did Marx.

For Lukács, the fundamental insight of the dialectic is that the whole exists prior to the parts and that the parts must be interpreted by the whole. But the only way to truly see the whole is by standing outside of it—only the proletariat can conceive of the social system in its entirety: "the proletariat represents the true reality, namely the tendencies of history awakening into consciousness" (Lukács, 1922/1971, p. 199). The working class by its very position of alienation is capable of seeing the true whole, the knowledge of class relations from the standpoint of the entire society and its system of production and social relations. Bourgeois thought is simply an ahistorical acceptance of its own pertinent parts and an acceptance of the status quo.

But in producing a true consciousness the proletariat is faced with two problems: the problem of reification, "the necessary, immediate reality of every person living in capitalist society," and the "overwhelming resources of knowledge, culture and routine which the bourgeoisie undoubtedly possesses" (Lukács, 1922/1971, p. 197). Thus, though the working class is capable of grasping the whole, it is susceptible to both psychological false consciousness and the cultural resources of the elite. It is only through constant and conscious critical reflection on the obdurate totality of economic relations that these two problems can be overcome and the "reified structure of existence" be disrupted (Lukács, 1922/1971, p. 197). Lukács thus places the production of a critical consciousness and culture at the center of Marxian theory.

The work of Antonio Gramsci marks a clear break with the model of economic determinism and adds a sense of agency with reference to the culture-producing organizations that Lukács missed. While Marx argues for a one-to-one relationship between material and mental production, Gramsci recognizes that the organizations and institutions that chiefly create and maintain the general cultural tenor of a society are relatively autonomous of the economic sphere. In this formulation, hegemony and language are the principal conduits of false consciousness. Gramsci, like Weber, recognized that coercive power cannot be used in the long term as the ordinary means of social control; it is the last trump of the elite. Power must be legitimated, and the concept of hegemony captures Gramsci's notion of the process of legitimation. The hegemonic process is the effective synthesis of political, intellectual, and moral leadership through which a group moves from defending its own interests to unifying and directing all other social groups through a taken-for-granted ideology.[3] The concept of hegemony moves the focus of a critical study of class relations from the economy to culture.

Because consciousness is formed through language, Gramsci also identified language as a key determinate in creating false consciousness. But, Gramsci argues, language can never be a reflection of social reality and is thus ideological: at any historical moment the accepted form of language is a "fossilised and anachronistic" conception of the world (Gramsci, 1971, p. 325). In their ascent, each new class of elite develops a language that reflects the material relations in their own time. Once in power, however, the language of the elite turns from its reflective function to establish and maintain the interests of the elite. Thus false consciousness is the unreflective acceptance and use of a language created during a past set of class relations. It is historically regressive and reflects only the political interests of the ruling class. The masses participate in their own oppression through the unreflected use of language; they unknowingly perceive and replicate a social world based on ideology rather than reflected knowledge. By using this "verbal conception" of the world, the masses tend to become morally and politically passive. But it is not the case, Gramsci argues, that the masses are completely uncritical in their view of the world. They have what he termed "two theoretical consciousnesses," the awareness that is based in ideology and another consciousness which is implicit in their work-activity and links all fellow-workers together (Gramsci, 1971, p. 334). But in most circumstances, during "normal times," the oppressed act and speak as subordinate. This act of self-subordination "holds together a specific social group, it influences moral conduct and the direction of will . . . and produces a condition of moral and political passivity" (Gramsci, 1971, p. 332). Thus both Lukács and Gramsci conceptualize the working class as having the possibility of true consciousness but also having severe limitations.

Like Lukács, Gramsci also recognizes that the ability to rule does not depend on material relations alone—social change will involve a war of cultural positions, a battle for people's minds, not simply nor necessarily overt conflict. Revolution for Gramsci is not just the product of external economic forces as in classic Marxism, but revolutions are preceded by intense work of cultural penetration in which the elite classes participate. This cultural revolution is Gramsci's process of hegemony. And like Lukács, Gramsci posits that a critical consciousness, that of being among a particular hegemonic force on the part of the proletariat, is the first stage toward a cultural revolution. A philosophy of praxis begins with a critical, reflexive examination of self and the current world in which one lives. This philosophy will affect one's outlook, speech, and practice. The first fruits of this critical consciousness will be a sense of being different and apart, an intuitive sense of independence. But Gramsci ultimately ties cultural revolution to resources outside the proletariat. He argues that the diffusion of a new hegemonic culture requires intellectual and moral organization. In particular, it requires the support of intellectuals and the cooperation of the culture-producing sectors in the society, much like Wuthnow's concept of cultural change.

The institutions and organizations of education, religion, polity, and the mass media, while dominated by the ruling class, are nonetheless autonomous, private entities that enable the oppressed to articulate and defend their own interests. Intellectuals, defined by Gramsci (1971) not as an elite group, but producers of knowledge and ideologies that reject the cultural traditions of a whole people as well as the dominant group, give to a subordinated group a "homogeneity and an awareness of its own function not only in the economic but also in the social and political fields" (p. 5). Thus, through the use of intellectuals and autonomous institutions, the working class has the ability to construct its own culture and saturate civil society with its distinct values of universalized socialism.

CULTURAL STUDIES AND BOURDIEU: IDEOLOGY AND SIGN SYSTEMS

Cultural Studies expands the logic of Gramsci's hegemonic process and sees a "dominant" ideology as the result of a negotiated social order. Though not explicitly addressed, the Birmingham School's definition of dominant ideology counters Abercrombie, Hill, and Turner's (1980) argument against the dominant ideology thesis. Abercrombie and his associates claim that modern Marxists argue that capitalist societies maintain and reproduce themselves through the effects of a dominant ideology. They argue against this view and state that the critical element for subordinating one class to another is found in the organization of social production. Thus they espouse a return to Marx's economic determinism. The chief difficulty that the dominant ideology school must face is establishing that there is in fact a pervasive, dominant culture that incorporates all of society. Abercrombie et al. posit that, historically, the ruling class ideology never became dominant either because the mechanisms of transmission were weak, as in feudalism and early capitalism, or the dominant ideology could not be well defined because of fragmentation, as in late capitalist societies.

This criticism of the dominant ideology misses one of the prime functions of culture: to constrain the conceptualization of what is possible, what is normal, and what is real.   While Abercrombie, Hill, and Turner are correct when they identify modern culture as fragmented, fragmentation by itself does not necessarily imply the lack of a dominant ideology or a general framework for reality. The fragmentation of culture allows a broader range of choices, but the choices of what is seen, heard, or felt are still limited. It is the limitation of choices that provides a necessary reality base for a collectivity. In this sense, culture functions more as an orienting paradigm than an oppressive ideology. And it is this concept of ideology upon which the Birmingham School focuses.

Cultural Studies has made a clear break with the classic dominant ideology thesis of Marxism, while still maintaining the critical perspective of ideology and culture. Culture in an industrial society is never a homogeneous structure. Rather, it is multifaceted, reflecting different methods of coping with peculiar constellations of social and material life experiences. The Birmingham School thus argues that it is more accurate to speak of cultures rather than culture. Though these cultures are differentially ranked according to the carrier social group, even the "dominant culture" is in truth fragmented and negotiated: "Almost always it requires an *alliance* of ruling-class fractions—a 'historical bloc'" (Hall & Jefferson, 1976, p. 39).

The Birmingham School also explicitly moves to viewing oppression as a "cooperative achievement. Hegemony and the acceptance of the dominant ideology is not achieved through coercion alone but requires some degree of consent from the subordinate class. Consent may be accomplished in two ways. One method is through a cultural process of co-optation. By providing the limits within which ideas and conflicts can move and are resolved, the hegemonic cultural order attempts to embrace all competing ideologies. As a consequence of accommodation, the "bourgeois culture" ceases to be entirely bourgeois, and the subordinated groups and their cultures are never directly confronted with or oppressed by a pure class culture. But the principal method through which dominant groups elicit the subordinate's cooperation is by co-opting their lived experiences. "It works *primarily* by inserting the subordinate class into the key institutions and structures which support the power and social authority of the dominant order. It is, above all, in these structures and relations that a subordinate class *lives its subordination*" (Hall & Jefferson, 1976, p. 39). The Centre thus distances itself from the Marxian dominant ideology thesis and from class determinism. Any specific ideology can never be understood as exclusively belonging to any one elite group. Though certain classes do exert more influence than others, the ideology that prevails in a society is the result of negotiation at every level.

Taking their cue from Gramsci and drawing on Saussure, Lévi-Strauss, Barthes, Volosinov, and Berger and Luckmann, Cultural Studies argue that ideology does not consist of ideas, images, or concepts, but ideology is the underlying structure of a society's knowledge/reality base. For Cultural Studies, ideology consists of the structure through which humans code reality. It is the deep structure of unchallenged premises upon which any human experience or discourse is based. The work of reality construction is "profoundly unconscious" and is ideological because it "does not adequately grasp all the conditions which make [its own reality claims] possible" and because "it offers a partial explanation as if it were a comprehensive and adequate one—it takes the part for the whole (fetishism)" (Hall, 1982, p. 86).

This change from content to structure is indicative of the shift that has occurred throughout the analysis of culture, and it gives Cultural Studies many of the same concerns as semiotics. Emphasis is placed on the sign and the discourse as outward manifestations of the underlying code. The struggle over ideology is thus not simply class conflict but a struggle over meaning construction. The struggle over meaning can become an arena for any societal conflict, for example, class, gender, ethnicity. When a sign becomes part of a conflictual discourse, it is considered part of the living "social intelligibility." But if a sign is withdrawn from conflict, it simply becomes part of the taken-for-granted association between meaning and sign, an ideology (Hall, 1982, p. 77). This definition of vital signification is like Gramsci's quest for a historically relevant language and Bellah's definition of culture: a culture is most alive when it is the subject of conflict. Generally, the dominant definition of a word, its taken-for-grantedness, is achieved as powerful individuals or groups give credibility to the association of sign and meaning and as the association is repeated by others over time. These repeated meanings become part of the "sedimented" memory of the collective and form a reservoir of themes and premises from which participants may draw. Thus the Centre's notion of how taken-for-granted reality is constructed puts a critical twist on Berger and Luckmann's process of institutionalization by identifying the controlling work of the elite.

Conflict over the meaning of a sign or a discourse is most likely to occur during times of problematized meanings. Meanings become problematized through unexpected events, events that break the social frame, when powerful interests are involved, or when a striking ideological conflict becomes apparent. The social struggle may be manifest in two ways: disarticulation and/or conflict over the means of signification production. Following Barthes, the Centre considers the connotative field of reference for a word to be the chief location through which ideology, and thus social conflict, enters a language. The connotation of a sign is usually challenged through either an inversion mechanism (Black = despised; Black = beautiful) or a metonymic mechanism, sliding along a chain of negative connotations (pig = disgusting animal; pig = police).

The struggle over meaning also entails conflict over the means of production of signification. In modern societies, Cultural Studies considers the mass media to be of primary importance. Culture requires communication, and in industrialized collectives the bulk of communication transmission occurs through the media. Early work at the Centre focused on the commodification of communication. In modern capitalist societies, the prime issues are who owns the means of communication and the manner in which the recipients of the "communication" are defined. The means of communication are owned by capitalists for the purpose of profit. And thus advertising has increasingly taken more and more communicative space, thus defining the transmission process. This advertising, and all forms of large-scale transmission, are aimed at the "masses," the "gullible, fickle, herdlike, low in taste and habit" (Williams, 1958, p. 303).

Yet, unlike the traditional Marxian approach, it does not appear that Cultural Studies blames advertising for creating "previously unsatisfied appetites." But advertising takes existing appetites and creates around them a fantasy that tends "towards a view of the world in which progress is conceived as a seeking of material possessions, equality as a moral leveling and freedom as the ground for endless irresponsible pleasure. These productions belong to a vicarious, spectators' world" (Hoggart, 1957, p. 277). The "false consciousness" produced by advertising results in a trivialization of the real issues of life, where nothing is concrete and personal, and increased uniformity of culture implies a leveling to the lowest common denominator. In this view of the effect of mass media and advertising, Cultural Studies is most like the postmodern critique.

But Hall (1982) moves away from this critique of advertising and recognizes, without succumbing to the disillusionment of postmodernism, that ideology is part of the taken-for-granted assumptions upon which society's knowledge is based. Ideology therefore demands the same reification as other cultural elements. He argues that even if access to the mass media were granted to disenfranchised groups, they would have to *"perform with the established terms of the problematic in play"* (Hall, 1982, p. 81). In other words, argumentation must take place within the confines of a structured ideology. An argument may make an opposing case, but in doing so, it *"also reproduces the given terms of the argument"* (Hall, 1982, p. 81). Additionally, the media in replicating ideological premises and at the same time attempting to influence the premises become "part and parcel of that dialectical process of the 'production of consent'—shaping the consensus while reflecting it" (Hall, 1982, p. 87).

Initially, Cultural Studies had a fairly clear sense of social change. Both Hoggart and Williams argue that through the Industrial Revolution the working class had gained materially but had lost culturally. The culture of the working class had quietly become a classless, faceless culture. The problem lay in the fact that the different forms of mass media were owned by and used for capitalists. Hoggart and Williams's solution was to encourage public ownership of the means of mass communication and to provide public support for different types of artists. Thus the producers of culture would not be driven by subsistence and profit, and a public forum could be created for the discussion of this freely produced work.

While it is not clear to what degree this brand of socialist reformation has been abandoned, it is apparent that Hall's work on ideology and signification has moved the focus of the Centre to decoding the symbolic articulations of oppressed groups' social predicament, much like the program espoused by Denzin. There is thus an emphasis on ethnography and "telling the tale." Using the same method that Hoggart and Williams employed, the history behind a particular symbolic representation is traced and brought into the complex relations of today's world. That is, the function of the sign as both distancing from and based upon the dominant culture is explicated.

A telling example of the Centre's approach is found in Hall and Jefferson's (1976) *Resistance Through Rituals; Youth Subcultures in Post-War Britain.* It is a wonderful book with two introductory theory sections, a methods section that clearly sets out their nonpositivistic methodology, and a series of enlightening excerpts from the Centre's work in progress. The emphasis in the ethnography is the symbolic style of the disenfranchised group. What is striking to me, in light of the title of the book, is the absence of any consideration of real interaction or ritual. There is no doubt that the symbols the subgroups use may constitute a center for ritualized behavior, but this use is never demonstrated; it is enough for the Centre to simply decode the symbolic structure. The book illustrates the main thrust of the Birmingham School and the view it has of its role in social change. The symbolic styles of the disenfranchised are decoded through a type of semiotic analysis in order to provide a "truer" version of a disenfranchised group and its culture than the "official" one transmitted by the mass media. The work of telling the tale seems to fit in with Gramsci's vision of hegemony and the process of defining a sign/symbol/discourse as problematic. In exposing the ideological interpretation of the media, the system is brought into question and crucial meanings problematized.

The Birmingham School and Pierre Bourdieu's formulation share a common ground in their emphasis on systems of symbols. There is a sense in which Bourdieu's theory may be seen as the mirror image of Marx's. Marx saw the economy as determinative, and while Bourdieu's theory begins with class, it is the symbolic field and the relations expressed by and through habitus that have the greater causal force. Like Marx, Bourdieu defines the social world as the place where the competition for scarce resources takes place. But unlike Marx, Bourdieu conceives of this competition as taking place in a symbolic realm. Bourdieu argues that Marx ignored symbolic struggles, and he sees his theory as a corrective that is more Marxian than Marx. There are three concepts central to Bourdieu's theory: field, habitus, and capital.

The field is Bourdieu's orienting concept. It denotes a set of objective positions and relations that are tied together by the "rules of the game" and by the distribution of four "fundamental powers" or capitals: economic, cultural (informal social skills, habits, linguistic styles, and tastes), social (networks), and symbolic (the use of symbols to recognize and thus legitimate the other powers). Agents are hierarchically distributed in the field initially through the overall volume of capital they possess and subsequently by the relative weight of the two particular "species of capital": symbolic and cultural. While the parameters of any field cannot be determined prior to empirical investigation, the important consideration for Bourdieu is the correspondence between the empirical field and its symbolic representation. The objective field corresponds to a symbolic field which is given legitimation and reality by those with symbolic capital. It is the symbolic field that people use to view, understand, and reproduce the objective; the symbolic field is also the field of symbolic violence and cooperative oppression. This conceptualized correspondence between reality construction and oppression has much in common with the Birmingham School.

Bourdieu (1989) argues that social groups and classes exist only because of the symbolic power of constitution, that is, the exercise of symbolic capital: "a group, a class, a gender, a region, or a nation begins to exist as such, for those who belong to it as well as for the others, only when it is distinguished . . . through knowledge and recognition" (p. 23). Bourdieu refers to this symbolic power as the power of world-making. The power of constitution is based on two elements. First, sufficient recognition to impose recognition. The group must be recognized and symbolically labeled by an agent that is officially legitimized as having the ability to symbolically impart identity. While Bourdieu seems to acknowledge that this recognition of the empowering agent must come from both an institutional source and the group itself, it is the institutional ordination upon which Bourdieu concentrates. Accreditation, particularly in the form of an educational credential (the school operates as a representative of the state), "frees its holder from the symbolic struggle of all against all by imposing the universally approved perspective" (Bourdieu, 1989, p. 22).

Yet Bourdieu (1989) does recognize that "symbolic efficacy depends on the degree to which the vision proposed is founded in reality" (p. 23). That is, there must be some substance behind the symbolic representation of existence. Thus the power to symbolically recognize is the "power of consecration or revelation" (Bourdieu, 1989, p. 23), the power to reveal the substance of the social space. But granting a group symbolic life "brings into existence in an instituted, constituted form . . . what existed up until then only as . . . a collection of varied persons, a purely additive series of merely juxtaposed individuals" (Bourdieu, 1989, p. 23). And, because legitimated existence is dependent upon symbolic capacity, the important conflict in society is the struggle over symbols and classifications.

The other salient form of capital is cultural capital. Bourdieu argues that cultural capital is differentially distributed through the dynamics of education and distance from necessity, both of which are ultimately functions of economic capital. Education is the chief institutional mechanism for cultural reproduction in the late twentieth century. Culture, in particular language, is standardized through the education system. Schooling is used to impose restrictions on popular modes of speech and to propagate the standard language. Further, Bourdieu argues that higher levels of education are associated with a particular kind of language and thinking. Individuals with higher levels of education tend to be disposed to see multiple levels of meaning in objects and to classify and experience them abstractly.

Generally, the use of language takes place within the structural confines of a linguistic market which acts as a system of sanctions and censorship. Individuals in a given market recognize their institutional position, have a sense of how their habitus relates to the present market, and anticipate differing profits of distinction. This anticipation acts as a self-sanctioning mechanism through which individuals participate in their own domination. Bourdieu thus adds a behavioral component to Gramsci's notion of cooperative oppression through unreflected language use.

The market itself is constituted by the symbolic relations of power in social space, that is, the totality of multiple, overlapping fields. For Bourdieu, power is seldom used as coercive force, but it is translated into symbolic form and thereby given a type of legitimacy: legitimacy through misrecognition. Misrecognition occurs as actors use language in accordance with their market and symbolic position. The actors do not recognize the violence that they are participating in by acknowledging and recreating their objective, oppressed position. The market can, within certain limits, be subject to negotiation, but the capacity to negotiate in the market is directly related to the amount of cultural and symbolic capital one possesses. Bourdieu (1991) also recognizes that the linguistic market is not omnipresent and thus not omnipotent: "It is also true that the unification of the market is never so complete as to prevent dominated individuals from finding, in the space provided by private life, among friends, markets where the laws of price formation which apply to more formal markets are suspended" (p. 71). But even in these circumstances "the reality of linguistic legitimacy" places individuals under the potential jurisdiction of formal language. Sanctions are always available to be called upon, and thus people generally recreate their symbolic position.

In addition to education, cultural capital is differentially distributed in social space through distance from necessity. Distance from necessity enables people to experience a world that is free from urgency and to practice activities that constitute an end in themselves. This ability to conceive of form rather than function, aesthetics, is dependent upon "a generalized capacity to neutralize ordinary urgencies and to bracket off practical ends, a durable inclination and aptitude for practice without a practical function" (Bourdieu, 1979/1984, p. 54). The upper-class aesthetic of luxury, or the pure gaze, prefers art that is abstracted, while the popular taste wants art to represent reality. Additionally, distance from economic necessity implies that all natural and physical desires are to be sublimated and dematerialized. The working class, because it is immersed in physical reality and economic necessity, interact in more physical ways than the distanced elite.

Thus cultural capital enables individuals to experience the world differentially and to classify their experiences differently. This function of cultural capital manifests itself as "taste." A particular taste is exhibited and recognized only by those who have the proper cultural code. Thus when individuals express a preference or classify an object, they are simultaneously classifying themselves. Taste may appear as an innocent and natural phenomenon, but it is an insidious reveler of position: "Taste classifies, and it classifies the classifier" (Bourdieu, 1979/1984, p. 6).

Bourdieu argues that cultural capital is internalized and ordered by habitus. Habitus is located in the body, not in the mind: "the notion of habitus expresses first and foremost the rejection of a whole series of alternatives into which social science . . . has locked itself, that of consciousness (or of subject) and of the unconscious" (Bourdieu, 1985, pp. 12–13). Habitus consists of dispositions which are impalpably and durably inculcated. It is a certain organization of one's body and its deployment in the world: posture, walking, speaking, eating, laughing. Habitus is both a system whereby people organize their own behavior and a system whereby people perceive and appreciate the behavior of others. Habitus works below the level of the conscious and outside the control of the will:

> The schemes of the habitus, the primary forms of classification, owe their specific efficacy to the fact that they function below the level of consciousness and language, beyond the reach of introspective scrutiny or control by the will ... in the most automatic gestures or the apparently most insignificant techniques of the body ... and engage the most fundamental principles of construction and evaluation of the social world, those which most directly express the division of labour ... or the division of the work of domination. (Bourdieu, 1979/1984, p. 466)

The degree to which Bourdieu's theory includes agency and social change has been the focus of debate. His method for accounting for both structure and agency is habitus. Bourdieu (1985) argues that in order to break away from the structuralist paradigm without falling into the subjectivity of the consciousness he "put forward the <<creative>>, active, and inventive capacities of habitus" (p. 13). But I have difficulty in seeing habitus as a form of creative agency.[4] Habitus is the direct expression of the structure contained in a field of power, durably inculcated during the time of primary socialization into the body, and it operates at a level below the consciousness and outside the immediate access of the will. What freedom Bourdieu's theory does seem to allow is obtained through circumscribed symbolic markets and expected rewards and sanctions.

Additionally, having recognized the central location of culture in producing human reality, Bourdieu has fallen into the trap of accentuating the stability of the macro-level system. He wants to talk about agency and change, but he has given himself little theoretical room in the concepts of habitus and field. On the possibility of social change, Bourdieu states:

> *The dominated, in any social universe, can always exert a certain force,* inasmuch as belonging to a field means by definition that one is capable of producing effects in it (if only to elicit reactions of exclusion on the part of those who occupy its dominant positions).... [But] the dominated seldom escape the antinomy of domination. For example, to oppose the school system ... is to exclude oneself from the school, and, increasingly, to lock oneself into one's condition of dominated. On the contrary, to accept assimilation by adopting school culture amounts to being coopted by the institution. The dominated are very often condemned to such dilemmas, to choices between two solutions which, each from a certain standpoint, are equally bad ones. (Bourdieu & Wacquant, 1992, pp. 80–82)

Bourdieu allows that there are two methods by which a symbolic struggle may be carried out. Objectively, individuals or groups may act in such a way as to display certain realities. His example of this method is group demonstrations held to manifest the size, strength, and cohesiveness of the disenfranchised. Subjectively, individuals or groups may try and transform the categories through which the social world is perceived. On the individual level this may be accomplished through insults, rumors, and the like. Groups may operate by employing more political strategies. The most typical of these strategies is the redefinition of history, that is, "retrospectively reconstructing a past fitted to the needs of the present" (Bourdieu, 1989, p. 21). Bourdieu's conceptualization of social change is a type of functional change within the confines of legitimacy. DiMaggio (1979) probably sums it up best: "Despite the political tensions that pervade his work, Bourdieu's is a world not of revolutions or even of social change, but of endless transformations. Symbolic violence and domination persist; only the disguises are altered" (p. 1470).

CULTURALLY BOUND IDEOLOGISTS AND THE CONSTRUCTION OF CULTURAL CHANGE

Unlike other perspectives of culture, the ideological school has maintained a consistent concern for the individual and his/her experience and perception of reality. At the heart of Marx's material dialectic is a philosophy of knowledge, though it was later theorists that linked this concern with how people know explicitly to theories of culture. Even Bourdieu's theory which attempts to de-center consciousness through his concept of habitus still contains implicit references to ways of perceiving with the concepts of language, education, and distance from necessity. And this concern with consciousness is logically focused on the issue of sense-meaning and not affect-meaning: the culture of a society is seen as constituting the taken-for-granted reality of the people, with culture consisting of language and such reified entities as commodities, categories, and ideas. Humans use these elements of culture to perceive and make sense of their world. Culture thus forms the underlying structure, content, and method of thought, and is seen as ideological in that the foundations are unknown, the content does not reflect current class conditions, the production is unduly influenced by the elites, and the culturally constrained perception of reality is accepted as the whole rather than a part. In keeping with an emphasis on sense-meaning, there has also been an explicit turn by contemporary theorists toward a semiotic analysis of culture.

While the ideological perspective has a better sense of individual and small group agency, it is nonetheless circumscribed by false consciousness and ideology. Like the subjective approach, reality is a construction that is influenced by the internalized culture. But unlike the work of Weber, Schutz, and Berger and Luckmann, ideologists conceive of the taken-for-grantedness of reality construction as problematic and constituting a false consciousness. In the final analysis, this consciousness is false because of the imposition of a value judgment by the theorists using this perspective. Many of the processes specified by these theorists are the same processes identified by others, the only difference is a value-driven critique of exclusion.

What the ideologists have missed is that the questions that occupy their analysis serve eventually to reify their own culture system. In one sense they appear to be blind to the empirical regularities of, and the theoretical need for, categorical inclusion and exclusion. Human reality is based on categorical distinctions which, by definition, exclude an infinite number of options to a finite few. All knowledge and knowledge-producing systems, including science and critical knowledge, are cultural products. Critical studies of culture in general have tapped into a logic whose conclusion they do not recognize. To argue or speak within the confines of a given paradigm is to accept and recreate its premises, and so there is a clear-cut attempt to stand outside the system. But in *maintaining* a critical stand, they fail to take the final step and acknowledge that every set of values, every social reality, and every symbolic field, including their own, is by its very nature a cultural construct and has no inherent claim to superiority. Further, every system of culture exists on the foundation of those who have been excluded. It can never be the case that a culture can exist without the process of exclusion, the exercise of what Lyotard terms "terror." Even the ideological stand can only exist because of the people and ideas of which they are critical and seek themselves to oppress.

But not only is cultural reality premised on the act of exclusion; the ability of any large-scale collective to survive is based on the same premise. Putting aside the question of inequality for the moment, collective goods— for example, communication and transportation technologies, law and interinstitutional dialogue and mediation—must be produced. If these are not produced on a national level, then they will be produced locally; and if locally, then the problem of linking these local productions one with another will have to be solved, which will, in turn, necessitate some larger structure. Regardless of whether the line of collective identity and decision making is drawn locally or nationally, there will be some interests that will be slighted in favor of others. One of the prime methods that humans use to systematically favor some and slight others is through distinctions created by cultural categories. By definition, then, any ruling group or paradigm will, in order to facilitate the smooth running of a large system, use categorical distinctions to exclude some knowledge systems and subgroups.

Inherent within this perspective, then, is a kind of blindness that is part and parcel of a sectarian view, that is, blindness to one's own process of reification and blindness to any "truth" that lies outside the dogma. A critique can add to what we know as long as it stands outside the existing structure, but as soon as the critique seeks to offer an alternative knowledge system, it becomes subject to the same dynamics that it criticized: it must reify and invest meaning in its own knowledge schema to the exclusion of others. Lemert offers the Soviet Union as an illustration of this problem. He argues that the dilemma of Marxism is how to keep the critique separate from the power that ideology has "to dull the mind and heart into quiet acceptance of the apparent reality of things. . . . [The Soviet Union] failed finally to escape the dulling effect of its own ideology" (Lemert, 1994, p. 143).

Criticizing a historic social system and trying to improve the lot of humanity is not wrong; it is, I believe, the responsibility of every human to reach for a more humane existence. But when we invoke a critical stand in our research, we run the danger of becoming blind to the very processes that humans use to create their world and may, in the end, reify our own system. For example, every critical view starts with an agenda and a definition of who constitutes the oppressed and the oppressor. These are typifications that in the normal process of group formation may become symbolic categories to the critiquing group. These group symbols may, in turn, be invested with a high degree of affect-meaning through ritualized interaction which the group may use to construct and guard its identity. The oppressed can thus become a sacred symbol rather than a group of real people in a real world. There is a danger in the culture-as-ideology perspective that the oppressed will continue to be defined as oppressed no matter what structural changes occur—being "oppressed" becomes a cultural value that people use to create their self and group identities. Additionally, the oppressor is a typification that ignores individual differences. It too is subject to the same process of affect-meaning and intense interaction and group boundary maintenance and may take on a reified existence in need of deconstruction.

Some of my comments thus far sound decidedly postmodern: in essence I have reduced the ideological approach to relativistic texts and have enjoined the ideologists to engage in a reflexive deconstruction of their perspective. And to this extent I agree with the postmodernists: the construction of cultural reality always entails socially determined values, and those values ought to be subject to deconstruction and should be lightly held until further notice. But it is also my position that there are certain general processes at work when humans produce a cultural reality and that these processes occur every time humans construct culture. And, because of the relativism brought to light by philosophers, symbolic interactionists, phenomenologists, ethnomethodologists, and postmodernists, these dynamics of reality construction are probably the most important theoretical arena of our time. Further, it is just those principles that must be understood and employed if the goals of the ideological perspective are to be realized in the long run.

The strength of this perspective is that it does recognize that culture can be put to ideological use, for the disenfranchised as well as the elite. Culture, by its very nature, is political. My use of the term is guided by the feminist emphasis on "the personal is political." In using the term, I am referring to the relationships among culture, identity, and interests. Culture is rarely free from the issues of identify and interest and thus always has the potential for use in conflict. One of the principal effects of culture is the creation of group identity. If a group has a self-conscious identity, it will always create symbolic borders in order to protect its interests and to define members and nonmembers. Groups, even symbolic ones, are endowed with the power of exclusion. As Goffman (1951) states, "status symbols visibly divide the social world into categories of persons thereby helping to maintain solidarity within a category and hostility between different categories" (p. 294).

What the ideologists have missed is that groups will always create symbolic borders, and *those borders will be subject to affect-meaning and ritualization.* By definition, borders always exclude, but the manner in which rituals are conducted around group borders is important. If the borders of a subgroup within a society become sacred and able to elicit high levels of emotional energy, the amount of tension between groups will increase and so will the likelihood of overt conflict. Group borders can become conflictual through two basic processes. First, the level of network density has a general effect on the emotional energy level of the group's borders. Thus the higher the network density of any group, the greater will be that group's sense of sacred identity and the greater will be its tendency to protect its boundaries. Additionally, the group's tendency to protect will be augmented by an outsider's sense of exclusion and self-sanctions. When in the presence of groups with strong borders, individuals tend to sense those boundaries and their exclusion and will stop themselves from offering a presentation of self for group acceptance; it is less damaging to their ego-identity to be self-sanctioned than to have it objectified by the group.

Second, the ritual work around cultural borders may be antagonistic. The content or the intent of the ritual becomes important at this point. Rituals may be defined in terms of their exclusionary practices: the focus of attention may be exclusively against another group and/or the common emotional mood may be exclusively negative with reference to another group. These two processes form the axes to a typology of conflict-group identity. Groups that are high on both network density and exclusionary practices are the groups most likely to engage in cultural violence and overt conflict. These groups actively define themselves against others and have the emotional energy to engage in antagonistic behaviors. The group identity of those who are low on both density and practice will tend to be experienced by those members as diffuse with borders that are permeable and not highly specified. These diffuse identity groups are unlikely to be involved in any type of cultural or group conflict. Groups that are high on exclusionary practices but low on network density will have a high sense of specificity with regard to their identity but will lack the needed emotional energy to bring about consistent, overt conflict. For these members, identity itself is generally viewed as complimentary—existing because of and in a functional fashion with other identities. Those high on network density but low on exclusionary practices generally have a segmented but shared identity. People with segmented identities have a number of identities available with some of them constructed through highly dense networks. Members of these groups are very aware of their group membership and have numerous identifying symbols, but they are willing and oftentimes anxious to share their culture with others. Thus it is theoretically possible for culture to be exclusionary and yet not lead to overt conflict or value imposition. And it is possible for a group to have a high degree of sacredness surrounding their identity without having the need or means (due to the content of their ritual) to exclude others to the point of antagonism. Both these forms provide a sense of group identity and inclusion and would also be "functional" in achieving the desired end of the ideologist: the demise of oppression, at least culturally speaking.

My intent thus far in this section has been to point out what I perceive to be a problem with this perspective's view of culture—the unreflexive reification of their own value system and concept of oppression/oppressor—and to offer a theoretical beginning point for the possibility of cultural change apart from the practice of violent exclusion or overt conflict. But it is not the case that ideologists are interested simply in cultural change: most of the theorists in this perspective want social change, though the contemporary position acknowledges the place of culture in such transformation. And, if equality is a value that a society wishes to pursue, then the ideologists are correct, and it is necessary that an alteration in social structure must take place: the entire issue of nonexclusionary ritual practices as noted above is predicated upon the assumption that people have relatively free choice with regard to their group membership. For those groups requiring social change, it is undoubtedly the case that change must be preceded by the cultural work of exclusion.

Drawing on theories from both the moral and ideological perspectives, we may posit that there are three general types of cultural change: gradual, punctuated, and revolutionary. Gradual change is associated with long-term changes in the size and diversity of a collective's population, with production dynamics that affect the division of labor and institutional differentiation, and with improvements in communication and transportation technology. Generally, increases in population size and diversity, and increases in the division of labor and institutional differentiation, create high levels of particularized culture in a society and selection pressures for the production of generalized culture.[5] The selection process is facilitated by increases in communication and transportation technology. Generally, expansion in communication and transportation technology produces a higher rate of symbol circulation. As symbols circulate among different groups, the particularized affect-meaning tends to diminish, the sense-meaning tends to become less specified, and the symbols are capable of being embraced by a more diverse collective.

A different kind of gradual change may be instigated by a disenfranchised group. As Cultural Studies points out, the struggle over ideology is not simply a class conflict but a struggle over meaning construction. Berger and Luckmann argue that institutions are legitimated through the accounts or myths that are told concerning their origin and purpose. And because the legitimation of an institution is a product of history, one that is a cooperative achievement, the legitimation itself may become the subject of conflict without upsetting the institutional arrangement themselves. Thus a group may challenge the myth surrounding an oppressive institution or group through attempts at redefining history, controlling the means of cultural production, or by organizing group demonstrations that objectively display the meanings that are thrown in question. Individuals may challenge cultural meanings through such devices as insults, rumors, and meaning inversions (see hooks, 1989). Additionally, as communication technology becomes increasingly more affordable and available, additional avenues of cultural production are presented to individuals and small groups. These displays, devices, and new cultural elements upset the taken-for-grantedness surrounding any discourse or element within a meaning system. Cultural meaning can then be renegotiated, in a manner similar to the symbolic interactionist concept of emergent meaning (Blumer, 1969), and social change brought about.

As W. Lloyd Warner (1959) notes, the passage of time allows a community's stock of symbols to become independent and malleable because they are no longer under the immediate control of the originating group.

These independent signs are subject to delayed attribution of meaning where each successive generation and its social and status structure can influence the meaning of its culture. And because there is a symbiotic relationship between an institutionalized arrangement and its myth, if the myth or legitimation of an institutional arrangement can be successfully reinterpreted, the social structure itself will change in response.

While this discourse over meaning may take place gradually, it will be more effective when performed during times of punctuated change. Punctuated change is a function of system shock, cultural innovation, and elite support and occurs sporadically and locally, though the effects may become diffused throughout the system. The concept of system shock comes from Wuthnow's work; Cultural Studies also has a notion of it, but it is couched in terms of "problematized meanings." Wuthnow's use of the term is very similar to Neil Fligstein's (1991). Applying the concept to institutional analysis of organizations, Fligstein hypothesizes that the institutional environment can experience a diffuse "turbulence" that is the result of sudden changes in the state or macroeconomic conditions. This "institutional shock" affords actors an opportunity for innovative behavior. Additionally, from the social movement literature, Doug McAdam (1982) addresses this opportunity for agency. McAdam argues that expanding political opportunities and indigenous organizations are necessary but not sufficient causes of insurgency. What is also needed is the "cognitive liberation" that these produce. Thus system shocks stimulate change and innovation by creating turbulence in the institutional field which, in turn, creates gaps in the normative, accounting, and cognitive structures of the actors. These cultural gaps create pressures for competing ideologies to explain and normalize the situation and may be strategically used by individuals and groups to engage in cultural disarticulation.

For example, during times of rapid economic expansion, changes occur in the institutional arrangements of the society and the cultural environment is disturbed. Economic expansion generally facilitates a growth spurt in firms, and they expand both vertically and horizontally. New types of firms emerge as well as new power relations among firms. These organizational changes tend to produce responses in the state and educational institutions, thus paving the way for general institutional changes. During these times of change, portions of the normative and symbolic culture are disturbed. Within and between firms and institutions new ways of doing business are introduced. These institutional and cultural changes create a level of uncertainty and competing ideologies—or new business methods or innovations—are created in response to the uncertainty (see Stearns & Allan, 1996).

Success of an ideology is dependent upon the carrier movement's access to elite resources—for example, power, money, networks—and upon favorable local conditions for selection. Local selective pressures depend on preexisting ideological diversity, conditions affecting the ease of ideological diffusion (communication and transportation technology, the degree of ecological integration, and the level of value and interest consensus), the presence of heterogeneous moral niches, and the state's perception of locally enacted ideology as constituting a threat or an enhancement to its mission. After an ideology is selected for, the access to elite resources and the mechanisms for the production and dissemination of the discourse must be routinized.

Revolutionary, system wide change is predicated on cultural opportunities: inconsistencies in either the "logic" of the system or in the discriminatory manner in which it is applied. Thus the likelihood of overt conflict increases due to two types of cultural opportunities. First, in highly differentiated societies, tension always exists in the cultural system due to the presence of value-inconsistencies. The presence of stark ideological contradictions affords disenfranchised groups a point of exploitation. Second, Doug McAdam (1994) argues that a social movement may, as a result of its own success, create a master critical frame that other social groups may use to define their own grievances. But both these opportunities must be culturally maximized before conflict can erupt. A subgroup must become organized in terms of creating its own culture and ideological symbols, putting forth leadership that can become the focus of ritualized behavior, and connecting with and utilizing elite resources. Additionally, a group's identity must become salient enough for members to make the necessary sacrifices.

In order to act, members of an interest group must have a sense of shared identity that excludes others from membership, and they must be "charged up with emotional energy to carry on battles on behalf of their group" (Collins, 1993, p. 291). The higher the level of emotional energy a group is able to create and maintain, the greater will be the intensity and duration of the conflict. Conflicts will tend to diminish as resources, including cultural, are used up. Because conflict is dependent upon ritual performance and interaction intensity, and because interaction intensity is a function of the focus of emotional energy, conflict tends to be around single issues: "An interaction ritual can reach a high degree of emotional intensity only if there is a single focus of attention" (Collins, 1993, p. 297).

It is important to note as a qualifying statement that it is not my purpose to present here a general theory of revolutions or conflict. The likelihood and ability of a group to participate in overt conflict is dependent upon more than culture; although it is a function of the level of cultural resources and mobilization, particularly in the early stages of a movement. But it is equally important to note that the bulk of social change in advanced industrial societies is more likely to take place in incremental phases rather than through a revolution (see Weber, 1968). High levels of bureaucratization and institutional complexity tend to be able to co-opt most social movements before they reach the stage of revolution. In such cases, the place of culture in social struggle and change becomes paramount.

NOTES

1. Because of its diversity, a complete rendering of the Centre's empirical work and theory falls outside the scope of this book. I focus on what appears to me to be the central orienting ideas for Cultural Studies. For a more complete overview of Cultural Studies, see Graeme Turner, *British Cultural Studies; An Introduction* (Boston: Unwin Hyman, 1990); and Ben Aggar, *Cultural Studies as Critical Theory* (London: Falmer, 1992).

2. But Mahar, Harker, and Wilkes depict this categorization of Bourdieu's as simply "an attempt to situate himself within an arena known to his American audience" (1990, pp. 23–24n). They prefer to call Bourdieu's work "generative structuralism." One can only assume that their categorization is somehow excluded from the role of gate-keeping that they accuse all other labels of playing.

3. From a functionalist's point of view, Parsons referred to this last stage of revolutionary social change as "institutionalization."

4. This critique is not original with me, and it is shared by others (e.g., Richard Jenkins, *Pierre Bourdieu*, London: Routledge, 1992; Paul DiMaggio, "Review Essay: On Pierre Bourdieu," *American Journal of Sociology*, 1979, 84 [6]:1460–1474).

5. The concept of selection pressures comes from Jonathan H. Turner's (1995) recent work on macrodynamics. Turner attributes the concept to Spencer and argues that these pressures are dynamic in the sense that they "cause" things to happen. I use the term in a Durkheimian sense: in the presence of high levels of particularized culture, a collective will tend to seek out and create more generalized symbols to represent the group. But, as I have argued, these symbols do not have to be the object of continual or periodic intense interaction. They may be held in reserve as long as they do not become the subject of dispute. This conceptualization avoids the problems associated with consensus and high moral density.

5

The Production of Meaning and Reality in Postmodernity

> One might even make out a case that they spend *more* of their daily hours in meaningful activities than their forebears did. The reason is precisely the "commercialized" culture that now exists. . . . What modern intellectuals usually fail to see is that the technology of ritual-production has gotten much more decentralized. People who carry around cassette recorders or radios blaring out popular music are literally wrapping themselves in a cocoon of self-chosen meaning almost every moment of the day.
>
> —Randall Collins (1986, p. 254)

The purpose of this book is twofold. First, the book presents a critique of the way in which culture is approached by most contemporary analyses, in particular, postmodernism. Many of the arguments presented in this book by the different perspectives are weakened by their overemphasis on the structural relations among elements in a culture system, their underconceptualization of how culture is created and reproduced at the micro-level, the ramifications of that process, and their neglect of affect-meaning. Perhaps this structuralist turn in the social sciences has been motivated by an attempt to grant culture an independent, theoretical effect on human behavior; alternatively, it may be due to the influence of postmodernism on the culture of cultural studies. Either way, there have been some positive results. I believe that establishing a separate analytical domain has resulted in a number of powerful insights into the makeup of culture, has once again fixed culture as a legitimate field of inquiry in sociology, and has prompted an increase in the use of culture as a variable in a diverse array of research projects. But disconnecting theories of culture from humans in interaction has serious theoretical consequences, most notably the conclusion that reality and meaning are rendered less viable for the subject due to some macro-level changes.

The second goal of this book is to generalize some of the dynamics and effects that postmodernism has identified and place those elements within a well-defined theory of meaning construction. It is my position that postmodernism has correctly identified some important cultural dynamics but that their conclusions are incorrect. My goal, then, is to move some of the issues raised by postmodernism out of the realm of critique and into a general theory of cultural meaning and reality. In order to be constructively effective, a critique must eventually be couched in positive terms—something must be built, not simply torn down. I admit that this move would be considered an anathema by unadulterated postmodernists—generalizing their statements does violence to the epistemological assumptions undergirding their work. But there are some issues that must be considered when weighing those suppositions.

Postmodernism's philosophy of knowledge represents a critique of the modernist assumption of representation, that a language can be developed that corresponds exactly to brute reality: it is claimed that this assumption has allowed science to blindly attempt discovery of the general laws that lay in back of the operation of the universe. Further, a connection is made between Western, colonizing culture and science: representational knowledge assumes an objective stand in order to dominate and manipulate the environment toward some predetermined goal, oftentimes at the expense of "less advanced" peoples. Even if the claim that science enables a colonizing culture is seen as too extreme, there are those that point out that it is impossible for humans to use knowledge without infusing it with some kind of value, thus obfuscating the goal of discovery. It is argued, then, that science is a value-laden knowledge system and thus cannot claim intrinsic superiority over other languages. However, it is not the case that postmodern knowledge is value-free nor that it exists apart from its own grand narrative.

Postmodernism wants to relinquish the goal of representational knowledge—some making the claim that it is an impossible dream—and move toward a paralogy of knowledge where all forms of discourse are equally valid. Lyotard (1979/1984) claims that "consensus has become outmoded and suspect value. But justice as a value is neither outmoded nor suspect" (p. 66). Rorty's (1979) hope is that we can abandon the notion of "permanent mutual frameworks" (p. 315) and move toward an epistemology without constraint or confrontation, where the final criteria by which any language is judged are its own pragmatics, much like Lyotard's language games. Bauman (1992, pp. xxi–xxii) advocates a kind of cultural tolerance that calls for equivalence, dialogue, and the legitimate fulfillment of all interests. And Seidman (1994) presents the postmodern call to ministry when he declares that social theorists ought to become advocates performing a kind of moral analysis and that "our broader social significance would lie in encouraging unencumbered open public moral and social debate and in deepening the notion of public discourse. We would be a catalyst for the public to think seriously about moral and social concerns" (pp. 136–137).

There is, then, a value-based desire in postmodernism to move away from the grand narratives that act as cultural centers to which every other cultural claim is compared and to move toward inclusion—postmodernism wants to level the cultural playing field. This value may indeed be a laudable one, but there are difficulties associated with it, at least from a postmodern view. This ethic is simply offering a new center, a new Durkheimian generalized culture, a new grand narrative—something that postmodernists claim they want to abandon. Nor is it the case that postmodernism offers a way to be free of the constraints and exclusions of reality construction. Human reality will be produced through the same methods whether in a traditional, modern, or postmodern society: "information must be selected, edited, and interpreted; anomalies must be explained; heretics from within and critics from without must be discounted, dissuaded, managed, or avoided" (Pollner & McDonald-Wikler, 1985, p. 241). Philosophically it may be possible to bracket the processes necessary to producing a firm reality, but sociologically it is not feasible. Reality construction *in situ* requires the use of constraint and confrontation; a beginning step toward this end is made when a culture or value center is established, much as postmodernism has done.

To the degree that divergent ideas and realities are not excluded in practice, reality becomes amorphous and fragile, as postmodernists have noted. Yet, because culture intrinsically demands it, postmodernists themselves participate in exclusionary practices, as a general theory of meaning construction would predict. For example, a great deal of proverbial ink has recently been spilled in the debate over what form theory should take and whether or not sociology is a science (for a set of concise statements, see Seidman & Wagner, 1992). Brown (1994) argues that the theories of sociology are themselves "the practices through which things take on meaning and value, and not merely as representations of a reality that is wholly exterior to them" (p. 229). Lemert (1990) claims "that the empirical reality in relation to which

theoretical texts are discursive is without exception textual" (p. 244).
Hence social scientific theories are simply texts about texts, without
any explanatory power whatsoever, and scientific discovery, according
to Brown (1994), is an honorific term that is ideological in intent because it disguises the very practices whereby it establishes its knowledge and authority—the very practices that postmodernists seek to
deconstruct. Seidman (1992) claims that the notion of scientific theory
in sociology ought to be abandoned because "it promotes the intellectual
obscurity and social irrelevance of theory, contributes to the decline of
public moral and political discourse, and furthers the enfeeblement of
an active citizenry" and because "modern human studies never have
been able to avoid the suspicion that their products—concepts, explanations, and theories—are imprinted with the particular prejudices
and interests of their creators" (p. 64). Finally, Gottdiener (1988) refers
to theory cumulation that is based on the work of classic theorists as
"logocentrism," the domestication and legitimation of new ideas, and
sees it as a political ploy by established theorists to maintain their
privileged position. But the work of theory cumulation is not new; it is
a basic tenet of scientific work. Yet Gottdiener is correct in asserting
that there is a political ploy involved.

At the core of this issue brought forward by postmodernists is the
definition of theory and sociology as a science. Most of the thinkers
that self-consciously founded the discipline—for example Comte,
Spencer, Durkheim—explicitly argued that sociology could be a science. It was upon that premise that the discipline was born and found
an institutional niche, and it has been the historical-institutional
definition of sociology that it falls within the category known as social
science. And theory, within the realm of science, has a particular definition and function. But some have become convinced that sociology
cannot and should not attempt to be a science; still others have posited
that science itself is a failed project. These critiques are not new, nor
are they restricted to postmodernism (e.g., Weber, 1904/1949; Dilthey,
1961; Kuhn, 1970; Feyerabend, 1975/1988). Yet a tension arises in that
many postmodernists still want to continue calling what they do theory. If the accumulation of abstract, general principles that are
thought to reflect the underlying laws of the universe is called theory
and the explication of a text found in a movie or a clarion call to social
change is called theory, then a problem of meaning exists. Gottdiener is
correct, the debate over the place of the classics in theory is a political
ploy, but it is not a ploy by social scientists, it is a ploy by those who
are not convinced that sociology can be scientific and yet continue to call
what they do "theory." This ploy is their quest for legitimation and is
a function of cultural group boundaries. The battle over the definition
of theory is a cultural war for legitimation upon which turns the allo-

cation of institutional and material resources. And, based on a generalized understanding of how culture functions within and between groups,
as advocated in this book, the behavior of both sides in this cultural
war is understandable and predictable.

On one level, then, the postmodern critique of science simply represents a contention for social power and its redistribution in a more equi-
table manner. Thus, from a sociology of reality perspective, the
postmodern problem is not whether science can exist as the most valid
knowledge system, but, as with all culture, the issue is one of group
boundaries and the ideological justification of unequal benefits. To the
extent that the postmodern critique of knowledge represents a bid for
legitimation and power by a disenfranchised group, it is, from a theoretical standpoint, an uninteresting statement; in that the postmodern
critique is an academic inquiry into the foundations of knowledge, it is
limited because it has failed to take into consideration the socially
based ramifications of culture. My intention here is not to condemn the
work of postmodernists or their value-system but, rather, simply to
point out that their knowledge system functions like any other culture,
according to generalizable features and processes.

Nor is it my intent to present an apologia for positivistic social theory; that has been adequately done by others (e.g., Collins, 1989;
Turner, 1993), and the issue of whether or not science can be *successful* is
not necessarily the critique of postmodernism. For example, Robert
Wuthnow (1995)—who does not claim to be a postmodernist, but has
clearly been influenced by the postmodern turn in the social sciences—
argues that since sociology is no longer considered a science, theory's
principal role is simply to provide a "lexicon of valuable concepts,
terms, and ways of talking about human behavior" (p. 2). Wuthnow's
(1995) reasons for considering sociology a nonscience do not involve the
claim that the theories of positivistic social science were proven wrong,
but, rather, "somehow, we are no longer convinced that master theories
of this kinds [sic] make sense. Perhaps we are even doubtful that they
are worthwhile" (p. 1). Wuthnow's comments are particularly noteworthy as he was then the chair of the theory section for the American
Sociological Association. Seidman (1992) echoes the same basis for rejecting scientifically based theorizing when he admits that he does not
offer "any arguments ruling out success in the quest for foundations in
sociology" (p. 64). While I do engage in a positivistic type of theorizing, it is a reflexive choice. I view science as a cultural creation with a
particular set of assumptions. These assumptions, like the assumptions
undergirding every knowledge system, cannot be proven (or disproved);
rather, they are simply accepted or rejected. One of the more important
bases upon which science stands is the pragmatic motive—the test of
any scientific theory consists of a simple question: does it work? And,

so, to this extent science agrees with Rorty's point concerning the validity of a knowledge system.

Postmodernism, like many other perspectives, is hindered by its value-system in its approach to understanding culture and reality. Reality construction, the production of identity and self, and the current unequal distribution of scarce resources demand that cultural borders be drawn and some forms of knowledge be delegitimated or excluded, as postmodernists have tried to do with science. Even under conditions of complete equality, it is questionable whether exclusionary practices could be abandoned—cultural meaning, reality, identity, and self would still demand the practice. The issue is not whether we can do away with these practices, the issue is where the lines will be drawn. Under conditions of threat or uncertainty, those lines will be drawn hard and fast, as many postmodernists have done in their quest for legitimacy.

As postmodernists have pointed out, humans are surrounded and constituted by culture. As such, one of the more important arenas of theorizing lies in the area of cultural reality. This chapter contains my best effort to extract general, cultural principles from the work of prominent theorists and postmodernists. Because, from my perspective, any analysis of culture must be based on a theory of how meaning is produced, I begin by presenting a theoretical model of the production of symbolic meaning. This model is followed by a generalization of the cultural dynamics of postmodernity and a critique of the postmodern model based on the theory of meaning construction. As I have noted throughout the book, the forces of postmodernity have pushed the production of meaning and reality to the micro-level. In the critique of the postmodern model, then, I explicate the microdynamics of meaning and reality construction in propositional form. The implications of the relations among the production of meaning, the dynamics of postmodernity, and the microdynamics of culture and identity are then examined. In creating the theory of meaning production and the critique of the postmodern model, I draw from and synthesize elements presented in previous chapters. It is my hope that by taking seriously the postmodernist's emphasis on culture, and noting the dynamics that they have pointed out, and then placing those processes within an abstract theory of meaning production, we will be able to ground the postmodern model in a generalized understanding of culture and move forward in our efforts to find out how meaning and reality work in technically advanced societies.

A THEORY OF MEANING PRODUCTION

In order to clarify the essence of culture, I want to separate analytically, for the moment, the mutually constitutive nature of culture and
human reality. Essentially, culture is the signed representation of a
perceived reality. The perceived reality may be of the brute/obdurate
universe or of the social world. This signed representation is by its very
nature an abstraction from reality. Culture is not equal to the obdurate
universe, nor is it equal to the social world (in its primitive form);
rather, it is a representation that comes to constitute the lived-verity
of human beings. This lived-verity renders meaningful the social and
obdurate worlds and is used to produce shared sense—and affect-
meaning.

And since culture is an abstraction, it is by its very nature contingent.
It is a human creation and an abstraction of reality and not reality itself; thus it is contingent upon continual reproduction. Cultural meaning
is reproduced through two primary mechanisms: the focus of psychic or
emotional energy, or through the process of associating one symbolic
element with another by perceiving them as being in the same meaning
context or denotative field. The focus of psychic energy is most clearly
related to the production of typified or sense-meaning, while the focus
of emotional energy is associated with the creation of affect-meaning.
Generally, the perpetuation of sense-meaning is aided by the structure
of culture, but people must attend to the relationships among signs to
produce meaning. The process of association is a tertiary level of meaning production. An element of culture that is not produced through the
explicit focus of attention but comes to be associated with another symbol that has been "infused" with psychic or emotional energy will tend
to carry only an echo of sense—or affect-meaning. Such elements constitute the tertiary culture of a collective. Primary and secondary levels
of meaning are both dependent upon the active work of people; the difference between the two is the level at which the interaction takes
place and where the control rests. Primary culture is produced and controlled at the micro-level and secondary at the meso-level.

Because culture comes to be the human animal's immediate, and con-
ceivably primary, reality, the contingent nature of cultural reality
produces a general sense of diffuse anxiety. This anxiety may be understood as insecurity over the ontological existence of lived-verity or as
uncertainty over the shared facticity of lived-verity. This anxiety is
generally not perceived by individuals participating in successful interactions. But, as Garfinkel's (1967) breaching experiments indicate,
this uncertainty lies close to the surface. Cultural reality thus produces
in human individuals and collectives the needs for ontological security
(the need to know that the world I am experiencing really does exist)

and facticity (the need to know that my experienced world is shared by others). Ontological security and facticity become issues for humanity because *culture intrinsically produces reflexivity*. For a symbol to be a symbol it must have meaning other than the direct experience of an object. Culture separates an object from its experience and demands the act of interpretation, that is reflexivity (Mead, 1934/1962, p. 67). And reflexivity implies the question or problem of meaning: the symbol itself can become the object of reflection, through what I have elsewhere in this book termed third-order reflexivity.

I have modeled the general dynamics that symbolic meaning produces in Figure 5.1. The model indicates that there are two primary processes set in motion due to the presence of symbolic meaning. One, pressures arise to produce factors that will ensure the repeatability of symbolic meaning (stabilization). And, two, pressures emerge that generate factors that will create a sense of reality with regard to a symbol (reification). Though both ontological security and facticity push for reification and stability, ontological security is more closely related to reification and facticity to stability.

Reification

The focus of psychic and emotional energy as well as the process of association determine the level of meaning production. The production of meaning is conceptualized as being of three types: primary, secondary, and tertiary. The lines surrounding tertiary meaning in the model are broken in order to indicate that it is contingent upon primary or secondary culture—association cannot take place without a primary or secondary element—and to indicate that the influence of tertiary culture on the needs for facticity and ontological security is limited. The doubled-headed arrow between culture and reflexivity indicates that these elements, though analytically distinct, are mutually constituted. The relationship between the level of meaning production and reflexivity eventually levels off, and further increases in the production of culture do not increase the level of reflexivity; this relationship is indicated by the +/= path. Reflexivity has a positive relationship with the needs for facticity and ontological security. But usually people operate with only a diffuse sense of these needs, as reflexivity is dampened by the stability and reification of culture, as noted by the long feedback arrows. Though not contained in this model, this diffuse sense can become acute in response to rising levels of uncertainty.

The needs for ontological security and facticity create pressures for interaction intensity (a positive, multiplicative function of physical proximity, common focus of attention and emotional mood, and pace). The relationship is positive: the greater the felt need for ontological

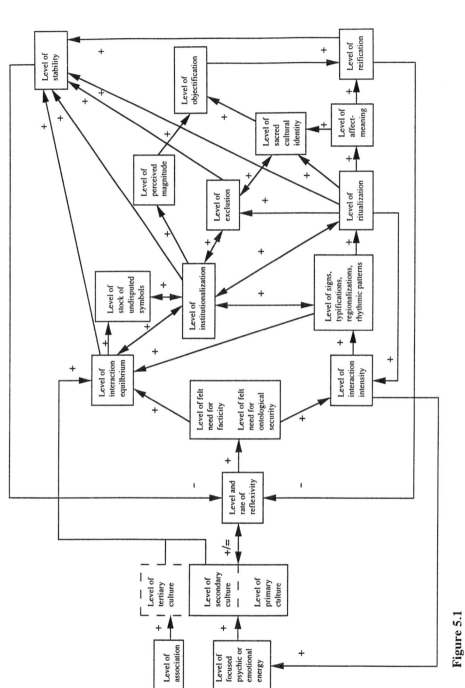

Figure 5.1
The Production of Cultural Meaning

security and facticity, the more that individuals will tend to seek out and participate in intense interactions.[1] The level of interaction intensity directly influences the production of signs, typifications, regionalizations, and rhythmic patterns: the more people encounter one another in intense interactions, the more likely they are to produce symbols that represent some aspect of the group, encounter, or immediate environment.

Typification refers to the process of linking expectations with types or categories. When a limited number of actors find themselves in repeated encounters that take place in similar situations, they tend to develop sets of sequenced actions that can be performed out of habit rather than conscious thought. Habitualized action provides psychological relief by narrowing the field of choices and emotional relief by mitigating the accumulation of tension that may result from undirected drives; it also provides a predictable sense of meaning that may be stored in the group's shared stock of knowledge. Typification occurs when habitualized action becomes expected for types of actors. That is, when more actors are added to an original intimate group, they tend to be understood as types. As this open group develops a past, typifications are built up in the course of a shared history, and habitualized actions become reciprocally attached to types of actors. As more and more people come into the repeated situation, an ever-expanding circle of taken-for-grantedness is created to relieve tension and uncertainty. Taken-for-granted typifications allow action to be predicted, and meaning and motive to be attributed, in a fairly consistent manner.

In addition to types of actors, situations or social settings tend to be typified. I am using Jonathan H. Turner's (1988, pp. 144–145) term "regionalization" to indicate this process. Generalizing from Goffman (1959), Turner defines regionalization as the number and distribution of available physical props, the span of available space, the division of that space into regions by objects, and circumscribed movement of people in those regions. These regions are symbolized in that they have an agreed upon meaning, and there is an association between typifications and regions that tends to stabilize meaning and make interactions repeatable.

The rhythm of an intense interaction also tends to be symbolized and ritualized. Rhythm refers to recurrent patterns in the use of personal space and nonverbal cues during interaction and is a principal method through which culture becomes embodied: "rhythm is a way of transmitting a description of experience, in such a way that the experience is re-created in the person receiving it, not merely as an 'abstraction' or an 'emotion' but as a physical effect on the organism—on the blood, on the breathing, on the physical patterns of the brain" (Williams, 1961, p. 24). Each distinct culture will have its own set of rhythmic patterns depending on, among other things, the degree of social differentiation among the groups.

The degree to which interactions are symbolized in terms of typification, regionalization, and rhythm has a direct effect on the level of ritualization. As interactions are understood and performed vis-à-vis typifications, regionalization, and rhythmic synchronization, the greater will be the degree to which patterned and stereotypical gestures come to be associated with explicit symbolic meaning. Ritualized behavior has a direct effect on the degree of affect-meaning a symbol can evoke in an encounter: the greater the level of ritualized behavior with respect to a given symbol, the greater the level of interaction intensity in response to the symbol, and thus the greater the degree of affect-meaning the symbol triggers.

The level of symbol reification is directly effected by two elements: the degree of affect-meaning and objectification. As symbols become associated with high levels of affect-meaning, they tend to appear more real to people than symbols with lower levels of affect-meaning. Symbols also vary in their perceived reality by the degree to which they are believed to exist independently of the individual, that is, objectified. The objectification of a symbol is a function of the degree to which a cultural identity is sacred: symbols that are associated with a cultural identity that has been infused with high levels of emotional energy tend to be perceived as something external to and independent of the individual.

The degree of objectification is also a function of the perceived magnitude of a symbol, magnitude being an additive function of the macro-elements of the number of people, length of time, and the amount of geographic space associated with the symbol. The association of macro-elements with a symbol is a direct function of institutionalization. Institutionalization is the process whereby certain solutions to collective problems become associated one with another. In order to survive, a collective faces problems that it must overcome, for example, cultural and biological perpetuation. But the content of the solution is immaterial; ultimately, it does not matter if a collective perpetuates itself biologically through the institution of family (however it is defined) or through an institutionalized hatchery. What is important is that the perceived solutions are a set of highly ritualized behaviors that are typified and regionalized and are perceived to meet collective problems, and indeed do meet those problems within the limits of sufficing. These solutions are ritualized in order to ensure their survivability, and the solutions tend to be understood by people as types of institutional forms, for example, religion.[2] These institutional forms tend to be bordered with high levels of affect-meaning, or sacredness, as the path from affect-meaning —>cultural identity —>exclusion —>

institutionalization indicates. Generally, the greater the association between the ritualized solution and the collective problem, the greater the level of institutionalization. Institutionalization thus implies perceived magnitude: large numbers of people and relatively long periods of time and geographic space.

In addition to symbolization and ritualization, institutionalization is a direct function of the tendency toward interaction equilibrium, the level of a stock of undisputed symbols, and the degree of exclusionary practices. Each of the elements that produce institutionalization is mutually constitutive with institutionalization, as is noted by the double-headed arrows. Additionally, it is important to note that the needs of facticity and ontological security are indirectly driving institutionalization. People have a need to avoid uncertainty concerning the solutions to problems that allow their collective to survive. These solutions are typified and are taken-for-granted and have high levels of affect-meaning in order to prevent people from being reflexive about the symbolic-contingency of their survival.

Stabilization

The needs for facticity and ontological security also create pressures for stabilization. Stabilization is a function of interaction equilibrium, institutionalization, exclusion, ritualization, and reification. Interaction equilibrium conceptualizes the work people perform in order to maintain a certain level of status quo in encounters. Part of this interactional status quo is produced through what Goffman (1967, p. 45) refers to as ritual equilibrium. According to Goffman (1967, pp. 5–45), the work of ritual equilibrium basically consists of avoidance and accommodating techniques. These avoidance and accommodating procedures are most clearly identified by ethnomethodology. Interactants assume a reciprocity of perspectives that unless it is breached provides the basis for the equilibrium. In an encounter, accounts are offered and accepted if a breach does occur; meaning is generally indexical, assumed to be taken-for-granted, and when in doubt, meaning is glossed over or filled in using an et cetera principle. The production of these avoidance and accommodating procedures is facilitated by a group's typifications, regionalizations, and rhythmic patterns.

Additionally, the model indicates that the level of secondary and tertiary culture present in a collective will facilitate the production of interaction equilibrium. Tertiary culture consists of cultural elements that have been created through the passive process of association and thus do not have high specificity with regard to sense-meaning, nor do they have high levels of affect-meaning. As a result, these symbols do not represent group boundaries and hence cannot present a threat to the equilibrium of an encounter. Secondary culture contains elements of primary meaning, but because of its association with organizations and professional groups, it tends to provide a meaning set that is taken-for-granted by the general public and thus promotes interaction equilibrium as well.

The importance of the concept of interaction equilibrium is that the needs for facticity and ontological security create pressures to maintain a certain level of status quo in an encounter and a collective. Because the stability of human reality is contingent upon the satiation of facticity and ontological security needs, conflict and exchange generally take place within the confines of an already produced equilibrium, and this equilibrium produces cultural stability. The concept of equilibrium has fallen into disrepute, but the concept must always be considered in the light of time. I agree with Turner (1995) that, in the long run, societies are disintegrating; there is not a single society that has lasted throughout time. But in the short run, people work hard at maintaining cultural equilibrium. In fact, as Goffman (1967, p. 10n), Bourdieu (1991), and Collins and Annett (1975, pp. 161–224) note, equilibrium holds even under some conflict-oriented situations: people are more likely to maintain interaction equilibrium when in the company of those with more power than with equals.

This tendency toward equilibrium also produces an environment in which collective symbols may be left relatively unchallenged. It is important for a society to maintain a certain level of undisputed collective symbols that may be used to elicit high levels of emotional energy through intensified interaction. The importance of this stock of symbols is the occasional need for unusual levels of commitment and sacrifice from the members of the collective. The greater majority of these symbols are produced through the process of institutionalization, but a minimal level of interaction equilibrium allows the stock to be maintained. The level of undisputed collective symbols has an indirect influence on the stability of the cultural system through institutionalization and ritualization. In order to elicit the high levels of emotional energy that are necessary for unusual commitment and sacrifice, the collective symbols must be used in ritualized interaction. Institutionalized settings generally provide the arena for such interaction. Institutionalization and ritualization also have independent effects upon the level of cultural stability simply due to their inherent processes: ritualization is the patterning of stereotypical behaviors, and institutionalization is an effect of a particular type of collective ritualization.

Stability is also influenced by the degree of exclusion. Exclusion refers to the practices through which a social group bars certain cultural elements that are perceived to be in conflict with their own culture.

This act of exclusion is an intrinsic part of culture. By definition, exclusion is the result of typification: types exclude from consideration some particulars and subsume others under a generalizing rubric. Exclusion is also a function of the degree of sacred cultural identity and ritualized behavior. The more sacred is an identity, the more likely is a group to defend its particularized culture; exclusion and cultural identity are mutually constituted, as indicated by the double-headed arrow. But most of the work of exclusion is part and parcel of maintaining an interaction equilibrium. That is, exclusionary tactics are generally glossed over or taken-for-granted as part of the institutionalized setting. This aspect of exclusion is recognized by the contemporary theorists of the ideological perspective, and it is what may be termed "cooperative oppression." And, finally, the level of reification influences the level of stability. The more real a cultural element is perceived to be, the greater will be the stability of the element.

THE CONTOURS OF POSTMODERNITY

Previously, the theories of postmodernism were reviewed in the context of the people who wrote them. In this section, the theoretical principles will be extracted, rendered abstract and general, and placed in propositional form. Two statements concerning this project are in order. First, it is not the case that I will be presenting a theory that completely explicates the issues raised by postmodernists. They assume a number of conditions that predate or form the preconditions for postmodernity. My desire is to remain within the confines of the postmodern project as much as possible. Thus the scope conditions of this theory are that it applies to societies that are advanced technologically, are based on democratic ideals, and are practicing an advanced form of capitalism. And the second caveat that I want to make is that although I hope to limit myself to the central factors as presented by the postmodernists, I will be furnishing more generalized explanations of those factors than do the original theorists. Thus, even though I believe what follows is an accurate model of the dynamics of postmodernity, it has been stated in terms not necessarily found within postmodernism itself. The primary motivation behind this restatement is to render the model amenable to empirical research and social, scientific theory.

Postmodernity is a time of complexity. Intricate social and cultural forces combine to produce antagonistic or perhaps dialectic effects in two arenas: culture and subjective identity. Culture has become supremely important in postmodernity. It is consequential not because it is the source of value orientations, norms, and other unifying forces; on the contrary, postmodernists regard with suspicion the whole notion of integrating cultural factors. Rather, culture is seen in a more general way as texts that provide meaning to the human universe. But at the same time that cultural meaning has risen in prominence, it has also become unstable and null. Many of the processes that promote cultural stability and reification are mitigated in postmodernity. And, with the rise of culture, the individual has ascended as the focus of cultural forces. In place of the collective, and grand narrative, the individual has become the locus of social organization in postmodernity; but at the same time the individual has lost viability through a postmodern consciousness.

Cultural Prominence

Culture is paramount in postmodernity due to four social processes: the level of credentialing, the level and rate of commodification, the level of imaging technology, and the relative importance of cultural space in a society, Table 5.1; Proposition I. Credentialing increases the relative importance of culture because of its association with formal education—higher levels of credentialing tend to increase the sheer size of both particularized and generalized cultural capital—and because credentialed knowledge becomes an important basis for job acquisition and social standing. The level of credentialing in any society is a positive and additive function of the level and rate of the division of labor and the level of intellectual technology, Proposition II. In societies where the rate of the division of labor and the level of intellectual technology are both high, there will be a corresponding increase in the general level of credentialing. Typically, the division of labor has been understood as a bounded factor. That is, the division of labor was bounded by both national barriers and the lifespan of the worker: labor would divide within the confines of a labor market or industry which, in turn, was contained within a given society; and, once an individual found his or her niche within that division, they would maintain that position for most of their life. But under conditions of multinational capitalism and global markets—a decrease in the spatial concentration of capital (Proposition II.A.1)—the division of labor has transcended the boundaries of nation and lifespan: individuals may have more than seven different careers within their lifetime, and the labor needed to produce any given commodity is divided up globally. This decrease in the spatial distribution of capital is in response to the problem of over-accumulation, increased communication and transportation technologies, and the level of abstraction and rate of circulation of money. Thus in places like the United States where the international division of labor has increased the size of the service class, the training and reskilling of the workforce takes place within educational institutions,

Table 5.1
Propositions Concerning the Relative Importance of Culture in Postmodernity

---

I. The relative importance of symbolic culture in any society is a positive, additive function of
    A. the level of credentialing
    B. the level and rate of commodification
    C. the level of imaging technology
    D. the relative importance of cultural space

II. The level of credentialing in a society is a positive, additive function of
    A. the level and rate of the division of labor, which is a negative function of the level of spatial concentration of capital and a positive function of
        1. the level of competition
        2. the level of manufacturing technology
        3. the level of intellectual technology
    B. the level of intellectual technology, which is a positive, multiplicative function of
        1. the level of scientific inquiry and ideology
        2. the interactive effects of the level of scientific inquiry and ideology, and the level of capitalist practice and ideology

III. The level and rate of commodification is a positive function of the level and rate of market velocity and expansion, which is a positive, multiplicative function of
    A. the interactive effects of the level of scientific inquiry and ideology, and the level of capitalist practice and ideology
    B. the level of production
    C. the level of commodify distribution, which is a positive, additive function of
        1. the level of the rationalization of the distribution process
        2. the level of communication and transportation technology
    D. the level of money abstraction and circulation, which is a positive, additive function of
        1. the level and rate of market velocity and expansion
        2. the level of communication and transportation technology
    E. the level of advertising, which is a positive, additive function of
        1. the level and rate of market velocity and expansion
        2. the level of communication and transportation technology
        3. the level of imaging technology importance of cultural space in a society

IV. The level of imaging technology is a positive, additive function of
    A. the level of communication and transportation technology
    B. the level of advertising

V. The relative importance of cultural space is a positive, additive function of
    A. the level of communication and transportation technology, which is a positive, additive function of

Table 5.1 Continued:

          1. the interactive effects of the level of scientific inquiry and ideology and the level of capitalist practice and ideology
          2. the level and rate of market expansion and velocity

  B. the degree of time/place compression, which is a positive function of the level of communication and transportation technology, and a negative function of the level of spatial concentration of capital, which is a negative function of
          1. the level and rate of accumulation
          2. the velocity and abstraction of money circulation
          3. the level of communication and transportation technology

  C. the number and diversity of available cultural identities, which is a positive, additive function of
          1. the decreasing viability of grand narratives
          2. the rate of social and cultural differentiation, which is a positive, additive function of the level and rate of the division of labor and the level of circumvention of symbolic boundaries, which is a positive, additive function of
               a. the level and rate of commodification
               b. the level of communication and transportation technology
               c. the level of discretionary spending

---

increasing the level of credentialing and the importance of symbolic culture.

The constant change, expansion, and competition in the job markets have resulted in an increase in the speed at which labor is divided, moving and dividing jobs in and out of societies, requiring individuals to reskill at increasing rates. As job market competition becomes a dominant feature of a society, it constitutes a driving force behind the selection of human skills—technical, social, and psychological (Proposition II.A.2). In addition to a decreasing spatial concentration of capital and increased competition, the rate of the division of labor is influenced by the level of manufacturing technology and intellectual technology (Propositions II.A.3 and II.A.4). Manufacturing technology generally increases the division of labor in society and results in a differentiation of social experiences and the development of specialized languages, or particularized culture. The term "intellectual technology" comes from Daniel Bell (1976, pp. 27–33), but the concept is one that is important to David Harvey. Like Bell, Harvey argues that, in late capitalism, organizational technology—the knowledge and ability to coordinate the actions of people in new and more productive ways—becomes as important as manufacturing technology in determining the level of productivity and the division of labor. Intellectual technology is generally produced and diffused in educational settings that result in higher levels of credentialing and greater importance given to symbolic culture; thus intellectual technology also has an independent effect upon the level of credentialing in a society, Proposition II.B.

Another factor that influences the importance of culture in any society is the level and rate of commodification. Commodification is a traditional Marxian concern, but as many postmodernists point out (e.g., Baudrillard, Denzin, Kellner), this dynamic eventually pushes production past use—and exchange-value and creates products whose main attribute is symbolic. Thus, as commodities become valued more for their symbolic or status significance rather than their actual use, and as people designate an increasing proportion of their available income for the purchase of status—and image-commodities, cultural meaning increases in importance. As noted in Proposition III, the level of and speed at which elements of human life are turned into commodities are a direct function of the rate that markets are moving products and the level of their expansion.

Postmodernism is fundamentally a critique of capitalism and science, and the two are generally conceptualized as mutually reinforcing one another. Accordingly, the level of scientific inquiry and ideology and the level of capitalist practice and ideology are prime dynamics in the postmodern model and have an interactive effect on the level of markets and thus commodification, Proposition III.A. Increasing commodification is an intrinsic element of capitalism. Capitalism is driven by profit, profit is dependent upon scarcity, and scarcity is a function of an expanding economy and expanding markets (see Dowd, 1989). Thus the process of commodification is driven by an inherent, capitalistic mechanism of expansion. As the practice and ideology of capitalism expand though markets, so does the overall proportion of the human lifeworld that is perceived as products or commodities. This effect is exponential in that the mere existence of items with exchange—or commodified sign-value prompts and justifies further commodification at a faster rate. And while it is probably true that for any individual the effect levels off, because there are limits to the size of the lifeworld that any human can perceive and with which they can interact, the overall rate of commodification continues to increase as old products are discarded and new ones needed and acquired. The effect of science on markets and commodification is twofold: science not only produces the technologies necessary for increased production, but it also provides products for commodification—in capitalist and technically advanced economies, much of what becomes commodified for general use is technology.

In addition to capitalism, science, and the level of production, the level and rate of market velocity and expansion are a function of the level and rate of money circulation and abstraction, the rate of the distribution of commodities, and the level of advertising. Markets that are pushed by the capitalist imperative for expansion require higher levels of production, faster rates of distribution, increased advertising, and more fluid forms of generalized media of exchange; and as each of these elements increase, they, in turn, expand the existing markets. These relations create a reinforcing cyclical process that has a multiplicative effect on the rate of commodification. Furthermore, money circulation and abstraction, distribution, and advertising all have independent effects on commodification: they tend to make commodities more abstract, ephemeral, and volatile in terms of turnover.

The relative importance of symbolic culture also increases due to the effects of imaging technology, Proposition IV. Imaging technology, the ability to produce and project images across time and place, increases the importance of image with regard to identity formation and cultural space: as the sheer number and quality of imaged symbols increases, people become more and more infatuated with image and visual pleasuring. With the concept of imaged symbols and its effect of visual pleasuring, I am attempting to capture and generalize the postmodernist concern with simulacrum and the fascination people have with media images. Though the jump from advertising and media images to the conclusion that these images have "no relation to any reality whatsoever" (Baudrillard, 1981/1994, p. 6) is not warranted, it does seem reasonable to conclude that in a cultural system with high levels of mass media (e.g., television, tabloids, magazines), the proportion of imaged symbols in relation to speech and written symbols with which people must contend will increase. But the level of imaging technology does not simply refer to an absolute proportion but also to the quality of the images. Changes in technology have improved the images produced on a mass scale, and there is a continual push for improvement through the demands of the market and advertising, Proposition IV.B. Since the dominant sense in the human animal is sight, imaged symbols are generally preferred over auditory and probably written symbols, though the latter is visually discerned. The postmodern model hypothesizes that in the presence of increasing levels of imaged symbols, both in terms of quantity and quality, humans respond by increasingly finding these images pleasurable, thus increasing the importance of symbolic culture.

The fourth influence on the importance of culture in a society is the relative significance of cultural space, which is a positive and additive function of the level of communication and transportation technology, the degree of time/place compression, and the number and diversity of available cultural identities, Proposition V. The concept of cultural space refers to the postmodern concern with the decreasing significance of physical place (e.g., Lash & Urry, Harvey, Jameson, Gottdiener, Bauman, Virilio [1991]). Historically humans have been rooted in a place. Their life, identity, and symbols were organized and understood with reference to a particular place in time. But as the level of communication and transportation technology increased, place became less and less important. People could begin to move about almost at will, and the natural barriers that moored people in place no longer represented restrictions. Today, faraway places are not only more physically accessible but culturally more available as well through communication technologies. People and cultures may be known and never seen or experienced in a face-to-face encounter. Thus, in the face of increases in the technologies of communication and transportation, the actual physical place that people occupy becomes relatively less important when compared to cultural space.

The level of communication and transportation technology also has an indirect effect on the level of cultural space through the degree of time/place compression, Proposition V.B. If the culture symbolizing the relationships among humans and time and place cannot keep pace with technological innovations, then a period of liminality will ensue, and the meaningfulness of time and place will recede. In that void the relative importance of cultural space increases, as individuals use space and identity rather than place and time to organize their meaning structure. In addition to transportation and communication technologies, the degree of time/place compression is a positive function of the spatial decentralization of capital, Proposition V.B.2. Capitalists are motivated to spread out their capital in terms of both money and labor as the level and rate of capital accumulation increases, decentralization tends to offset the market/profit stagnation that develops out of overaccumulation, and the process is facilitated by improvements in a society's ability to move money, information, product, and people at faster rates. Decentralization tends to lessen the importance of place just as did early urbanization, but in a potentially more profound manner.

Cultural space also becomes important in a society due to the decreasing viability of grand narratives and the rate of social and cultural differentiation, Propositions V.C.1, 2. These processes create new cultural identities, and the plurality of cultural identities and lifestyles presented to an individual not only allows for choice but necessitates choice as well; it becomes the case that not choosing constitutes a choice. Thus the individual is "forced" to choose among cultural identities which, in turn, increases the importance of cultural space within a society. With the concept of available cultural identities I have tried to capture the idea of social saturation and at least part of the postmodernist argument concerning the loss of grand narratives. One of the primary effects of culture is to provide a sense of identity. Since culture is a collective production, there appears to be a positive, symbiotic relationship between a collective identity and the legitimation of the cultural system: the higher the sense of collective identity, the greater will be the legitimation of the cultural system, and the inverse is true as well. Postmodernism tends to talk about collective identities and legitimation in terms of grand narratives and argues that grand narratives are no longer possible due to the fragmentation of the cultural system. And, as grand narratives are no longer able to suppress cultural diversity, the number and diversity of cultural identities expands, again increasing the importance of culture generally.

The diversity of available identities also increases in response to the rate of social and cultural differentiation. Classically, cultural and social differentiation has been viewed as the result of the division of labor, Proposition V.C.2. As the division of labor responds to changes in the levels of intellectual and manufacturing technology, the spatial decentralization of capital, and increased competition, people have to acquire new knowledge and create particularized cultures and new identities. Thus the number and diversity of cultural identities is mutually constituted with the rate of social differentiation through the division of labor. But in postmodernity, another factor becomes equally if not more important: the level of symbolic boundary circumvention, a positive and additive function of the level and rate of commodification, the level of communication and transportation technology, and the level of discretionary spending.

The concept of symbol circumvention is based on the assumption that social groups identify with and are defined by the symbols they use. Goffman (1951) refers to such identifiers as status symbols: "Status symbols visibly divide the social world into categories of persons thereby helping to maintain solidarity within a category and hostility between different categories" (p. 294). Because of the importance of identity, there are restrictions that inhibit the use of particular status terms; but the original meaning can only be guaranteed as a symbol if it is kept within its group and context (see Warner, 1959). Thus, as status symbols are lifted out of an originating group and commodified, they are released from their original constraints and able to be modified and made accessible to the broader society (V.C.2.a). Capitalists interested in expanding their markets, or keeping their market share, continually seek new items to commodify. One successful technique is to lift these elements out from an already existing "cutting edge" group and commodify them, thus increasing the number and diversity of cultural identities available to the general public. Capitalists also create new cultural identifiers by linking them to already established status symbols, thus producing not only increases in the number of identities but also additional circumvention of and differentiation within the already existing ones.

The process of circumvention is facilitated by the level of communication and transportation technology (V.C.2.b) and discretionary spending (V.C.2.c). As people travel and communicate over vast distances, they are exposed to additional commodified symbols as well as localized group identities. The exposure of local culture tends to diffuse the particularized elements, again making them available to diverse others. Symbolic barriers are truly circumvented when people are able to buy cultural identities and markers; thus commodification, travel, and communication must be linked with increases in the general public's level of discretionary spending. As the amount of discretionary spending increases, people are more able to avail themselves of the commodified symbols at faster rates which, in turn, influences the level of market expansion and commodification.

It is my opinion that symbol circumvention is one of the primary processes with which postmodernists are concerned. As a result of symbols being lifted out of an originating group, they are released from the constraints that the group can impose, and the symbols are thus rendered modifiable and available to the general collective. When this process occurs, groups can no longer protect the sense—or affect-meaning of a symbol and it becomes a "free-floating signifier." As with many of the postmodern dynamics, symbol circumvention is a dual-edged sword: it not only increases the importance of culture in a society; it also makes it less stable and appear less real. Ironically, under postmodern conditions, the rising relative importance of symbolic culture in a society is accompanied by a decrease in the relative level of cultural stabilization and reification.

Cultural Inconsistency and Illusion

Because of the nature of culture, humans tend to stabilize and reify their symbols and sign systems. Culture always imposes a meaning upon an object beyond the thing-in-itself; hence meaning has an arbitrary relationship with the object and is thus dependent upon social action and interaction to maintain its connection with the object. Culture, then, always has about it a sense of unreality, a separation from brute reality. And humans, by virtue of culture, can be, and indeed are compelled to be, reflexive about the arbitrary existence of their reality. Thus the meaning of every sign that humans use, and the foundation for constructed reality, are continually uncertain and create a general level of diffuse anxiety that at times may become acute.

From a Marxian point of view, or in terms of the emergent interaction as conceptualized by symbolic interactionism, reification may be understood as assuming a false reality behind a concept or symbol. But if we take seriously the insights that social constructivism, ethnomethodology, and the sociology of knowledge bring us, then it becomes apparent that in interaction and in daily life humans must believe in and act as if their symbols and concepts constitute reality in and of themselves. My use of the concept of reification attempts to capture the dynamics at work in making a modicum of culture appear real to people. Additionally, because culture is not intrinsically linked to anything other than social interaction, the meaning of culture must be stabilized across time and space; otherwise, every encounter and action will be subject to extreme levels of uncertainty.

But in postmodernity, factors have emerged that render this reification and stabilization problematic (Table 5.2). Culture tends to become unstable and transient in response to the deinstitutionalization of time-honored centers, Proposition I.A, and the increased circumvention of symbolic barriers, Proposition I.B. I have modified the postmodernist concern with decentering somewhat by indicating a loss of time-honored centers. It is not the case that there are not "centers" in postmodernity around which humans organize their activities and meaning production. Bauman (1992) affirms this position when he argues that the only visible vehicle for continuity and cumulative effects in postmodernity is the human body. But the centers are different, and they and their content are shifting, relative to the stability of a modernist society. Theorists such as Robert Bellah and Thomas Luckmann have pointed out that this kind of decentering occurs as people lose institutionalized places for special kinds of interaction, for example, rituals and interaction over moral issues. The loss of institutionalized place and center is a positive and additive function of six factors: the level of structural differentiation, the level of communication and transportation technology, the level of social and cultural diversity, the level of institutionalized doubt, the level of market velocity and expansion, and the level and rate of commodification.

Institutionalization occurs as collective problems are met through ritualized action and interaction. In addition to ritualization, institutions require legitimating myths—histories and stories that produce a sense of tradition, rightness, and reality through the perception of long lengths of time and large numbers of people. Deinstitutionalization occurs as the structures that pattern interactions weaken, legitimating myths are challenged, doubt becomes institutionalized, and as the greater proportion of a collective's symbols become emotionally flat with unspecified meanings. Thus, as the level of structural differentiation (I.A.1) and communication and transportation technology (I.A.2) increase, people are disembedded from local contexts of social relations and interactions, and their ability to interact in patterned ways de-

Table 5.2
Propositions Concerning Cultural Destabilization and Dereification in Postmodernity

---

I. The relative level of cultural destabilization and dereification in any society is a positive function of
    A. the level of deinstitutionalization of time-honored centers, which is a positive, additive function of
        1. the level of structural differentiation
        2. the level of communication and transportation technology
        3. the level of social and cultural diversity
        4. the level of institutionalized doubt, which is a positive, additive function of
            a. the level of scientific inquiry and ideology
            b. the level of credentialing
            c. the rate of knowledge turnover
        5. the level of market velocity and expansion
        6. the level and rate of commodification
    B. the level of circumvention of symbolic boundaries

---

creases. Structural differentiation also tends to produce particularized cultures—social diversity—which, in turn, serves to create value inconsistencies and conflicts over meanings and histories (myths) in a society, thus lowering the legitimacy of an institutional structure. The level of social diversity in a society also increases due to such factors as participatory democracy, immigration, and communication and transportation technology, thus producing an independent effect for diversity upon the deinstitutionalization of time-honored centers, Proposition I.A.3.

Legitimacy is further lowered as doubt becomes normative (I.A.4). Postmodernity is characterized by expert systems and high levels of credentialing. Expert, scientific, and academic knowledge is designed to be continually revised (I.A.4.a); thus intellectual doubt is considered part and parcel of knowledge acquired through the education system (I.A.4.b), and "doubtful" knowledge constitutes the knowledge of most worth. This doubt tends to influence every area of life, thus lowering institutional legitimacy, and it is reaffirmed as the rate at which new knowledge replaces old increases (I.A.4.c). Additionally, the level of market velocity and expansion (I.A.5) coupled with the level and rate of commodification (I.A.6) produces sets of symbols that are not tied to any group or collective need—not institutionalized. Because of the rate of circulation and permutation of these commodified symbols, it is unlikely that they can be tied to a traditional, institutionalized center;

and as the proportion of these commodified symbols increases, they may tend to lower the legitimacy of time-honored centers.

The second factor in producing a relative level of cultural destabilization and dereification in any society is the rate of symbol circumvention. As noted above, one of the qualities of extricated symbols is that they tend to be affectively flat and definitionally generic—or free-floating. But the presence of a stock of diffuse signs does not necessitate a break with social reality, as many postmodernists argue. What the presence of a fragmented culture does imply is that the reification and stabilization of culture is, at best, problematic at the institutional level, due to a collective's inability to sufficiently border and protect the meaning of their signs and reality. In addition to its direct effect, circumvention decreases cultural stability and reification through the level of communication technology by lifting symbols, images, and information out of the constraints of situated activities and subordinating them to the dictates of presentation rather than information validity, which in turn renders stability and reification problematic.

The Central Organizing Feature of Postmodernity

The second arena of postmodern complexity concerns the individual subject: the self becomes the locus of social action and is simultaneously disabled as an individual subject. There is, of course, an intimate relationship between the self and culture. Culture and individual identity are linked: though identity devolves to the person, it and the self are both cultural constructions. On one level, the self or the subject is a "natural" result of culture and one of the defining characteristics of humanity. In order for culture to be culture (a system that endows objects with meaning), there must be a reflexive subject; meaning must always be interpreted. On another level, the construction of self as a particular kind of entity is contingent upon the culture of the self. That is, the essence of the object that is constructed is determined by the category of the self that is culturally available; the self as a personal and social object has always existed, but the meaning of that social category has changed in response to modernizing and cultural processes (see Williams, 1976; Mauss, 1938/1985; Collins, 1988, pp. 256–259; Marske, 1987; Shweder & Bourne, 1984).

In a gross simplification, there has been a movement from a we-self to a me-self. The we-self is a subject that is organized with preference to the group and has been the principle understanding of the self through history: the individual perceives herself to be a role within a densely knit group of roles. The me-self is a fairly recent category, and it sees itself as an individual among other individuals. This recent concept of the subject functions, from a Durkheimian perspective, as a kind

Table 5.3
Propositions Concerning the Relative Importance of the Individual in Postmodernity

---

I. The relative level of importance given to the individual in any society is a positive, additive function of
   A. the relative level of cultural destabilization and dereification in a society
   B. the multiplicative effects of the level and rate of market velocity and expansion, the level and rate of commodification, and the level of advertising
   C. an interactive effect of the level of social and cultural diversity and the level of communication and transportation technology

---

of generalized culture providing social integration and may be understood as the result of the relative level of cultural destabilization and dereification in a society (Table 5.3, Proposition I.A). As a culture institutionally loses its center and the rate of symbol circumvention increases among groups, there is a tendency to search for alternatives; and the category of the individual subject provides just such a locus of organization and stabilization between groups. As Marske (1987) argues, in a highly differentiated society the individual becomes one of the few collective symbols that segmented groups can hold in common. Additionally, under conditions of social differentiation and change, the self becomes, for the individual, the most trustworthy, stable element in the environment.

In addition to the relative level of cultural destabilization and dereification in a society, the importance of the category of the individual has been influenced by historical processes (e.g., political democratization, the Protestant Reformation) and two distinctly postmodern factors: the multiplicative effects surrounding the level and rate of market velocity and expansion (I.B), and an interaction effect of the rate of social and cultural differentiation and the level of communication and transportation technology (I.C). Expansive markets in capitalistic countries require the creation and recreation of consumer needs and wants. This process of need fabrication also promotes individuation, as it is individuals that are the ultimate consumers, particularly under conditions of increasing discretionary spending. Individuals also represent the last line of expansion—from marketing to group influenced needs to individual lifestyles, expanding markets thus drive the process of commodification so that it intrudes further and further into issues of lifestyle and personal choice. Advertising facilitates the market/commodification dynamic as well as shifting the concerns of individuals and identity formation to abstract and aesthetic images.

These kinds of images are amenable to rapid change and reorganization, which, in turn, tends to produce expanding markets, commodification, and further advertising images.

Increasing social and cultural diversification and levels of communication and transportation technology produce an interaction effect that politicizes the individual. As cultural differentiation increases, so does the possibility of value inconsistencies, both for the individual and the collective. In a differentiated society, the individual has to move among different social settings and communicate with differentiated social groups. This movement tends to create the possibility that some of the values that the individual adopts will be inconsistent one with another, as a reflection of the differentiated settings and groups. Individuals develop crosscutting value structures, and it becomes increasingly difficult for groups to develop a consistent focus of attention—a necessary precondition for groups becoming political entities (see Collins, 1993). As Bauman (1992) states, the group is "unable to override the diversity of its supporters' interests and thus claim and secure their *total* allegiance and identification" (p. 197). Rather, these polity concerns are diffused to agents who adapt them in a self-reflexive manner.

As a result of increases in communication technologies, people have what Anthony Giddens (1991) terms "mediated experiences." Mediated experience is created as people are exposed to accounts of situations and others with whom they have no direct association in time and place. Media, then, brings an intrusion of distant events into the everyday consciousness of people. This intrusion functions as a dialectical movement between local and global domains, where the concerns of individuals reach beyond the level that they can directly influence through social movements (e.g., global warming, ethnic cleansing). There is thus a tendency for the focus to move from group politics to choices of lifestyle and life politics. A lifestyle consists of a more or less integrated set of practices that a person might embrace. In this sense, lifestyles are seen to be political: the effects of how one chooses to live their daily life reach beyond the micro-level practices themselves. As individuals choose politically informed lifestyles, they participate in life politics, a lifestyle that is concerned with issues that flow from the practices of self-actualization within the dialectic of the local and global spheres, where self-realization and the practice of lifestyles is seen to influence global issues. Taken together, social-cultural differentiation and the mass media form an interactive effect that elevates the category of the individual to a political position: people live at crosscutting intersections where it becomes increasingly difficult to mobilize collectives for social change, but at the same time, they are politically enabled through the conceptualization of global problems as issues of lifestyle.

The Decentered Subject

As the individual is becoming more important in terms of being the locus of social and cultural organization, there is a relative decline in the degree of viability of the individual subject. Some postmodernists, like Baudrillard, Gergen, and Jameson, have concluded that the subject is dead and that the category of the self no longer exists. Others, like Bauman, Harvey, and Douglas Kellner (1992), take a more moderate position. Like Baudrillard and Gergen, Kellner sees the media as the vehicle par excellence of postmodern culture but adds that rather than dulling the senses, the plethora of cultural images provides an opportunity for greater reflexivity concerning self-identity.   But, unlike Jameson and Baudrillard, Kellner argues that there are affective and behavioral proscriptions concerning the self and identity in postmodern culture; they are simply ever changing and in greater number. Thus people in postmodernity are much more aware of identity issues and can experiment with different identities without running the risk of traditional sanctions. And, as Bauman notes, this ability to experiment is due to the loss of a culturally legitimated center around which a self can be organized.   For Kellner, then, identity formation in postmodernity is akin to a game played with a myriad of possible roles. But, both Kellner and Harvey agree, the game has possible side effects in the form of uncertainty and instability of identity, and sensory overload due to the sheer numbers of stimuli.

Generally, then, the postmodern subject is defined in terms of sensory block, an inability to invest emotionally, and an increased rate of reflexivity (Table 5.4, Proposition I). The concept of sensory block comes from Harvey and generalizes Gergen's issue of social saturation. Due to an increase in the absolute number of stimuli with which individuals have to contend, people must cognitively select and edit information. As the number of available stimuli continues to rise, the individual will tend simply to shut off his or her ability to apprehend more information; people reach a satiation point and merely suffice in their choice and level of information. And, as Proposition II states, in postmodernity new stimuli are produced (II.A), required (II.B), made available (II.C), and unfettered and extricated (II.D) at increasing rates.

The postmodern subject is also disabled emotionally. With the concept of the inability to invest emotionally, I am generalizing Harvey's concern with the blasé attitude, Jameson's emotional flatness, Baudrillard's death of the subject, Gergen's inauthentic emotions, and the con-

Table 5.4
Propositions Concerning the Relative Viability of the Subject in Postmodernity

---

I. The relative decline in the degree of viability of the individual subject is a positive, additive function of the degree of sensory block, the degree of inability to invest emotionally, and the rate of reflexivity.

II. The degree of sensory block any individual experiences is a positive function of the absolute number of stimuli with which that individual has to contend, which is a positive function of
   - A. the level of commodification
   - B. the level of credentialing
   - C. the level of communication and transportation technology
   - D. the level of circumvention of symbolic boundaries

III. The degree of inability to invest emotionally is a positive, additive function of the level and rate of environmental change and the level of divergent interactions.
   - A. the level and rate of environmental change is a positive function of
       1. the rate of technological innovation
       2. the level and rate of the division of labor
       3. the level and rate of market velocity and expansion
       4. the relative level of cultural destabilization and dereification
   - B. the level of divergent interactions is a positive function of
       1. the level and rate of the division of labor
       2. the level of deinstitutionalization of time-honored centers
       3. the level of circumvention of symbolic boundaries

IV. The rate of reflexivity is a positive, additive function of
   - A. the level of communication and transportation technology
   - B. the level of institutionalized doubt

---

cept reflects the initial side of Bauman's tribal politics, with the need for spectacular emotional displays—emotion must soar irregularly because it cannot be invested. People are able to invest their emotion in symbolic entities that have a degree of stability about them and around which they can achieve some level of interaction intensity. In postmodernity, both those conditions are less likely to be fulfilled. The environment within which the individual lives is subject to high rates of change: technology builds, grows, and changes exponentially (III.A.1), the division of labor fragments and shifts with a greater flexibility (III.A.2), markets expand and change products at ever-increasing rates (III.A.3), and the cultural world in which people live is no longer institutionally moored (III.A.4). Interaction intensity is linked to people's interaction patterns, which tend to be organized and rendered repeatable by the occupational and institutional structures.

Thus, as these factors change and become flexible, the opportunities for patterned interactions are diminished, and with them the ease of emotional investment in signs and symbols, Propositions III.B.1, 2. Additionally, in those cases when people are able to pattern interactions and produce an emotionally meaningful culture, that culture is subject to circumvention due to commodification, increases in the level of communication and transportation technology, and discretionary spending (III.B.3).

And, finally, the postmodern subject is created through an increased rate of reflexivity. Postmodernists generally do not conceptualize reflexivity as a variable but note that it becomes problematic due to the influence of the mass media and institutionalized doubt (IV.A, B). As Kenneth Gergen argues, due to massive increases in communication and transportation technologies, and the defusing of the postmodern critique of knowledge, the self has become reflexive and is embedded in an institutionalized field of doubt. These processes have created problems for the social construction of the self: the postmodern self experiences a decreased commitment to the self as an objective and stable entity, and multiphernia (personal inadequacy built around a vertigo of self-values) increases.

POSTMODERNISM IN PERSPECTIVE

According to the postmodern model, culture has simultaneously become increasingly important and yet inconsistent and illusionary; and the individual subject has become the locus of social organization, but at the same time has been affectively disabled. However, the postmodernists have overstated the case by concluding that there is a crisis, that reality consists only of text, and that the self is necessarily decentered and fragmented, and they have erred in their exclusive concern with the structure of culture. The postmodern model misses four essential and interrelated elements. First, it does not consider the basic processes through which meaning is created; second, it misses the effect that the contingent nature of culture has upon human beings; third, the model leaves unexplicated the micro-level dynamics of culture; and, fourth, the postmodern model contains an unarticulated, and deficient, social psychology.

The Process of Meaning Production

While I applaud the emphasis on cultural meaning, the issues of how and where culture is created, and the ramifications of culture's mode of production, are not sufficiently considered by postmodernists. The production of meaning and reality are not direct effects of the structure of culture; rather, the meaning potential of the structure must always be enacted by people. And there are only two methods through which meaning is enacted: the focus of emotional and cognitive energy and/or through the process of association. Association is only able to produce a tertiary level of meaning, a set of symbols available to a group whose sense-meaning is diffuse and affect-meaning is flat. It is this tertiary meaning with which the postmodern model is specifically concerned—the forces identified in the postmodern model have collectively produced a stock of available signs that do not directly arise from the interaction of the social groups that can potentially use them; and they achieve their initial level of meaning and reality with humans through the process of association. These cultural elements are fragmented in the sense that they are not meaningfully related one to another by the system. As a result, humans have at their disposal a stock of signs whose meaning is diffuse (i.e., not highly specified), or free-floating. Thus far the postmodern model is correct. But the presence of a stock of diffuse signs does not necessitate a break with social reality, nor does it necessarily segment the large collective or completely do away with grand narratives. What the presence of a fragmented culture does imply is that the reification and stabilization of culture is at least problematic at the institutional level. Yet, in order for culture to be functional, a certain level of meaning and reality must be maintained, and thus, if meaning is not reified and stabilized at the system-level, then these processes will tend to occur at the micro-level of interaction.

There are three possible results from the presence of sets of diffuse cultural signs, but each of these possibilities is tied to humans in interaction. First, if a commodified sign is used by many diverse groups, there will be a tendency to keep the meaning of the sign unspecified, in terms of both affect—and sense-meaning; it is difficult for a group to "own" a sign if other dissimilar groups employ it. Individuals will tend to relate meaningfully to such signs only through association. Since such signs are unable to elicit strong emotion from the interactants, the use of such signs in group interaction could create a "thin and meager"[3] conscious life for its members (Goffman, 1951, p. 304)—a sense of the postmodern self. Second, commercialized signs could be adopted by a group or individual which would, in turn, attempt to define the sign exclusively in symbolic/collective terms, leaving the conscious life of the group and the self far from emotionally flat or without meaning. Third, the forces of mass marketing, coupled with the general use of a term by an intermediary group (e.g., a profession), could create a general social category that is adopted and used by many diverse groups. This social category could have an equally intense meaning for all concerned groups, giving them a general and meaningful sign. For example, the profession of counseling and the mass marketing of self-help books have given a categorical opportunity to social groups and individuals to relate meaningfully to the category of victim-self and addict-self.

This final process supplies a stock of secondary culture that theoretically may provide for a certain degree of cultural consensus and cohesion. While the system-level culture may indeed be fragmented and grand narratives difficult to maintain, it is not the case that grand narratives are necessary for the integration of a social system, any more than high levels of moral culture is necessary. As I have argued, the legitimacy of any grand narrative is dependent not so much upon the structure of the culture but on the affect-meaning in back of the narrative, and high levels of emotional energy surrounding a collective identity are difficult to sustain in any but a traditional society—they require continual, ritualized interaction. What is necessary for a society to be integrated, culturally speaking, is *some degree of consensus* about its culture and identity. But where that threshold level is has yet to be explicated. It is theoretically possible that secondary culture, formed and maintained at the level of organizations and professions, can provide just such a level of consensus. Additionally, if large-scale projects that require commitment and sacrifice are in the making, then a society also needs a stock of collective symbols that are undisputed; but, again, it is not necessary that these symbols be continually invested with emotional energy nor that they coalesce into a recognizable grand narrative at all times—it is simply required that these be available to form such a narrative around which people may ritually interact and form a collective sacred identity when necessary (under conditions of threat, for example).

Note that each of the above possibilities concerning the presence of tertiary culture is dependent upon the manner in which groups in real social interaction respond to and use symbols. It is indeed possible to view culture as an artifact and make inferences about the society from which it originated, as does postmodernism—the field of cultural anthropology makes inferences of this type, as it is the only way to understand a dead culture. But if culture is to be analyzed in real time, in a living society, it ought to be examined *in situ*: culture does not exist as an amorphous, ethereal entity that is not dependent on human interaction and "indulges in manifestations with no purpose or utility of any sort, for the mere pleasure of affirming itself" (Durkheim, 1912/1995, p. 471). Thus it is ultimately the microdynamics of interaction that determine what influence the macroforces of postmodernity will have on culture.

Therefore the mechanisms through which meaning and reality are produced remain the same, but the emphasis is different in postmodernity than in the early stages of modernity: the micro-level dynamics

have become more important than the macro-level. But, it is important
to note, there is a potential danger when meaning/reality construction
and stabilization are more dependent upon the micro-level, when individuals are free to create and sustain culture and the structure of culture
is in continuous flux. The use of too many different cultural elements in
too short a period of time will tend to unmask the arbitrariness of culture, which may in turn lead to a feeling of disillusionment—a state of
the postmodern. But this problem exists as a potential, not a given: due
to the needs for facticity and ontological security, people work hard a t
avoiding cultural disruption and this third level of reflexivity.   Further, the model of cultural meaning production indicates that increases
in the level and rate of reflexivity will tend to increase the overall
level of interaction intensity which will promote higher levels of reification, thus mitigating problematic levels of reflexivity and disillusionment. Additionally, the presence of secondary culture mitigates
the potential difficulty associated with the micro-level, by increasing
the level of interaction equilibrium.
     The importance of this conceptualization of the production of mean-
ing is that it removes the emphasis from the sign/symbol and stresses
the social through interaction. Meaning, particularly affect-meaning,
is not a direct function of the system, nor is it a quality of the
sign/symbol; rather, it is a function and quality of the focus of psychic
and emotional energy and particular aspects of the interaction process.
Symbols and cultural structures act as a triggers for individuals and
groups to "remember" and "reenact" the meaning, though, as symbolic
interactionists have pointed out, the meaning emerges from the interaction. Further, people may or may not focus psychic or emotional energy
on an element of culture, depending upon the qualities of the interaction. An additional quality of symbolic meaning that places emphasis
on the interaction is the emotional decay factor: if a symbol ceases to be
the focus of regular group or individual interaction, then its ability to
initially elicit the same emotional response at the same level deterio-
rates and will require additional efforts to reestablish.

Facticity and Ontological Insecurity

     The second essential element missed by the postmodern model is the
effect that the contingent nature of culture has upon human beings. A
sign's relationship to the physical universe is arbitrary and abstract.
It is the arbitrary nature of signs that make their meaning ultimately
dependent upon continual interaction and thus uncertain.   Sign-
uncertainty is *an intrinsic feature of culture*; signs are by definition one
step removed from obdurate reality.   Baudrillard's (1981/1994, p. 6)
principle of equivalence is incorrect—signs have always been and a l-

ways will be essentially self-referential: each sign does not simply stand as a signifier of a single object, the sense-meaning of the sign is also a function of its relation to other signs. This self-referencing can vary, and signs can become more abstract, further removed from obdurate reality and the tendency to experience uncertainty will increase with abstraction.

Yet Baudrillard is correct when he argues that mass media and advertising have increased the self-referencing of the system and the abstraction of the sign. *But the process and problems associated with culture as a self-referencing system have always existed.* Cultural meaning is an abstraction from obdurate reality, essentially self-referential, and thus it is inherently contingent and must be recreated on an ongoing basis. This contingency creates in humans a diffuse sense of anxiety and the needs for ontological security and facticity. Because of sign uncertainty/anxiety, humans seek to reify and stabilize their signs and sign systems. *And the processes whereby humans seek to reify and stabilize culture have fundamentally been the same through time.* In an oversimplification, reification and stabilization of culture can occur at the macro-institutional level and/or at the level of small group interaction. And, while the loss of stabilization and reification at the system level does have cultural ramifications, it does not do away with the needs for facticity and ontological security. In fact, a decrease in the stabilization and reification of culture at the system level increases the need for facticity and ontological security and will push for certain kinds of interactions at the micro-level.

Meaning and Reality at the Micro-Level

The third factor that the postmodern model misses is the micro-level dynamics of culture. Postmodernism assumes reification at the institutionalized sign-system level. The postmodern view of reification comes from the structuralist assumption that meaning is constituted by sign-relations, and it is manifested in Baudrillard's rather simplistic jump from simulacra to nonreality: the state of the sign system could only influence reality construction to the degree that Baudrillard, and others, posits, if there were no other factors involved in reality construction. But constructed reality is not simply a systemic function; it is also determined by certain qualities of human interaction and perception. System-level stabilization and reification are primarily the results of institutionalization. But the effect of institutionalization on reification is indirect, and institutionalization is but one of five direct factors in producing stabilization. If there has been a postmodern fragmentation of the culture system, then the needs for facticity and ontological security that drive the processes of stabilization and reification will create pressures for increased cultural work at the micro-level.

Most of the dynamics of culture at the micro-level are delineated in the lower right-hand section of the model of meaning production and are discussed at length elsewhere. At this point, it becomes theoretically desirable to extract and clarify the microdynamics of culture. To summarize these processes I have listed the main elements in propositional form in Tables 5.5, 5.6, and 5.7. There are three basic issues involved with culture: the production, reification, and stabilization of symbolic meaning.

The production of cultural meaning at the micro-level. Cultural meaning is created through the focus of psychic and/or emotional energy or through the process of association. The assumption undergirding the approach in this book is that cultural meaning is a product of human action and interaction and is thus not a direct quality of the symbol nor of the structure; this assumption is reflected in Table 5.5, Proposition I. Association is a passive mechanism whereby the meaning of one symbol is transferred to another. Thus the more frequently symbols of dissimilar meaning are perceived together in the same meaning-context, the greater is the tendency to associate the meaning of one with the other, Proposition IV. Because it is passive, the depth and specificity of the meaning produced is limited. Both association and the focus of psychic or emotional energy may be used individually or in groups, but because culture presupposes shared meaning, Proposition I.A holds that interaction is the preferred method. Additionally, though affect-meaning may be created through private rituals, these private rituals will tend to need to be objectified through public performance.

As implied by Proposition I.A, interactions vary by their intensity, that is, how much emotional and psychic energy they can produce. The general level of interaction intensity varies by the degree of physical proximity, common focus of attention, common emotional mood, and pace. Proposition II indicates that the relationship among these variables is multiplicative. That is, proximity aids in the establishment of a common focus of attention, and a common focus, once established tends to reinforce a common emotional mood and both tend to bring people closer together. Collectively these work together to reinforce the pace or time sequencing of an interaction. It is important to note that the pace of an interaction has a curvilinear effect: initial increases will produce correspondingly higher levels of emotional energy, but, past a certain point, additional increases in the pace are difficult for humans to synchronize and will tend to break down interaction.

Proposition III submits that people are more likely to participate in intense interactions based on perceived similitude, a shared stock of rituals, and felt needs for ontological security and facticity. In consid-

Table 5.5
Micro-Level Propositions of Meaning Production

I. The level of meaning with which any symbol is associated at the micro-level is a positive function of
    A. the level of interaction intensity
    B. the process of association
II. The level of interaction intensity is a positive, multiplicative function of
    A. the level of physical proximity
    B. the degree of common focus of attention
    C. the degree of common emotional mood
    D. the rate of interactional pace, which is a positively curvilinear function of
        1. the read and response rate
        2. the level of rhythmic synchronization
III. The probability that people will participate in intense interactions is a positive function of
    A. the level of similitude
    B. the level of shared stock of rituals
    C. the felt needs for ontological security and facticity
IV. The level of cultural meaning produced through association is a positive function of the repeated spatial association among symbols of dissimilar meanings.

---

ering the micro-level production of meaning, I have intentionally set aside the issue of structure and its influence on the probability that people will participate in intense interactions. There are two reasons behind this move. First, if the postmodern model is correct when it posits the fragmentation of institutionalized ritual centers, then the influence of macro-level structures upon interaction intensity will be close to nil. Second, micro-level structures (e.g., friendship networks) do have an influence on the probability of intense interactions, but that effect is indirect through ritualization and I address ritual density in Table 5.6. Thus, the propositions in Table 5.5 assume a free-floating, postmodern like situation and hence provide a direct answer to the postmodern problem of meaning.

In unstructured situations, then, people's interactions are likely to achieve some level of intensity if they perceive a level of similitude with others. The perception of similitude does not necessarily imply cognitive awareness. In fact, the cognitive awareness of attraction or similarity is generally an accounting, a backward reconstruction, of the experience. Similitude is an emergent quality that arises out of initial and tentative interaction. It has the quality of a gestalt in that it is a complex and unconscious reading of rhythmic patterns, speech (e.g., words, construction, inflection, tone), and bodily dispositions (e.g., nonverbal cues, mannerisms). Bourdieu (1977), though conceptualizing art, clearly captures the essence of what I mean by similitude: it is "'pure practice without theory' . . . something *ineffable* . . . something which communicates, so to speak, from body to body, i.e., on the hither side of words or concepts, and which pleases (or displeases) without concepts" (p. 2). Similitude and ritualized behavior reinforce one another due to the influence that ritualization has upon the possession and perform-ance of similar acts, speech, and nonverbal cues. Intense interactions will also tend to take place when there is a noticeable level of shared ritual elements; the concept "the level of shared stock of rituals" thus refers to the degree of match among the various interactants' stock of rituals. People in the same general proximity tend to monitor one an-other for various cues, one of which is the level of shared ritualization.

These shared elements prompt and facilitate intense interactions. People will also tend to initiate and participate in intense interactions in response to the felt needs for ontological security and facticity. As noted previously, culture demands reflexivity and reflexivity intrinisi-cally produces ontological insecurities, experienced as a kind of general anxiety over the existence of the general properties of reality, accord-ing to Heidegger. Because ritualized, intense interactions tend to reduce reflexivity and to present symbolic meaning as carrying its own fac-ticity and thus taken-for-granted reality, intense interactions also tend to produce ontological security. Thus, as people experience felt needs for ontological security and facticity, they will seek out intense interac-tions that will produce the sense of reification necessary to meet onto-logical anxiety. Because these felt needs increase during times of change and uncertainty, and because postmodernity is characterized by fragmentation and flux, the theory predicts that individuals will tend to participate in higher levels of interaction intensity than in previous eras; thus producing a subjectively meaningful, complex reality, a real-ity that is distinctively different than the one with which postmod-ernists are concerned..

The reification of meaning at the micro-level. The second issue con-cerning the production of symbolic meaning is its level of reification. Because all cultural meaning is an abstraction from the obdurate world, the perception of the reality of a symbol can vary. The perceived real-ity of symbolic objects at the micro-level is the product of two qualities: the degree of affect-meaning the symbol is able to elicit and the per-ceived objectification of the symbol (see Table 5.6, Proposition I). As the model of meaning production indicates, the degree of affect-meaning has the greatest effect on the perceived reality of a symbol due to both its direct and indirect effects. This theoretical relationship may be empirically observed in that when a choice is required, culture that is reified through affect-meaning is preferred, rather than objecti-

Table 5.6
Micro-Level Propositions of Reification Processes

I. The level of reification produced for any cultural symbol at the micro-level is a positive function of the level of affect-meaning and the degree of objectification associated with the symbol.

II. The level of affect-meaning is a positive function of
      A. the level of ritual density, which is a positive function of
            1. the level of network density of an identifiable group
            2. the level of experienced uncertainty or threat among an identifiable group in an encounter

III. The degree of objectification associated with the symbol is a positive, additive function at the micro-level of
      A. the level of association between a symbol and a cultural identity
      B. the degree of the sacredness of the cultural identity, which is a positive function of
            1. the degree of affect-meaning and the level of ritualization associated with a cultural identity
            2. the degree of cultural exclusion practiced around the symbols of a group

---

fied culture. The degree of affect-meaning is an effect of interaction intensity and is most directly influenced by the level of ritual density, the proportion of individual or group behaviors that are performed ritually (II.A). This effect of ritual is due to its ability to recreate the same behaviors in response to a given symbol that leads to high interaction intensity, which in turn produces high levels of emotional energy in response to the symbol. As noted in Propositions II.A.1 and II.A.2, the level of ritual performance increases proportionally with the level of network density and/or uncertainty or threat.

Culture also appears real as it is objectified. When cultural elements are perceived to be objects existing outside of or apart from the individual, the element is objectified and its sense of reality increases. The objectification of a modicum of culture is principally the result of its association with other people. In other words, the more a symbol is perceived as being produced and shared by others, the more likely is it that the symbol will be understood as an object in the environment. Objectification is generally a function of macro-level processes: increasing amounts of people, time, and geographic space. But objectification can also occur at the micro-level: as a symbol is associated with a particular group of people, it will be perceived as having objective qualities. Thus the more a symbol is associated with a cultural identity and the more sacred is that identity, the more likely is the symbol to be perceived as an object in the environment, Propositions III.A and III.B.

Table 5.7
Micro-Level Propositions of Stabilization Processes

I. The level of stabilization produced for any cultural symbol at the micro-level is a positive, additive function of
   A. the level of reification
   B. the level of ritual density
   C. the degree of exclusion, which is a positive, additive function of
      1. the level of ritual density
      2. the degree of sacredness of cultural identity
      3. the level of particularized typifications, regionalizations, and rhythms
   D. the level of interaction equilibrium, which is a positive function of
      1. the level of assumed reciprocity of perspectives
      2. the number of avoidance and accommodation techniques
      3. the level of secondary and tertiary cultures available to people in an encounter

---

Cultural identities become sacred, reified, and thus salient as they are ritualized and a degree of cultural exclusion is practiced (III.B.1, 2).

The stabilization of meaning at the micro-level. The third meaning construction issue is stabilization. Because all cultural meaning is intrinsically contingent, the stability of the meaning associated with a symbol varies. As the model of meaning production indicates, the perceived stability of any cultural element is the function of four processes: reification, ritual density, exclusion, and interaction equilibrium; and these same factors operate to stabilize culture at the micro-level (see Table 5.7). Reification influences stability in a taken-for-granted manner: people assume that reified objects are real and unchanging. This assumption leads people to perform ethnomethods with regard to the item, thus producing a taken-for-grantedness and stability in practice. Ritual density is by definition a stabilizing factor; it is the patterning of stereotypical behaviors in relation to symbolic meaning in order to ensure the meaning's repeatability. Exclusion works to stabilize cultural meaning because it limits ambiguity and conflict over meaning. Every cultural system inherently excludes some assumptions and meanings, and to the degree that dissimilar assumptions and meanings are excluded, the meaning of culture is stabilized. Proposition I.C.1 indicates that the practice of exclusion increases as an individual's or group's level of ritual density increases. Rituals tend to create sacred borders that will be guarded (Proposition I.C.2), and they also produce particularized typifications, regionalizations, and rhythms, which exclude by default. Finally, interaction equilibrium is produced by, and acts to exclude divergent meanings through, the assumption of shared perspectives, the level of available avoidance and accommodation techniques, and the presence of secondary and tertiary cultures (I.D.1, 2, 3).

The Social Psychology of the Self in Postmodernity

Finally, the fourth problem with the postmodern model is that it is generally based on an unarticulated and incomplete social psychology. Most postmodernists rely on an assumed correspondence between the subject and the structure of culture. Generally the postmodern self is not constructed through social interactions per se, but is constituted culturally. So that if a problem exists in the culture of a society, then there will be a problem with the self that is produced from that culture, in terms of both the self-concept and the emotions surrounding the self. Thus, because the culture of postmodernity is fragmentary, disparate, changing, and ever expanding, it is impossible for people to establish a core conceptual identity. This problem is particularly salient with regard to the subjectivity of the self—the postmodern self is not only conceptually fragmented but also affectively flat: because these changing cultural images are presented to people at tremendous rates, individuals are unable to form any lasting emotional investment in them. But in order for a fragmented self to result simply from a fragmented culture, the system must be exclusively determinative, and it is not: the system informs and constrains, but it does not determine—the *primary* function of the culture system is to stabilize meaning, not create it. It is important, then, to consider the self *in situ*, in the process of its construction.

The clearest postmodern, theoretical statement concerning the development of the self comes from Kenneth Gergen (1971; 1991). Gergen argues that the self is best understood as a situated, linguistic process through which an individual categorizes his or her own behaviors. The self thus always tends to be experienced as fragmented and sometimes contradictory in that these conceptualizations are situational, a concept borrowed from Goffman. In postmodernity, the possibility of discordant self-images increases as the culture fragments—not only are the situations possibly isolated one from another but the culture informing each situation may be segmented and socially saturated with too many images of self from which to choose. This situation increases reflexivity to the point that a coherent self-image is impossible to achieve.

While I do agree that an individual can experience a self that is fragmented (see Allan, 1997), postmodernists in general, and Gergen's theory in particular, miss some theoretical implications that ought to inform our understanding of the self in postmodernity. Gergen is correct in asserting that the self is associated with the linguistic system and involves an act of reflexivity. Following Mead (1934/1962) and Goffman (1959), sociologists recognize that the formation of the self involves at least two processes: a reflexive, internal conversation, and the production of a symbolic object. Mead proposed that the self is fundamentally a particular kind of behavior: an internal conversation between what he termed the "I" and the "Me," the individual as actor and observer. The theme or object of the conversation, the organization of a particular biographical history, may encompass decades or milliseconds and might be global or quite specific. That is, the self arises when an individual considers his or her own conduct, thought, or emotion and then places these within a continuously built frame of reference. This understanding of the self parallels Schutz's theory of meaning construction in that it is constituted through a kind of backward glance. Thus the reflexive-self might emerge while the behavior or internal action is in process and therefore be a specific, situational self, or the self may arise in more comprehensive backward glances involving any number of circumstances, behaviors, interactions, and emotions. These more comprehensive glances are attempts to organize a coherent sense of self, a grand narrative of the individual.

But it is not the case that reflexivity is simply a straightforward behavior, either present or absent as Mead seems to imply. Rather, as Gergen notes, reflexivity can become problematic; what Gergen has left unexplicated is the variability of reflexivity. Proposition I from Table 5.8 explicitly states that the act of biographical reflexivity produces a coherent self-image up to a certain point; past that threshold limit, the reflexive act tends to break down and begins actually to challenge meaning rather than create it (see third-order reflexivity). Proposition I also posits that reflexivity can vary by its rate, how frequently the process occurs, and by complexity, the number of and connections among the conceptual considerations that the process must go through before the loop is concluded and a self emerges. Generally, the rate of reflexivity is a function of the level of uncertainty experienced by the individual, uncertainty being a function of the level and rate of environmental change, the level of institutional doubt, and the level of personal doubt, Proposition II. The concept of personal doubt is intended to capture the experience concerning a negative evaluation of one's response to past environmental change and uncertainty, which would increase uncertainty in a current, similar situation.

At the micro-level, the complexity of the reflexive loop is a function of the individual's cultural capital—Proposition III.A—and tends to increase in response to four factors: cosmopolitanism, change, distance from necessity, and education, Propositions III.A.1, 2, 3, 4. Cosmopolitanism refers to an interaction pattern that tends to be characterized

Table 5.8
Micro-Level Propositions of Self-Reflexivity

I. The self is a positively curvilinear function of biographical reflexivity, which varies by rate and complexity.
II. The rate of an individual's reflexivity is a positive function of the level of uncertainty, which is a positive, additive function of
    A. the level and rate of environmental change
    B. the level of institutional doubt
    C. the level of personal doubt
III. The complexity of an individual's reflexive loop is a positive function of
    A. the cultural capital of an individual, which is a positive function of
        1. the level of cosmopolitanism in the social network
        2. the level and rate of environmental change
        3. the level of the distance from necessity
        4. the level of credentialing

---

by diverse groups, dissimilar communications, and situational variety. In a dense network, individuals interact repeatedly with a relatively small group of people over extended periods of time, and their group symbols tend to become highly particular. Thus, in a more cosmopolitan network, an individual's cultural capital will tend to be less group specific and more complex, in order to handle the more diverse and changing social situations. In like manner, as the level and rate of environmental change increase, social groups must come up with symbolic means to manage the environment, thus increasing the level of cultural complexity. Additionally, the elaboration of one's cultural capital is influenced by distance from necessity and the level of credentialing or education. Distance from necessity is Bourdieu's concept and indicates that as a person is no longer directly concerned with physical survival, he or she will tend to conceptualize the world differently. Ideas about the world, and the connections among those ideas, will become more abstract, complex, and aesthetically inclined. Furthermore, individuals with high levels of education tend to see the world in terms of various levels of abstract meaning rather than as concrete objects.

Postmodernity contains two factors that tend to create what might be termed "hyper-reflexivity." Hyper-reflexivity is the result of the combination of a high rate of change coupled with a complex culture system. While the self is a construction based on reflexivity, if the level of reflexivity passes a certain breaking point, there is a possibility that the construction cannot be completed. That is, if the frequency of reflexivity is high due to change, and if there is a large number of disconnected conceptual considerations that must be encompassed before closure, then it is unlikely that a single, biographical narrative can be manufactured. Due to the influence of markets and commodification, the rate of the division of labor, the level of cultural destabilization, imaging technology, time/place compression, and symbolic circumvention, the rate of change is rapid, in terms of both social and cultural conditions; and, due to social and cultural differentiation, the level of available cultural identities, the level of intellectual technology, the level of communication and transportation technology, and the level of credentialing, an individual's cultural capital, taken as a whole, tends to be extremely complex. These factors collectively tend to produce the condition of hyper-reflexivity and a sense of a fragmented self. And, as noted by postmodernists, and some modernists (see Giddens, 1991), this increased rate and complexity of reflexivity takes place within a cultural frame of institutionalized doubt, an additional factor producing uncertainty.

Thus far my argument is not significantly different from the one found in the postmodern model. But there are at least two phases in the production of the self. The first phase entails the reflexive act and is subject to all the social and cultural pressures thus far noted; in the second phase, the self as a symbolic object is formed (Table 5.9). In his theory, Mead (1934/1962) noted that the self became an object to the individual and explicated the place of this object in the emergent social order and interactional meaning. But he failed to see the ramifications of the self as a symbolic object in cultural terms. As a result of the process of reflexivity, the self becomes a symbolic object, and like all symbolic objects, its level of reification and stability is a function of culture and can vary at both the macro—and micro-levels. The macrolevel processes correspond to the institutional factors noted in the model of meaning production and are of primary concern to most postmodernists; thus, like all culture, the macro-level objectification, stabilization, and reification of identity and self-concepts are not as solid as they possibly once were. But, as the theory of meaning production indicates, the loss of these institutionalized resources is not necessarily problematic for the subject nor for his or her self.

In general, during the act of reflexivity, the actor-self is observed and evaluated in terms of an existing and biographic-self and the categorical expectations of an encounter. The categorical or normative expectations are an emergent quality of culture, the situation, and the interactive process of presenting, imputing, and accepting identities. Thus, while culture informs the creation of self, the process is a complex of both structure and agency, a point undervalued by the postmodern model. A concept of the self emerges out of this process, a conclusion of "who I am" in this situation, and becomes a reflexively available part of the individual. This object-self corresponds to Mead's "Me" and po-

Table 5.9
Micro-Level Cultural Reality Propositions of the Self-Concept

---

I. The self is a positive function of the level of reification and stabilization associated with the symbolic object "Me."

II. The level of reification associated with the self-concept at the micro-level is a positive, additive function of the level of affect-meaning and the degree of objectification associated with the symbol.

III. The level of stabilization associated with the self-concept at the micro-level is a positive, additive function of the level of reification, the level of ritual density, the degree of exclusion, and the level of interaction equilibrium.

---

tentially to Goffman's sacred-self. Though Goffman is generally seen as conceptualizing the self as fragmented and situational, much like postmodernists, he also has a sense of the self in keeping with the concept of a core, transituational identity.

In *Stigma* (1963) Goffman proposes a threefold typology of identity: the social identity, the personal identity, and the ego identity. Both the social and personal identities fit in with the concept of a fragmented self; it is the ego identity that hints at something else. The ego identity is "first of all a subjective, reflexive matter that necessarily must be felt by the individual whose identity is at issue" (Goffman, 1963, p. 106). This identity is of the individual's own construction and made out of the same materials that others use to construct a personal and social identity. The ego identity is that which "distinguishes an individual from all others [and] is the core of his being, a general and central aspect of him, making him different through and through, not merely identifiably different, from those who are most like him" (Goffman, 1963, p. 56). Goffman (1963) likens his ego identity to that of Erikson and also refers to it as one's felt identity: "the subjective sense of his own situation and his own continuity and character that an individual comes to obtain as a result of his various social experiences" (p. 105).[4]

More important for the case at hand, in *Interaction Ritual* (1967) Goffman presents a twofold image of the self, the sacred self and self-as-player. The self-as-player is one who participates in a ritual game and performs honorably or dishonorably. Interaction is pictured as a ritual performance during which participants must present a face in keeping with approved social attributes. Interactants may be said to maintain face when the line they effectively take is supported by the judgments of those present and is confirmed by evidence given through impersonal agencies. "At such times the person's face clearly is not lodged in or on his body, but rather something that is diffusely located in the flow of events in the encounter" (Goffman, 1967, p. 7).

On the other hand, the sacred self is an "image pieced together from the expressive implications of the full flow of events in an undertaking" (Goffman, 1967, p. 31). This sacred self is the face to which feelings become attached and which may be slighted: "If an encounter sustains an image of him that he has long taken for granted, he probably will have few feelings about the matter. If events establish a face for him that is better than he might have expected, he is likely to 'feel good'; if his ordinary expectations are not fulfilled, one expects that he will 'feel bad' or 'feel hurt'" (Goffman, 1967, p. 6). The sacred self, like all sacred objects, has clear and unencroachable boundaries, so that it is subject to "slights and profanation" (Goffman, 1967, p. 31). And the sacred self is produced through the same process that any other sacred object is created: the infusion of affect-meaning, or emotional energy.

The culture of the self is particularly amenable to reification and stabilization at the micro-level because its social organization always entails the individual. Generally speaking, the level of stabilization and reification of the self-concept is a function of the same processes as any other symbolic object (Table 5.9, Propositions II and III). Of particular importance is the level of affect-meaning that any self-concept can elicit. Thus the sacred self is a symbolic object that is created in group interaction, and its experienced reality is dependent upon the individual's network density and ritual performance. In general, the greater the degree of network density and the greater the ritual density in an individual's life, the greater is the tendency to experience self as a sacred object invested with high affect-meaning and clear boundaries. And, as noted earlier, one of the primary functions of ritual and high levels of affect-meaning is to restrict reflexivity; and, under conditions of increasing uncertainty and ontological insecurity, people will tend to produce more ritualized encounters at the micro-level, thus producing not only a sense of reified culture in general, but also a sense of a sacred, reified self, which in turn will tend to reduce reflexivity and mitigate the problems associated with the fragmented subject. Additionally, the culture of the subject has become stabilized and reified at the meso-level through the production of a secondary culture focused on the self by professional organizations and moral entrepreneurs. This secondary culture in particular helps maintain cultural stability around the self through the production of interaction equilibrium (Proposition III).

BRINGING REALITY BACK IN

While it is more difficult to create a sense of reality and self in postmodernity, the processes through which these are produced continue to be essentially the same for humans as they always have been. On the whole, I agree with certain elements of the postmodern model:

both cultural meaning and the individual self have become more important in technically advanced, well-developed capitalist societies. But
based on the theory of meaning production, I contend that there are
problems with the assertion that culture has become fragmented—or, in
my words, destabilized and dereified—to the point that it constitutes a
crisis for the experience of meaningful reality for the general population. I have argued that the reification and stabilization of culture
will continue at the micro-level in the face of fragmentation at the system-level.

In terms of the structure of culture, the influence of the postmodern
dynamics come through institutionalization. But as may be concluded
from the model of meaning production, even if the influence of institutional spheres is completely removed, the model can still function—the
reification and stability of cultural meaning is secure. However, it is
not the case that the production of cultural meaning is without dilemmas. People must contend with time/place compression, the rapid circulation and change of aesthetic and ephemeral symbols, the loss of
time-honored centers, and so on. But the postmodern model has been
incomplete: people are not simply pliant receptors in the hands of the
wordmongers, they are cultural entrepreneurs themselves. Because of
the contingent nature of culture, humans will always tend to stabilize
and reify their culture, if not at the macro-level, then at the micro-
level. Meaning is and always has been in the hands of the actor at the
level of the encounter, and thus people have the mechanisms necessary
to reify and stabilize both culture and self at the micro-level. In particular, ritualization and interaction equilibrium need to be given
greater prominence in the study of cultural fragmentation.

I also agree that under conditions of postmodernity the individual
self becomes increasingly important as a site of social organization and
meaning construction; but the problems associated with the self are not
as dramatic as hypothesized by postmodernism. The dynamics of the
postmodern model have indeed reduced some of the viability of the
subject: there are increasing tendencies toward sensory block, a blasé
attitude, and reflexivity. But these tendencies are offset by the processes inherent in the production of cultural meaning and self. As I have
argued, the issues of hyper-reflexivity and the deconstruction of the
self-concept are mitigated by the reification and stabilization of the
self though ritually dense interactions and by the presence of a culture
of the personality at the secondary level. Individuals are prompted by
the needs for facticity and ontological security to objectify and emotionally infuse their identities. And while the time-honored centers
for performing the necessary rituals may have changed, people have
shifted to other arenas, such as spectator sport, to produce the necessary
emotional energy. That is not to say that the formation of the individ-

ual self is without difficulties in postmodernity. On the contrary, individuals are overwhelmed by the amount of available stimuli, tend to be very reflexive, and do have problems with depression and other such emotional issues, undoubtedly traceable to postmodern, social factors. But the postmodern model has been incomplete on this point as well. Issues of emotional energy, ritual enactment around the self, and the presence of secondary culture must be considered in order to make our understanding of the problems and their extent more robust and true to lived-experience.

Postmodernism is but the clearest contemporary example of the replication of the fundamental error of structuralism. Meaning is not produced nor directly reproduced through the structural relations of the cultural system but through human action and interaction. As I have demonstrated, each major perspective of culture has shifted its emphasis in analysis to the systemic/structural level and has simultaneously neglected affect-meaning. In light of the dynamics of postmodernity, this change is ill-advised. It is not enough simply to analyze a set of elements in terms of their relations one to another, nor is it enough to "tell the story" of a group's culture; rather, what is of paramount importance is what people do with their culture in interaction and how they produce cultural reality. Contemporary cultural analysis must focus on the processes of meaning production, reification, and stabilization at the micro-level. In particular, analysis must investigate the ritualized behaviors of people in encounters and the level of emotional energy that is consistently reproduced as a result of those behaviors vis-à-vis the emergent cultural identities.

NOTES

1. It should be noted that interaction intensity appears to be limited apart from the processes explicated in the model. Within an interaction there is an ebb and flow between intense and more relaxed sequences. If an individual's "chain" (to borrow Collins' [1975, pp. 133-160] term) of interactions were charted, a similar type of ebb and flow would be noted apart from the need for ontological security. There is apparently a satiation point for people vis-à-vis interaction intensity and emotional energy.

2. It is also true that organizational elements tend to cluster around institutional forms. For example, the perpetuation of a collective's culture through formal education is facilitated by the organizational attributes of the educational system. But it is not the case that the organization of a school and the institutional form of education are one and the same. The institution is a cultural phenomenon that consists of highly ritualized and regionalized typified behaviors.

3. Goffman's concern is with the symbols of class status. When there is consonance between the individual in an encounter using a status-sign and their status position, the individual experiences self-affirmation and group solidarity emerges

as well as a depth in the psychic life of its members. If, as the result of the circulation of symbols, an individual uses a symbol ill-suited for his or her status group, "conscious life may become thin and meager, focused as it is upon symbols which are not particularly congenial to it" (Goffman, 1951, p. 304).

4. Whereas Freud's ego is the moderator between the id and the super-ego, Erikson places emphasis on the ego rather than the id as a driving force in the human psyche. One result of this shift is that Erikson's actor appears more rational/logical than does the instinct-driven person conceptualized by Freud. Erikson conceives of the ego as using synthesizing methods to create and maintain a sense of I, "namely, a sense of being *centered* and *active*, *whole* and *aware*—and thus overcome a feeling of being peripheral or inactivated, fragmented, and obscured" (Erikson, 1982, p. 86).

References

Abercrombie, Nicholas, Stephen Hill, & Bryan S. Turner. 1980. *The Dominant Ideology Thesis.* London: George Allen & Unwin.

Allan, Kenneth. 1997. The Postmodern Self; A Theoretical Consideration. *Quarterly Journal of Ideology*, 20, 3–22.

Allan, Kenneth, & Jonathan H. Turner. 1998. Theories of Postmodernity. In Jonathan H. Turner, The *Structure of Sociological Theory*, 6th ed. Belmont, CA: Wadsworth.

Barthes, Roland. 1964/1967. *Elements of Semiology* (Annette Lavers & Colin Smith, trans.). London: Jonathan Cape.

———. 1964/1972. *Critical Essays* (Richard Howard, trans.). Evanston, IL: Northwestern University Press.

———. 1970/1974. *S/Z* (Richard Miller, trans.). New York: Hill & Wang.

Battershill, Charles D. 1990. Erving Goffman as a Precursor to Post-modern Sociology. In Stephen Harold Riggins (ed.), *Beyond Goffman: Studies on Communication, Institution, and Social Interaction.* New York: Mouton de Gruyter.

Baudrillard, Jean. 1972/1981. *For a Critique of the Political Economy of the Sign* (Charles Leven, trans.). St. Louis: Telos Press.

———. 1973/1975. *The Mirror of Production* (Mark Poster, trans.). St. Louis: Telos Press.

———. 1976/1993. *Symbolic Exchange and Death* (Iain Hamilton Grant, trans.). Newbury Park, CA: Sage.

———. 1981/1994 *Simulacra and Simulation* (Sheila Faria Blaser, trans.). Ann Arbor: University of Michigan Press.

Bauman, Zygmunt. 1991. *Modernity and Ambivalence.* Ithaca, NY: Cornell University Press.

———. 1992. *Intimations of Postmodernity.* New York: Routledge.

———. 1994. Is There a Postmodern Sociology? In Steven Seidman (ed.), *The Postmodern Turn: New Perspetives on Social Theory*. London: Cambridge.

Bell, Daniel. 1976. *The Cultural Contradictions of Capitalism*. New York: Basic Books.

Bellah, Robert N. 1970. *Beyond Belief: Essays on Religion in a Post-Traditional World*. New York: Harper & Row.

———. 1975. *The Broken Covenant: American Civil Religion in Time of Trial*. New York: Seabury Press.

———. 1980. *Varieties of Civil Religion*. San Francisco: Harper & Row.

Bellah, Robert N., Richard Madsen, William M. Sullivan, Ann Swidler, & Steven M. Tipton. 1985. *Habits of the Heart: Individualism and Commitment in American Life*. New York: Harper & Row.

———. 1991. *The Good Society*. New York: Alfred A. Knopf.

Berger, Peter L. 1967. *The Sacred Canopy*. Garden City, NY: Doubleday.

Berger, Peter L., & Thomas Luckmann. 1966. *Social Construction of Reality*. Garden City, NY: Doubleday.

Blumer, Herbert. 1969. *Symbolic Interactionism*. Englewood Cliffs, NJ: Prentice-Hall.

Bourdieu, Pierre. 1971. Systems of Education and Systems of Thought. In M.F.D. Young (ed.), *Knowledge and Control*. London: Collier-Macmillan.

———. 1977. *Outline of a Theory of Practice* (Richard Nice, trans.). Cambridge: Cambridge University Press.

———. 1979/1984. *Distinction: A Social Critique of the Judgment of Taste* (Richard Nice, trans.). Cambridge, MA: Harvard University Press.

———. 1983/1986. Forms of Capital. In John G. Richardson (ed.), *Handbook of Theory and Research for the Sociology of Education*. New York: Greenwood Press.

———. 1985. The Genesis of the Concepts of *Habitus* and of *Field*. *Sociocriticism*, 2, 11–29.

———. 1989. Social Space and Symbolic Power. *Sociological Theory*, 7, 14–25.

———. 1991. *Language and Symbolic Power*, ed. John B. Thompson (Gino Raymond & Matthew Adamson, trans.). Cambridge, MA: Harvard University Press.

Bourdieu, Pierre, & Loïc J. D. Wacquant. 1992. *An Invitation to Reflexive Sociology*. Chicago: Chicago Press.

Brown, Richard Harvey. 1987. *Society as Text: Essays on Rhetoric, Reason, and Reality*. Chicago: University of Chicago Press.

———. 1989. *Social Science as Civic Discourse: Essays on the Invention, Legitimation, and Uses of Social Theory*. Chicago: University of Chicago.

———. 1990. Rhetoric, Textuality, and the Postmodern Turn in Sociological Theory. *Sociological Theory*, 8, 188–197.

Calhoun, Craig, Edward LiPuma, & Moishe Postone (eds.). 1993. *Bourdieu: Critical Perspectives*. Chicago: University of Chicago Press.

Cassirer, Ernst. 1944. *An Essay on Man*. New Haven, CT: Yale University Press.

Chagnon, Napoleon A. 1992. *Yanomamö*. Fort Worth, TX: Harcourt Brace.

Clarke, D. S., Jr. (ed.). 1990. *Sources of Semiotic: Readings with Commentary from Antiquity to the Present.* Carbondale: Southern Illinois University Press.

Collins, Randall. 1974. Three Faces of Cruelty: Towards a Comparative Sociology of Violence. *Theory and Society,* 1.

———. 1975. *Conflict Sociology.* New York: Academic Press.

———. 1986. *Weberian Sociological Theory.* New York: Cambridge University Press.

———. 1988. *Theoretical Sociology.* San Diego, CA: Harcourt Brace Jovanovich.

———. 1989. Sociology: Proscience or Antiscience? *American Sociological Review,* 54, 124–139.

———. 1993. What Does Conflict Theory Predict About America's Future? *Sociological Perspectives,* 36, 289–313.

Collins, Randall & Joan Annett. 1975. A Short History of Deference and Demeanor. In Randall Collins, *Conflict Sociology.* New York: Academic Press.

Condon, William S., & W. D. Ogston. 1971. Speech and Body Motion Synchrony of the Speaker-Hearer. In D. D. Horton & J. J. Jenkinds (eds.), *Perception of Language.* Columbus, OH: Merrill.

Denzin, Norman K. 1986. Postmodern Social Theory. *Sociological Theory,* 4, 194–204.

———. 1991. *Images of Postmodern Society: Social Theory and Contemporary Cinema.* Newbury Park, CA: Sage.

———. 1992. *Symbolic Interactionism and Cultural Studies: The Politics of Interpretation.* Oxford: Blackwell.

———. 1993. *Rain Man* in Las Vegas: Where Is the Action for the Postmodern Self? *Symbolic Interaction,* 16, 65–77.

Derrida, Jacques. 1967/1976. *Of Grammatology* (Gayatri Chakravorty Spivak, trans.). Baltimore: Johns Hopkins University Press.

Dilthey, Wilhelm. 1961. *Meaning in History: W. Dilthey's Thoughts on History and Society* (H. P. Rickman, ed.). London, Allen & Unwin.

DiMaggio, Paul. 1979. Review Essay: On Pierre Bourdieu. *American Journal of Sociology,* 84, 1460–1474.

Dowd, Douglas Fitzgerald. 1989. *The Waste of Nations: Dysfunction in the World Economy.* Boulder, CO: Westview Press.

Durkheim, Émile. 1887/1993. *Ethics and the Sociology of Morals* (Robert T. Hall, trans.). Buffalo, NY: Prometheus Books.

———. 1893/1984. *The Division of Labor in Society* (W. D. Halls, trans.). New York: Free Press.

———. 1895/1938. *The Rules of Sociological Method* (Sarah A. Solovay & John H. Mueller, trans., ed. George E. G. Catlin). Glencoe, IL: Free Press.

———. 1912/1995. *The Elementary Forms of the Religious Life* (Karen E. Fields, trans.). New York: Free Press.

———. 1925/1961. *Moral Education: A Study in the Theory and Application of the Sociology of Education* (E. K. Wilson, trans.). New York: Free Press.

———. 1957. *Professional Ethics and Civic Morals* (Cornelia Brookfield, trans.). London: Routledge.

Engels, Frederick. 1885/1968. Feuerbach and the End of Classical German Philosophy. In *Karl Marx and Frederick Engels: Selected Works in One Volume.* New York: International Publishers.

———. 1893/1968. Engels to F. Mehring, July 14, 1893. In *Karl Marx and Frederick Engels: Selected Works In One Volume.* New York: International Publishers.

Erikson, Erik H. 1982. *The Life Cycle Completed.* New York: Norton.

Feyerabend, Paul. 1975/1988. *Against Method,* rev. ed. London: Verso.

Fligstein, Neil. 1991. The Structural Transformation of American Industry: An Institutional Account of the Causes of Diversification in the Largest Firms, 1919–1979. In Walter Powell & Paul DiMaggio (eds.), *The New Institutionalism in Organizational Analysis.* Chicago: University of Chicago Press.

Garfinkel, Harold. 1967. *Studies in Ethnomethodology.* Englewood Cliffs, NJ: Prentice-Hall.

Geertz, Clifford. 1966. *Person, Time, and Conduct in Bali: An Essay in Cultural Analysis.* New Haven: Yale University Southeast Asia Studies.

———. 1973. *The Interpretation of Cultures.* New York: Basic Books.

———. 1983. *Local Knowledge: Further Essays in Interpretive Anthropology.* New York: Basic Books.

Gergen, Kenneth J. 1971. *The Concept of Self.* New York: Holt, Rinehart & Winston.

———. 1991. *The Saturated Self.* New York: Basic Books.

Giddens, Anthony. 1984. *The Constitution of Society.* Berkeley: University of California Press.

———. 1990. *The Consequences of Modernity.* Stanford: Stanford University Press.

———. 1991. *Modernity and Self-Identity.* Stanford: Stanford University Press.

Goffman, Erving. 1951. Symbols of Class Status. *British Journal of Sociology,* 11, 294–304.

———. 1959. *The Presentation of Self in Everyday Life.* Garden City, NY: Anchor.

———. 1963. *Stigma.* New York: Touchstone.

———. 1967. *Interaction Ritual.* New York: Pantheon.

Gottdiener, Mark. 1985. Hegemony and Mass Culture: A Semiotic Approach. *American Journal of Sociology,* 90, 979–1001.

———. 1990. The Logocentrism of the Classics. *American Sociological Review,* 55, 460–463.

———. 1995. *Postmodern Semiotics: Material Culture and the Forms of Postmodern Life.* Oxford: Blackwell.

Gramsci, Antonio. 1971. *Selections from the Prison Notebooks.* London: Lawrence & Heinemann.

Grossmann, Reinhardt. 1992. *The Existence of the World: An Introduction to Ontology.* London: Routledge.

Hall, John R., & Mary Jo Neitz. 1993. *Culture: Sociological Perspectives.* Englewood Cliffs, NJ: Prentice-Hall.

Hall, Stuart. 1980. Cultural Studies and the Centre: Some Problematics and Problems. In *Culture, Media, Language: Working Papers in Cultural Studies, 1972–79.* London: Hutchinson.

————. 1982. The Rediscovery of "Ideology": Return of the Repressed in Media Studies. In Michael Gurevitch, Tony Bennett, James Curran, & Janet Woollacott (eds.), *Culture, Society and the Media*. London: Methuen.

Hall, Stuart, & Tony Jefferson, eds. 1976. *Resistance Through Rituals: Youth Subcultures in Post-War Britain*. London: Hutchinson.

Halle, David. 1984. *America's Working Man*. Chicago: University of Chicago Press.

Halton, Eugene. 1992. The Cultic Roots of Culture. In Richard Münch & Neil J. Smelser (eds.), *Theory of Culture*. Berkeley: University of California Press.

Harvey, David. 1989. *The Conditions of Postmodernity: An Inquiry into the Origins of Cultural Change*. Oxford: Blackwell.

Heidegger, Martin. 1926/1962. *Being and Time* (John Macquarrie & Edward Robinson, trans.). New York: Harper San Francisco.

Hoggart, Richard. 1957. *The Uses of Literacy: Aspects of Working-Class Life with Special Reference to Publications and Entertainments*. London: Chatto & Windus.

hooks, bell. 1989. *Talking Back: Thinking Feminist, Thinking Black*. Boston: South End Press.

Husserl, Edmund. 1913/1931. *Ideas: General Introduction to Pure Phenomenology* (W. R. Boyce Gibson, trans.). London: G. Allen & Unwin.

————. 1970. *The Crisis of European Sciences and Transcendental Phenomenology*. Evanston, IL: Northwestern University.

Jameson, Fredric. 1979/1984. *The Postmodern Condition*. Minneapolis: University of Minnesota Press.

Kellner, Douglas. 1992. Popular Culture and the Construction of Postmodern Identities. In Scott Lash & Jonathan Friedman (eds.), *Modernity and Identity*. Oxford: Blackwell.

Kuhn, Thomas S. 1962. *The Structure of Scientific Revolutions*. Chicago: University of Chicago Press.

Kurzweil, Edith. 1980. *The Age of Structuralism: Lévi-Strauss to Foucault*. New York: Columbia University Press.

Larrain, Jorge. 1979. *The Concept of Ideology*. London: Hutchinson.

Lash, Scott, & John Urry. 1987. *The End of Organized Capitalism*. Madison: University of Wisconsin Press.

————. 1994. *Economies of Signs and Space*. Newbury Park, CA: Sage.

Lemert, Charles. 1990. The Uses of French Structuralisms in Sociology. In George Ritzer (ed.), *Frontiers of Social Theory*. New York: Columbia.

————. 1992. General Social Theory, Irony, Postmodernism. In Steven Seidman & David G. Wagner (eds.), *Postmodernism and Social Theory: The Debate over General Theory*. Cambridge, MA: Blackwell.

————. 1994. Social Theory at the End of a Short Century. *Sociological Theory*, 12, 140–152.

————. 1995. *Sociology After the Crisis*. Boulder, CO: Westview Press.

Lévi-Strauss, Claude. 1949/1969. *The Elementary Structure of Kinship*. Boston: Beacon Press.

————. 1958/1963. *Structural Anthropology*. New York: Basic Books.

Luckmann, Thomas. 1967. *The Invisible Religion: The Problem of Religion in Modern Society.* New York: Macmillan.

——. 1973. Philosophy, Science, and Everyday Life. In Maurice Natanson (ed.), *Phenomenology and the Social Sciences.* Evanston, IL: Northwestern University Press.

——. 1991. The New and the Old in Religion. In Pierre Bourdieu & James S. Coleman (eds.), *Social Theory for a Changing Society.* Boulder, CO: Westview Press.

Luhmann, Niklas. 1985. Society, Meaning, Religion—Based on Self-Reference. *Sociological Analysis,* 46(1), 5–20.

Lukács, Georg. 1922/1971. *History and Class Consciousness.* London: Merlin Press.

Lyotard, Jean-François. 1979/1984. *The Postmodern Condition.* Minneapolis: University of Minnesota Press.

MacCannell, Dean, & Juliet Flower MacCannell. 1982. *The Time of the Sign: A Semiotic Interpretation of Modern Culture.* Bloomington: Indiana University Press.

Mahar, Cheleen, Richard Harker, & Chris Wilkes. 1990. The Basic Theoretical Position. In Richard Harker, Cheleen Mahar, & Chris Wilkes (eds.), *An Introduction to the Work of Pierre Bourdieu.* London: Macmillan.

Marske, Charles E. 1987. Durkheim's "Cult of the Individual" and the Moral Reconstitution of Society. *Sociological Theory,* 5, 1–14.

Marx, Karl. 1888/1978. Theses on Feuerbach. In Robert C. Tucker (ed.), *The Marx-Engels Reader.* New York: W. W. Norton.

Marx, Karl, & Frederick Engels. 1844/1978. Economic and Philosophic Manuscripts of 1844. In Robert C. Tucker (ed.), *The Marx-Engels Reader.* New York: W. W. Norton.

——. 1848/1961. The Communist Manifesto. In Arthur P. Mendel (ed.), *Essential Works of Marxism.* New York: Bantam Books.

——. 1932/1978. The German Ideology: Part 1. In Robert C. Tucker (ed.), *The Marx-Engels Reader.* New York: W. W. Norton.

Mauss, Marcel. 1938/1985. A Category of the Human Mind: The Notion of Person; The Notion of Self. In Michael Carrithers, Steven Collins, & Steven Lukes (eds.), *The Category of the Person: Anthropology, Philosophy, History* (W. D. Halls, trans.). Cambridge: Cambridge University Press.

McAdam, Doug. 1982. *Political Process and the Development of Black Insurgency 1930–1970.* Chicago: University of Chicago Press.

——. 1994. The Role of Activist Subcultures in the Emergence of Collective Action. Paper presented at the annual meeting of the Pacific Sociological Association, April 15–17, Portland Oregon.

McNeill, David. 1992. *Hand and Mind: What Gestures Reveal about Thought.* Chicago: University of Chicago Press.

Mead, George Herbert. 1934/1962. *Mind, Self, and Society,* ed. Charles W. Morris. Chicago: University of Chicago Press.

Mehan, Hugh, & Houston Wood. 1975. *The Reality of Ethnomethodology.* New York: Wiley.

Nöth, Winfried. 1995. *Handbook of Semiotics.* Bloomington: Indiana University Press.

Parsons, Talcott. 1951. *The Social System.* London: Free Press.

———. 1961. Culture and the Social System. In Talcott Parsons (ed.), *Theories of Society: Foundations of Modern Sociological Theory.* New York: Free Press.

———. 1966. *Societies: Evolutionary and Comparative Perspectives.* Englewood Cliffs, NJ: Prentice-Hall.

———. 1990. Prolegomena to a Theory of Social Institutions. *American Sociological Review,* 55, 313–345.

Parsons, Talcott, & Edward Shils, eds. 1951. *Towards a General Theory of Action.* Cambridge, MA: Harvard University Press.

Peirce, Charles Sanders. 1867/1991. On a New List of Categories. In Fames Hoopes (ed.), *Peirce on Signs.* Chapel Hill: University of North Carolina Press.

———. 1931–1958. *Collected Papers.* Cambridge, MA: Harvard University Press.

Peterson, Richard A. 1990. Symbols and Social Life: The Growth of Cultural Studies. *Contemporary Sociology: An International Journal of Reviews* 19(4), 498–500.

Pollner, Melvin, & Lynn McDonald-Wikler. 1985. The Social Construction of Unreality: A Case Study of a Family's Attribution of Competence to a Severely Retarded Child. *Family Process,* 24, 241–254.

Psathas, George. 1989. *Phenomenology and Sociology: Theory and Research.* Washington, DC: University Press of America.

Ritzer, George. 1997. *Postmodern Social Theory.* New York: McGraw-Hill.

Rorty, Richard. 1978. Philosophy as a Kind of Writing: An Essay on Derrida. *New Literary History,* X, 141–160.

———. 1979. *Philosophy and the Mirror of Nature.* Princeton: Princeton University Press.

———. 1994. Method, Social Science, and Social Hope. In Steven Seidman (ed.), *The Postmodern Turn: New Perspectives on Social Theory.* Cambridge: Cambridge University Press.

Ryle, Gilbert. 1971. *Collected Papers.* New York: Barnes & Noble.

Saussure, Ferdinand de. 1916/1959. *Course in General Linguistics,* ed. Charles Bally & Albert Sechehaye; in collaboration with Albert Reidlinger (Wade Baskin, trans.). New York: Philosophical Library.

Schmitt, Richard. 1969. *Martin Heidegger On Being Human.* New York: Random House.

Schutz, Alfred. 1932/1967. *The Phenomenology of the Social World* (George Walsh & Frederick Lehnert, trans.). Evenston, IL: Northwestern University Press.

———. 1962. *Collected Papers* (Maurice Natanson, ed.). The Hague, Netherlands: Martinus Nijhoff.

Schutz, Alfred, & Thomas Luckmann. 1973. *The Structure of the Life World.* Evenston, IL: Northwestern University Press.

Scott, Marvin B., & Stanford M. Lyman. 1968. Accounts. *American Sociological Review,* 37, 385–402.

Seidman, Steven. 1992. Postmodern Social Theory as Narrative with a Moral
    Intent. In Steven Seidman & David G. Wagner (eds.), *Postmodernism and
    Social Theory: The Debate over General Theory*. Cambridge, MA: Black-
    well.
———. 1994. The End of Sociological Theory. In Steven Seidman (ed.), *The Post-
    modern Turn: New Perspectives on Social Theory*. Cambridge: Cambridge
    University Press.
Seidman, Steven, & David G. Wagner. 1992. Introduction. In Steven Seidman &
    David G. Wagner (eds.), *Postmodernism and Social Theory: The Debate
    over General Theory*. Cambridge, MA: Blackwell.
Shweder, Richard A., & Edmund J. Bourne. 1984. Does the Concept of the Person
    Vary Cross-culturally? In Richard A. Shweder & Robert A. LeVine
    (eds.), *Culture Theory: Essays on Mind, Self, and Emotion*. Cambridge:
    Cambridge University Press.
Simmel, Georg. 1903/1971. The Metropolis and Mental Life. In Donald N.
    Levine (ed.), *Georg Simmel: On Individuality and Social Forms*. Chicago:
    University of Chicago Press.
———. 1908/1971. Group Expansion and the Development of Individuality. In
    Donald N. Levine (ed.), *Georg Simmel: On Individuality and Social Forms*.
    Chicago: University of Chicago Press.
———. 1922/1955. *The Web of Group-Affiliations* (Reinhard Bendix, trans.).
    New York: Free Press.
Snow, David A., & Leon Anderson. 1993. *Down on Their Luck: A Study of Home-
    less Street People*. Berkeley: University of California.
Soja, Edward. 1994. Postmodern Geographies: Taking Los Angeles Apart. In
    Roger Friedoland & Deirdre Boden (eds.), *NowHere: Space, Time and
    Modernity*. Berkeley: University of California Press.
Spencer, Herbert. 1873. *The Study of Sociology*. London: Kegan, Paul, Trench.
Stearns, Linda Brewster, & Kenneth Allan. 1996. Institutional Environments:
    The Corporate Merger Wave of the 1980s. *American Sociological Re-
    view*, 61(4), 699–718.
Swidler, Ann. 1986. Culture in Action: Symbols and Strategies. *American Socio-
    logical Review*, 51, 273–286.
Turner, Graeme. 1990. *British Cultural Studies: An Introduction*. Boston: Unwin
    Hyman.
Turner, Jonathan H. 1985. *Herbert Spencer: A Renewed Appreciation*. Beverly
    Hills, CA: Sage.
———. 1988. *A Theory of Social Interaction*. Stanford: Stanford University Press.
———. 1993. *Classical Sociological Theory: A Positivist's Perspective*. Chicago:
    Nelson-Hall.
———. 1995 *Macrodynamics: Toward a Theory on the Organization of Human
    Populations*. New Brunswick, NJ: Rutgers University Press for Rose
    Monographs.
van den Berg, Axel. 1995. Review of *Bourdieu: Critical Perspectives*. *Contempo-
    rary Sociology*, 24, 275–277.
Veblen, Thorstein. 1899/1953. *The Theory of the Leisure Class*. New York: Men-
    tor.
Virilio, Paul. 1991. *Lost Dimension*. New York: Semiotext.

Warner, W. Lloyd. 1959. *The Living and the Dead.* New Haven: Yale University Press.

Weber, Max. 1904/1949. *The Methodology of the Social Sciences* (Edward A. Shils & Henry A. Finch, trans. & ed.). New York: Free Press.

———. 1968. *Economy and Society* (Guenther Roth & Claus Wittich, ed.). Berkeley: University of California Press.

Weinstein, Deena, & Michael A. Weinstein. 1990. Simmel and the Theory of Postmodern Society. In Bryan S. Turner (ed.), *Theories of Modernity and Postmodernity.* London: Sage.

Williams, Raymond. 1958. *Culture and Society: 1780–1950.* New York: Columbia University Press.

———. 1961. *The Long Revolution.* London: Chatto & Windus.

———. 1976. *Keywords.* London: Fontana.

———. 1993. Advertising: The Magic System. In Simon During (ed.), *The Cultural Studies Reader.* London: Routledge.

Wittgenstein, Ludwig. 1936–1949/1973. *Philosophical Investigations.* New York: Macmillan.

Wuthnow, Robert. 1987. *Meaning and Moral Order: Explorations in Cultural Analysis.* Berkeley: University of California Press.

———. 1989. *Communities of Discourse: Ideology and Social Structure in the Reformation, the Enlightenment, and European Socialism.* Cambridge, MA: Harvard University Press.

———. 1992. *Vocabularies of Public Life: Empirical Essays in Symbolic Structure.* London: Routledge.

———. 1995. The Editors Talk with Robert Wuthnow. *Perspectives: The Theory Section Newsletter,* 18, 1–2.

Zerubavel, Eviatar. 1981. *Hidden Rhythms: Schedules and Calendars in Social Life.* Chicago: University of Chicago Press.

———. 1991. *The Fine Line: Making Distinctions in Everyday Life.* New York: Free Press.

Index

Abercrombie, Nicholas 108–109
Actor 27, 41–43, 78, 84, 167, 172,
    174
    disabled 31, 81, 82
    oversocialized 69, 81
Advertising 3, 21, 23, 25–26, 111,
    142, 145, 152–53, 160
Affect-meaning 62, 63
    commitment and 64
    consciousness and 117
    definition 4–5
    felt reality and 76, 80, 87–88,
        89–90, 137, 163
    forming group borders 119–20
    group sentiment 63
    institutions and 137–38
    neglect of 9–10, 71, 77, 81–82,
        117, 127, 173
    process of association and 138,
        157
    production of 89–96, 133, 137,
        159, 161–64
    reified self and 169–71
    sacred/moral force 69, 93
    symbol circulation and 117, 122,
        148
    tertiary culture and 133, 157
Agency 43, 58, 80, 106
    culture and 4
    disabled 32–36, 81–83

    neglect of 5, 10, 39, 45, 52, 116–
        17
    social change and 123
    structure and 32, 33, 169
Allan, Kenneth 9, 123, 166
Ambivalence 93–94
Arche-writing 33
Articulation problem of 77

Barthes, Roland 34–35, 58, 101,
    110–11
Battershill, Charles D. 14
Baudrillard, Jean 13, 24–28, 30, 31,
    144–45, 154, 159–60
Bauman, Zygmunt 14, 16–17, 28–29,
    79, 94, 129, 149, 153–55
Bell, Daniel 24, 143
Bellah, Robert N. 62, 71–73, 79, 81–
    82, 92, 110, 149
Berger, Peter L. 39–40, 45–52, 57,
    61, 75, 110, 118, 122
Blasé attitude 23, 31
Bourdieu, Pierre 100, 102–103, 108,
    113–17, 125–26, 139, 163,
    168
Bracketing 49
Breaching experiments 133
Brown, Richard Harvey 8, 19, 129–
    30

About the Author

KENNETH ALLAN is Assistant Professor of Sociology at the University of North Carolina, Greensboro.

ISBN 0-275-96124-9

HARDCOVER BAR CODE